And Still We Wait

Princeton Theological Monograph Series

K. C. Hanson, Charles M. Collier, D. Christopher Spinks,
and Robin A. Parry, Series Editors

And Still We Wait

Hans Urs von Balthasar's Theology of Holy Saturday and Christian Discipleship

RIYAKO CECILIA HIKOTA

PICKWICK *Publications* · Eugene, Oregon

AND STILL WE WAIT
Hans Urs von Balthasar's Theology of Holy Saturday and Christian Discipleship

Princeton Theological Monograph Series 229

Pickwick Publications
An Imprint of Wipf and Stock Publishers
199 W. 8th Ave., Suite 3
Eugene, OR 97401

www.wipfandstock.com

PAPERBACK ISBN: 978-1-5326-0559-8
HARDCOVER ISBN: 978-1-5326-0561-1
EBOOK ISBN: 978-1-5326-0560-4

Cataloguing-in-Publication data:

Names: Hikota, Riyako Cecilia

Title: And still we wait : Hans Urs von Balthasar's theology of Holy Saturday and Christian discipleship / Riyako Cecilia Hikota.

Description: Eugene, OR: Pickwick Publications, 2018 | Series: Princeton Theological Monograph Series 229 | Includes bibliographical references and index.

Identifiers: ISBN 978-1-5326-0559-8 (paperback) | ISBN 978-1-5326-0561-1 (hardcover) | ISBN 978-1-5326-0560-4 (ebook)

Subjects: LCSH: Balthasar, Hans Urs von, 1905–1988 | Jesus Christ—Descent into hell | Holy Saturday | Catholic Church—Doctrines

Classification: BT470 H44 2018 (paperback) | BT470 (ebook)

Manufactured in the U.S.A.   01/29/18

Dedicated to My Parents and Sister

Contents

Acknowledgments

THIS BOOK HAS BEEN DEVELOPED FROM MY PHD THESIS SUBMITTED TO the University of Edinburgh. First of all, I would like to express my deepest gratitude and appreciation for my primary supervisor, Dr. Nicholas Adams (now Professor of Philosophical Theology at the University of Birmingham), for his expertise, supervision, and support. His lucid and insightful feedback always helped me to have a fresh look at my whole project and writing. I am also deeply grateful for my secondary supervisor, Professor David Fergusson, who has always been a great source of help, support, and inspiration for me. I would like to thank him, in particular, for encouraging me to develop my thesis into a book and recommending me to Wipf and Stock Publishers. I am also grateful for his further advice on the last chapter of this book. I would also like to give thanks to the late Dr. Michael Purcell, without whom my studies in Edinburgh would not have been possible in the first place. I am also grateful to Professor Oliver Davies of King's College London and Dr. David Grumett of the University of Edinburgh, who agreed to become the examiners of my thesis, for their constructive feedback and insights. I am further indebted to Dr. Grumett for his helpful advice on the last chapter of this book.

I also owe gratitude to Professor Martin Kirschner (now Professor at Katholische Universität Eichstätt-Ingolstadt), who kindly invited me to his seminar at the University of Tübingen and gave me some helpful feedback during my research stay there. At the University of Tübingen, I am indebted to Dr. Paul Silas Peterson as well, who so generously shared his knowledge and expertise on Hans Urs von Balthasar and Adrienne von Speyr with me. Among my friends in Tübingen, I would like to give special thanks to Asuka Kimura for helping me to gain access to some important German sources after leaving Tübingen. I am also thankful to the late Frau Cornelia Capol and the sisters of the Community of St. John in Basel, Switzerland, for their hospitality at the Hans Urs von Balthasar Archive.

Among my friends in Edinburgh, first of all, I would like to give thanks to my friends at New College of the University of Edinburgh, especially Ichun Kuo, Wilhelmia Ko, Robert Afayori, Teodor Borz, Kengo Akiyama, Whitney Gamble, Michael Braeutigam, and Khay Tham Lim for all the lovely times and stimulating conversations we have had. I am also thankful to my friends at St. Mary's Roman Catholic Cathedral: Monsignor Patrick Burke, Brian Sibbald, Alina Armstrong, Godwin Enemali, Mary Christiansen, and the Legion of Mary at the Cathedral as they have been a great source of inspiration for my Catholic faith. Further, my special thanks go to Rev. Jaehun Park and Youngsook Park of the Edinburgh Japanese Church for their constant support and encouragement. This ecumenical friendship has been a great source for my spiritual growth. I am also thankful to my friends at the EJC, including Mio Yamagata, Stephen Price, and Soonju Kim for their prayer and support during my studies at Edinburgh. I would like to thank Norio Yamaguchi as well for his friendship and for all the interesting conversations we have had.

In Paris, where I have finished writing this book, my special thanks go to Jose Maria Nogales, who has sustained me emotionally and spiritually every single day after we met, especially during the most difficult stage of writing. I am especially grateful to Father Vincent Holzer at the Institut Catholique de Paris, who accepted me for his seminar, and whose outstanding expertise on Balthasar has further motivated and inspired me to deepen my knowledge of the Swiss theologian. I would also like to thank my friends at the Centre Catholique des Japonais de Paris, Shintaro and Sachiko Yuzawa in particular. As I have been developing my thesis into this book, the activities at the Centre have been a great source of inspiration and motivation for me.

Away from Europe, I am always grateful for my beloved parents and sister in Japan. Without their unchanging love, support, encouragement, and understanding, I could not have completed my studies or this book.

Last but not least, I would like to express my most sincere gratitude to Wipf and Stock Publishers for giving me this valuable opportunity to publish my revised thesis.

Paris, France 2017
Riyako Cecilia Hikota

Notes: All the translations from German to English in this book are mine unless stated otherwise. Special thanks to Michael Braeutigam, Georg Schauer, and Alexander Utkin for checking and proofreading my translations.

Introduction

The Context: The Debate Concerning Christ's Descent into Hell

IN RECENT YEARS, HOLY SATURDAY AND CHRIST'S DESCENT INTO HELL have been quietly gaining more and more scholarly attention,[1] but there is still more to be said about their significance. The most influential modern theologian who has seriously engaged with this doctrine is the Swiss Catholic theologian, Hans Urs von Balthasar (1905–1988). Inspired by the mystical visions of his collaborator and friend, Adrienne von Speyr, he has presented an innovative, but also controversial, interpretation that on Holy Saturday Jesus Christ suffered in utter solidarity with the dead in hell and took to himself our self-damnation. For Balthasar, this "act" of Christ reveals the full depth of our redemption. One of the most distinctive characteristics of Balthasar's interpretation is that he reads this doctrine as a Trinitarian event and emphasizes the passivity of the Son, who, in sheer "obedience of a corpse," underwent the godforsakenness in solidarity with the sinful humanity as the final point of his salvific mission received from the Father.

However, Balthasar's innovative interpretation has caused controversies, leading critics such as Alyssa Lyra Pitstick to argue that Balthasar's theology is even heretical.[2] On the surface, Balthasar's interpretation seems to be quite far from the mainstream Catholic teaching of the doctrine (known as the harrowing of hell), which obviously presents Jesus Christ in hell as being already crowned with the glory of Easter and emphasizes the salvation of the patriarchs from *Sheol* (or Hades, the realm of the dead, which contains both the righteous and the wicked). For example, the current

---

1. See, for example, Alfeyev, *Christ the Conqueror of Hell*; Lauber, *Barth on the Descent into Hell*; Lewis, *Between Cross and Resurrection*; Miles, "Obedience of a Corpse."

2. Pitstick, *Light in Darkness*; *Christ's Descent into Hell*.

Catholic Catechism, which was promulgated by Pope John Paul II in 1992, summarizes this doctrine as follows:

> By the expression "He descended into hell," the Apostles' Creed confesses that Jesus did really die and through his death for us conquered death and the devil "who has the power of death" (Heb 2:14). In his human soul united to his divine person, the dead Christ went down to the realm of the dead. He opened heaven's gates for the just who had gone before him.[3]

The Catechism also explains that Jesus "descended there as Savior, proclaiming the Good News to the spirits imprisoned there"[4] and also "Jesus did not descend into hell to deliver the damned, nor to destroy the hell of damnation, but to free the just who had gone before him."[5] This statement of the current Catechism of the Catholic Church basically reflects the teaching of the Catechism of the Council of Trent (1566; the so-called "Roman Catechism"), which had a dominant influence for more than four centuries. The Roman Catechism provides two reasons why Christ descended into hell: to liberate the just[6] and to proclaim his power.[7]

Turning to such authorities as these, Pitstick has summarized the traditional teaching by focusing on the following four points:

> First, Christ descended in His soul united to His divine Person only to the limbo of the Fathers. Second, His power and authority were made known throughout all of hell, taken generically. Third, He thereby accomplished the two purposes for the descent, which were "to liberate the just" by conferring on them the glory of heaven and "to proclaim His power." Finally, His descent was a glorious one, and Christ did not suffer the pain proper to any of the abodes of hell.[8]

---

3. *Catechism of the Catholic Church*, §636–37.

4. Ibid., §632.

5. Ibid., §633.

6. See *Catechism of the Council of Trent*, 64: "Christ the Lord descended in to hell, in order that, having despoiled the demons, He might liberate from prison those holy Fathers and the other just souls, and might bring them into heaven with Himself. This He accomplished in an admirable and most glorious manner; for His august presence at once shed a celestial lustre upon the captives and filled them with inconceivable joy and delight."

7. Ibid., 65: "Another reason why Christ the Lord descended into hell is that there, as well as in heaven and on earth, He might proclaim His power and authority, and that every knee should bow, of those that are in heaven, on earth, and under the earth."

8. Pitstick, *Light in Darkness*, 28.

In short, Pitstick has argued that there does exist a "traditional" Catholic doctrine of the descent and that the creeds, the magisterial teaching, the Scripture, the liturgy, the consensus of the saints, and the *sensus fidelium* expressed in sacred art all *unanimously* show that the descent is "glorious in the first and proper sense of the word," in other words, "glorious" in the sense of Easter, while Balthasar seems to interpret it in the sense of Good Friday.[9]

In response to Pitstick, Edward T. Oakes has taken the position to defend Balthasar, and the series of their debates on this topic has been published.[10] While admitting that "Balthasar is a disturbing theologian. Even among some of his most vocal enthusiasts, he seems 'not quite right,'"[11] Oakes has attempted to defend Balthasar against Pitstick's harsh critiques by mainly focusing on the following three points: Protestantism, papacy, and purgatory.[12] As it is well known, Balthasar is hugely influenced by the Reformed theologian, Karl Barth, in many areas of his theology, including his famous "hope" for universal salvation. Oakes criticizes Pitstick's curt dismissal of Reformed theologians in general. This point is worth noting because, as Oakes reminds us, it is nothing less than St. Paul's doctrine of atonement that Balthasar has tried to bring back into the center of Catholic theology through his engagement with Barth. Therefore, Oakes argues that it is actually St. Paul's teachings that Pitstick is denying by dismissing Barth's influence on Balthasar. Further, Oakes turns to the authority of the two popes, namely, St. John Paul II and Pope Emeritus Benedict XVI, who are known to have greatly commended Balthasar's contributions to the Catholic

---

9. Ibid., 22–29.

10. See Pitstick and Oakes, "Balthasar, Hell, and Heresy"; "More on Balthasar, Hell, and Heresy." Also see Oakes, "The Internal Logic of Holy Saturday in the Theology of Hans Urs von Balthasar"; "*Descensus* and Development"; and Pitstick, "Development of Doctrine, or Denial?"

11. Pitstick and Oakes, "Balthasar, Hell, and Heresy," 29.

12. See Pitstick and Oakes, "Balthasar, Hell, and Heresy" ;"More on Balthasar, Hell, and Heresy."

Church.[13] (The former is the one who insisted that Balthasar be a cardinal,[14] and the latter's own interpretation of Christ's descent into hell sounds similar to Balthasar's.[15]) Finally, as to Pitstick's treatment of purgatory, Oakes points out that Pitstick's argument admits a pre-Christian purgatory, which does not make sense, as not only Balthasar but also the traditional teaching states that the "hell" Christ descended into was *Sheol*.[16] In short, through a series of articles and responses on this topic, Oakes has tried to present Balthasar's

13. Speaking of papacy, naturally we wonder how the current Pope Francis views Balthasar and his treatment of Holy Saturday. So far we have not found any official comment made by him on Balthasar, but it is worth noting that the wording of the following Easter message he gave in 2013 more or less sounds like Balthasar's interpretation of Christ's descent into hell: "*This same love for which the Son of God became man and followed the way of humility and self-giving to the very end, down to hell—to the abyss of separation from God*—this same merciful love has flooded with light the dead body of Jesus, has transfigured it, has made it pass into eternal life." Pope Francis, *Urbi et Orbi*. Italics added.

14. St. John Paul II appointed Balthasar a cardinal in 1988, but Balthasar passed away two days before the ceremony.

15. For example, the following passage sounds very much like a summary of Balthasar's theology of Holy Saturday: "God himself suffered and died . . . He himself entered into the distinctive freedom of sinners but went beyond it in that freedom of his own love which descended willingly into the Abyss. While the real quality of evil and its consequences become quite palpable here, the question also arises . . . whether in this event we are not in touch with a divine response able to draw freedom precisely as freedom to itself. The answer lies hidden in Jesus' descent into Sheol, in the night of the soul which he suffered, a night which no one can observe except by entering this darkness in suffering faith. Thus, in the history of holiness which hagiology offers us, and notably in the course of recent centuries, in John of the Cross, in Carmelite piety in general, and in that of Thérèse of Lisieux in particular, 'Hell' has taken on a completely new meaning and form. For the saints, 'Hell' is not so much a threat to be hurled at other people but a challenge to oneself. It is a challenge to suffer in the dark night of faith, to experience communion with Christ in solidarity with his descent into the Night. One draws near to the Lord's radiance by sharing his darkness. One serves the salvation of the world by leaving one's own salvation behind for the sake of others. In such piety, nothing of the dreadful reality of Hell is denied. Hell is so real that it reaches right into the existence of the saints. Hope can take it on, only if one shares in the suffering of Hell's night by the side of the One who came to transform our night by his suffering . . . The doctrine of everlasting punishment preserves its real content. The idea of mercy . . . must not become a theory. Rather it is the prayer of suffering, hopeful faith." (Ratzinger, *Eschatology*, 217–18.)

16. In relation to Purgatory, Oakes argues that Balthasar's interpretation of Christ's descent into hell as *Sheol* provides the best solution regarding the possible salvation of unevangelized non-Christians. For a critical response to Oakes's argument concerning this issue, see D'Costa, "The Descent into Hell as a Solution for the Problem of the Fate of the Unevangelized Non-Christians."

interpretation as an authentic development of the doctrine which can stand the norms set by Blessed John Henry Newman.[17]

Another scholar whose response to Pitstick is worth noting here is Paul J. Griffiths.[18] His focus is not on Balthasar's interpretation itself but on the scope and doctrinal weight of what Pitstick has called the "traditional" teaching. Regarding her four-point summary of the "traditional" teaching, Griffiths has argued that Pitstick "drastically overestimates the extent to which there is settled doctrine on this topic, and therefore also misconstrues the nature of her own enterprise."[19] Pitstick herself clearly appeals to the *consensus fidelium* to support her argument. However, as Griffiths says, "Appeal to the *consensus fidelium* to support or rule out some doctrinal is, therefore, while quite legitimate, always difficult and never prima facie probative."[20] Specifically, Griffiths has pointed out that the technical language she uses in her summary (such as the phrase "limbo of the Fathers") "has never been the subject of definition by any council, that appears in no creed, and that, so far as I can tell, is almost entirely absent from ordinary magisterial teaching."[21] Further, concerning the meaning of "glory" in the sense of Easter which Pitstick emphasizes, Griffiths criticizes the way she uses the notion "to close thought down" rather than "to break open and suggestively expand the meaning of the descent in ways whose limits cannot be specified in advance."[22] As a conclusion he writes, "the church doesn't teach very much about that matter, which means that the scope for such discussion is wide."[23] In short, Griffiths has shown that the "traditional" teaching presented by Pitstick is "nothing that requires assent from Catholics."[24]

However, Griffiths's article is far from being the final word on this debate concerning Balthasar's innovative interpretation of Holy Saturday. While it has certainly helped us to see that Pitstick's accusation of Balthasar

17. See Oakes, "The Internal Logic of Holy Saturday in the Theology of Hans Urs von Balthasar."

18. Griffiths, "Is there a Doctrine of the Descent into Hell?"

19. Ibid., 258.

20. Ibid., 261.

21. Ibid., 262.

22. Ibid., 265.

23. Ibid., 268.

24. Ibid., 265. If we turn to the scholarship on Adrienne von Speyr, who has provided the inspirational source for Balthasar's theology of Holy Saturday, similar defenses have been done for her too. See Sutton, *Heaven Opens*, 179–84; Miles, "Obedience of a Corpse," 200–7. Also, for a debate concerning Speyr's orthodoxy (similar to Pitstick vs. Oakes), see Gardiner, "The Dubious Adrienne von Speyr"; "Anne Barbeau Gardiner Answers Jacques Servais"; Servais, "A Response from Jacques Servais."

of heresy may not be as solidly grounded as she claims, some of the serious concerns raised by Pitstick against Balthasar have been shared by others (mostly concerning his treatment of the Trinity, Christology, and universal salvation).[25]

Going back to the statement of the current Catechism on this doctrine, while it is true that it sounds far from Balthasar's interpretation on the surface, we should also note that when this Catechism was presented to the public at first some scholars actually said it should have left some room for interpretations like Balthasar's. For example, a Rahnerian scholar Peter C. Phan has written,

> There are, however, elements in the CCC's exposition of the Creed that are "old" in the pejorative sense of outmoded. For example, in its interpretation of the formula "he descended to the dead," the Catechism seems to take it literally to mean that Jesus descended into the realm of the dead . . .While such an interpretation is not to be ruled out of course, it would have helped matters immeasurably to state unambiguously that such a phrase need not be taken literally and that other interpretations (such as Hans Urs von Balthasar's or Karl Rahner's) are theologically plausible.[26]

It is further worth noting that Cardinal Christoph Schönborn, the editor of the Catechism, has specifically mentioned Balthasar in his introduction to the Catechism's teaching of this doctrine in quite a subtle way. He has said,

> The fifth article . . . concerns an equally central good of the Christian patrimony of faith. The brief paragraph on Jesus' descent into hell keeps to what is the common property of the Church's exegetical tradition. Newer interpretations, such as that of a Hans Urs von Balthasar (the contemplation of Holy Saturday), *however profound and helpful they may be, have not yet experienced that reception which would justify their inclusion in the Catechism.*[27]

25. For example, see Kilby, *Balthasar*; D'Costa, "The Descent into Hell as a Solution for the Problem of the Fate of the Unevangelized Non-Christians"; Reno, "Was Balthasar a Heretic?"

26. Phan, "What is Old and What is New in the Catechism?," 63.

27. Ratzinger and Schönborn, *Introduction to the Catechism of the Catholic Church*, 75. Italics added.

We should not read too much into this "not yet," but the subtle way that Balthasar is mentioned here is worth noting.[28] His interpretation has been neither received as orthodox nor rejected as heterodox. In other words, there is still room and even a need to evaluate Balthasar's theology of Holy Saturday critically.[29]

The Contributions of This Book in Terms of Its Approach, Scope, and Questions

Now let us clarify the position of this book and the contributions we aim to make in terms of critical evaluation of Balthasar's theology of Holy Saturday. Despite its polemical tone, there is no doubt that Pitstick's work has been a great achievement for it has certainly stirred much scholarly interest in this topic. As we have noted above, she has also raised some serious concerns about Balthasar's theology, which have been shared by other critics. First of all, does Balthasar's theology not bring some kind of a rupture into the Trinity? Secondly, does he not depart from the Chalecedonian Christology by confusing the divinity and humanity of Jesus Christ? Finally, does his theology not inevitably lead to admitting universal salvation in a systematic sense despite his insistence that it is merely a "hope"? We will discuss these questions as we expound his theology of Holy Saturday.

On the other hand, we find three significant problems with Pitstick's approach to Balthasar, which are directly related to the contributions this book aims to make. First of all, we have to note the huge genre difference between Balthasar and Pitstick. While Balthasar is known for his utter distaste for neo-scholasticism,[30] Pitstick's entire work is precisely written in a neo-scholastic style.[31] This genre difference should not be ignored, as it seems to be one of the causes which lead her to miss the exploratory nature

28. For example, Gavin D'Costa too appreciates this statement made by Cardinal Schönborn: "It is in this spirit of reception that Balthasar is to be critically evaluated, even if Pitstick has given good grounds for rejecting his reception." D'Costa, *Christianity and World Religions*, 208.

29. Recently, Pitstick has published another book to strengthen her argument further by clarifying that St. John Paul II and Pope Emeritus Benedict XVI do not share Balthasar's interpretation of Christ's descent into hell and also that this particular passage written by Cardinal Schönborn is not an official anticipation by the Church of an eventual embrace of Balthasar's interpretation. See Pitstick, *Christ's Descent into Hell*. We do not oppose her argument on these points, but we do not believe either that this further clarification affects the thesis of this book.

30. For this point, see Kilby, *Balthasar*, 16–23.

31. See Ibid., 11.

of his treatment of Holy Saturday and to misread him as if he attempted to reshape the Catholic dogma in a radical way. Throughout this book, our position is that Balthasar does *not* try to present a radical reinterpretation of the doctrine of the descent into hell in contrast to the traditional teachings but rather tries to appreciate the "in-between" state of Christ in *Sheol* on Holy Saturday more seriously than any other theologian has ever done. We will argue for it while paying full respect to the genre he is working within, which we understand to be a contemplative combination of theology and spirituality.

This point leads us to the second point: the problem concerning the sources. First of all, in order to evaluate Balthasar's theology of Holy Saturday fully, we believe that it is important to see Adrienne von Speyr's mystical visions and to examine how he has developed his own theology by using them as an inspirational source while also turning to various sources for support. In contrast to Pitstick, who almost entirely ignores her writings, throughout this book we will refer to Speyr's mystical visions when it is relevant. We will also emphasize the importance of the spiritual writings of saints in history for him: St. John of the Cross and St. Thérèse of Lisieux in particular.

Finally, the entire scope and angle of this book differs from Pitstick's work and the other previous studies on Balthasar's theology of Holy Saturday. In the last analysis, our focus is on Holy Saturday itself, the day between the cross and the resurrection, which includes Mary's Holy Saturday and the Christian's Holy Saturday experience today as well as Christ in hell. We believe that this angle is significant in order to do full justice to Balthasar's treatment of this subject. After all, he himself has preferred this liturgical term "Holy Saturday" to the more doctrinal term "Christ's descent into hell." His preference for this liturgical term also implies the wide scope his theology potentially has. It is not only about what Christ did or where he was on this particular day in what condition, but it also has in its scope the whole "Holy Saturday experience," which can be characterized by silent waiting. For example, the Roman Missal clearly states, "On Holy Saturday the Church *waits at the Lord's tomb* in prayer and fasting, meditating on his Passion and Death and on his Descent into Hell, and awaiting his Resurrection."[32] We also believe that this element of waiting is important to understand the way Balthasar remains faithful to the Catholic tradition. In his own words,

> We could, simply put, distinguish the two great movements
> of the tradition: that of the East and that of the West. For the
> East, the icon of Christ's descent makes the main representation

32. *The Roman Missal*, 374. Italics added.

of our salvation. Christ strides over the gates of hell which lie across under his feet, as victor over death, and extends His saving hand to those waiting in the darkness of *Sheol* . . .In the West, theology and liturgy mainly honor the silence of death, so the church watches quietly and prayerfully with Mary at the grave. However, both traditions have an inner limit. The Eastern tradition shows us not the dead but the one who is fully alive, namely the Christ of Easter . . .The Western tradition with their pure silence remains somehow eventless, and nothing seems to happen between Good Friday and Easter. Is there a possibility to reconcile both theologies by criticizing their weak points?[33]

This passage helps us to see why Pitstick's main question (whether the descent was glorious in the sense of Easter or Good Friday) can be actually misleading for evaluation of Balthasar's theology of Holy Saturday. His own concern does not lie so much in clarifying the meaning of the glory as in fully appreciating this strange pause between death and life, or between suffering and victory. This point can be further justified by noting that Pitstick's argument does not really answer the question why the church actually waits a whole day before the celebration of the Easter Vigil mass on Holy Saturday night.[34] To underline this point, we will conclude this book by exploring the profound relation between the mystery of Holy Saturday and the mystery of the Eucharist, which is "the source and summit of the Christian life."

Once we note Balthasar's emphasis on the "in-betweenness" of Holy Saturday, we start to see the possibility to widen its scope and explore its implications for Christian life. In addition to his innovative treatment of Holy Saturday, Balthasar is also regarded as a pioneer in the area of theological engagement with tragedy, but the profound connection between these two areas has not yet been fully examined. Balthasar fundamentally sees something "tragic" in an in-between state. We will present a close connection between his theology of Holy Saturday and his tragic view of the paradoxical existence of the Christian by focusing on the element of waiting.

With this approach and within this scope, we will explore the following questions in particular: what kind of implications Balthasar's theology

33. Balthasar, "Theologie des Abstiegs zur Hölle," 140–41.

34. Regarding this point, we have to note that even though the Easter vigil mass had been celebrated on the Saturday morning after the 8th century, the time for this celebration was restored to the night preceding Easter Sunday in 1955 (after the restoration was started *ad experimentum* by *Dominica Resurrectionis Vigiliam* from 1951 and continued as an experiment until confirmed in 1955), as a result of recognizing "the original symbolism" and "authenticity," as well as a great number of petitions sent to the Holy See. See Reid, *The Organic Development of the Liturgy*, 159–69.

of Holy Saturday can provide for Christian discipleship? In relation to this, we will also explore the implications for the question of Christian suffering as well: how does Balthasar's theology of Holy Saturday help Christians to find meaning and hope in their suffering while avoiding the pitfall of systematized theodicy, that is, avoiding presumptuously theorizing or explaining away the reality of suffering? In fact, Christian discipleship and suffering are closely interlinked in Balthasar's theology, so in the last analysis these questions become virtually inseparable. This point will be made clear as we expound his theology.

We will try to explore the implications for Christian suffering and discipleship by connecting the in-between state of Christ in *Sheol* and the in-between existence of the Christian in this world. Such an exploration is quite relevant when we critically evaluate Balthasar's theology of Holy Saturday while doing full justice to the genre within which he is working. After all, Balthasar's own concern does not lie so much in how to clarify the dogmatic aspects of the mystery of Holy Saturday as how to enrich Christian discipleship by contemplating on its profound mystery. This point is clear from the following passage which appears at the end of his article on Christ's descent into hell:

> What follows from all this for us? Let us leave it to the theologians to discuss the dogmatic aspects. *We, however, like Mary and most Christians, cannot follow Christ on this last way. We remain awake at the grave with the other holy women*: What can we do? Many things. In our lives, revive the spirit of solidarity, this power to share the burden of another, to pray with fervor—and such prayer is unfailing—so that our brothers and sisters would not be lost in the end . . . We simply attempt to put into action the small things that are possible for us.[35]

The Outline of the Chapters

Finally, let us explain the structure of this whole book and specify the contents and issues we will discuss in each of the chapters:

In chapter 1, we will prepare the setting for the subsequent chapters. Based on Balthasar's Trinitarian theology and Christology, we will narrate Christ's descent into hell on Holy Saturday as the event in which Christ the Savior went through the transition from the old to the new aeon in hell,

---

35. Balthasar, "Theologie des Abstiegs zur Hölle," 146.

while emphasizing the aspect of "waiting" as well as how it does not necessarily contradict the traditional teachings.

In chapter 2, we will explore the descent into hell as "the dark night of the soul," which is a crucial concept for Balthasar's theology of Holy Saturday. For Balthasar, hell is first and foremost a christological concept. As the main influences on Balthasar on this topic, we will examine Adrienne von Speyr's mystical vision of hell, "the dark night of the soul" of St. John of the Cross, and "the night of nothingness" of St. Thérèse of Lisieux. We will also make reference to St. Mother Teresa as one contemporary example of the descent into hell persevered for the sake of brethren.

In chapter 3, the focus is on Mary, for Balthasar presents Mary as the perfect role model of Christian discipleship. We will discuss how Mary obediently participated in her son's suffering of the sinner's godforsakenness. We will also criticize Balthasar's view of the feminine, which is revealed in his Mariology. In relation to this point we will discuss his critics' concern that Balthasar's theology does not really serve the cause of social justice.

In chapter 4, we will try to locate Balthasar's theology of Holy Saturday within his "tragic" view of Christianity. We will argue that the element of waiting which characterizes Holy Saturday between the cross and the resurrection represents the fundamentally "tragic" state of Christian existence (understood as "tragedy under grace"). In the last analysis, if we locate Christian suffering in the in-between existence represented by Holy Saturday, we could somehow interpret the meaning of suffering into "tragic waiting." This could help us to avoid simply explaining away the reality of suffering while also leaving the hope to find meaning in suffering. The "tragic" waiting in our lives, which is represented by the in-betweenness of Holy Saturday, now can be seen in a christological light.

In chapter 5, we will try to put together the discussions of all these chapters by exploring the mystery of the Eucharist, which constitutes the central part of the life of the church, in light of the mystery of Holy Saturday. Liturgically speaking, Holy Saturday is the day on which we do not celebrate the Eucharist, but without the empty and silent pause of Holy Saturday, we cannot truly appreciate the mystery of the Eucharist.

I

Christ in Hell on Holy Saturday

Introduction

IN CHAPTERS 1 AND 2, OUR FOCUS WILL BE ON HANS URS VON BALTHASAR'S interpretation of Christ's descent into hell. In chapter 1, we will expound and evaluate Balthasar's interpretation of Christ's descent into hell by focusing on its Trinitarian framework and its christological significance. As we expound his theology, we would like to note two points in particular; first, Balthasar tries to appreciate the "in-between" state of Christ in *Sheol* on Holy Saturday instead of departing far from the "traditional" interpretation that seems to emphasize Christ as victor over death and sin; and secondly, Balthasar seems to show a deep interest in the reality of human suffering. Both points will be of particular importance for chapters 3 and 4, where we will widen the scope and discuss Mary's Holy Saturday as well as the Christian's Holy Saturday today in order to explore the implications of Balthasar's theology for Christian discipleship and suffering.

The section titles of this chapter are as follows: under the heading of the Trinitarian framework of Christ's descent into hell, 1) The overview of Balthasar's Trinitarian theology, 2) the cross and the descent into hell as Trinitarian events, 3) the question concerning the beatific vision, 4) the Trinity and the problem of suffering, and under the heading of the christological significance of the descent into hell, 5) *kenosis* as the essence of Balthasar's Christology grounded in the Trinity, 6) mission, 7) the Son's obedience—the economic expression of the eternal love within the immanent Trinity, 8) the descent into hell as the center of kenotic Christology, 9) the importance of "analogy" in Balthasar's theology, and 10) conclusion.

The Trinitarian Framework of Christ's Descent into Hell

In this section, we turn to Balthasar's Trinitarian theology. We will explore it as a fundamental framework to understand the cross and the descent into hell, as well as a basis for our argument concerning Christian suffering, which we will develop in the later chapters. Our focus will be placed on the Trinity revealed on the cross and in hell, while reference will be made to relevant topics. First, we will start by describing Balthasar's subtle and nuanced approach to the relationship between the immanent and economic Trinity. Then, following his thoughts, we will discuss *kenosis* as the essential characteristic of the immanent Trinity. After this preparation, we will examine his interpretation of the cross and the descent into hell as the abandonment of the Son by the Father, which is actually the radical form of mutual love between them. We will also examine the problem concerning the beatific vision. This point seems to be at the core of the difference between Balthasar's interpretation of the descent into hell and the traditional teachings of the doctrine, and it gives Pitstick one of the reasons for concluding that his interpretation is heretical. Then we will pause to evaluate his Trinitarian theology by considering the serious concern raised against his treatment of the Trinity, namely that he has *the tendency to* bring a rupture within the eternally blissful unity within the Trinity and eventually ends up elevating and divinizing suffering as well.

The Overview of Balthasar's Trinitarian Theology

Regarding the relationship between the immanent and economic Trinity, Karl Rahner uttered a now-famous dictum: "The 'economic' Trinity is the 'immanent' Trinity and the 'immanent' Trinity is the 'economic' Trinity."[1] This axiom, now often dubbed "Rahner's Rule," is a result of Rahner's intention to present the Trinity "*as* a mystery of salvation (in its reality and not merely as a doctrine)."[2]

On the one hand, Balthasar agrees with this axiom in the sense that it is only through the economic Trinity that we can have knowledge of the immanent Trinity. It is only through the figure and disposition of the incarnate Son, Jesus Christ, that we can encounter the Father, Son, and Holy Spirit

---

1. Rahner, *The Trinity*, 22.

2. Ibid., 21–22. This is because Rahner thinks that neoscholaristic, manualistic theology of the Trinity (what he calls *Schultheologie*) has turned the Trinity into an object of psychological and metaphysical speculation which is isolated from the history of God's self-communication. See Phan, "Mystery of Grace and Salvation."

as the divine persons of the Trinity. On the other hand, Balthasar departs from Rahner's rule and strongly insists that the economic and immanent Trinity cannot be simply identified with each other. He is especially critical of the way Rahner treats the immanent Trinity, even when distinguished from the economic, merely as "a kind of precondition for God's true, earnest self-revelation and self-giving."[3] Balthasar ascribes such a treatment to Rahner's "concern to preserve God's inner, triune nature as the mystery of mysteries."[4] In Rahner's model, "God" refers to the Father, who communicates himself in history as the Son and the Spirit, while he himself remains the unoriginate source, in other words, the incomprehensible mystery. According to Balthasar, Rahner makes the divine self-communication within the immanent Trinity appear to be "strangely formal,"[5] as Rahner admits no reciprocal "Thou" within the immanent Trinity because God has only one self-consciousness.[6] As a result, in Balthasar's view, the immanent Trinity becomes "hardly credible as the infinite prototype of God's 'economic' self-squandering."[7] Instead, Balthasar himself proposes a very lively interpersonal "drama" within the immanent Trinity, which can ontologically ground and support the drama in the economic Trinity.

Balthasar is extremely careful to maintain a clear distinction between the immanent and economic Trinity, so that immanent does not "dissolve into the economic."[8] In other words, he believes we must not let God "be swallowed up in the world process."[9] He says this as a criticism of a Hegelian process theology, the position allegedly taken by such theologians as Jürgen Moltmann. Moltmann's position is also based on Rahner's rule. However, Moltmann not only blurs the distinction between the immanent and economic Trinity, but goes further to claim that the economic Trinity *becomes* the immanent Trinity. In Moltmann's own words, "The economic Trinity completes and perfects itself to [the] immanent Trinity when the history and experience of salvation are completed and perfected."[10] For Moltmann, the cross in history is the fulfillment of the Trinity. His utmost concern is to show God's intimate involvement with the world and eventually to claim that God himself suffers in the midst of all the sufferings of his creation. He

---

3. Balthasar, *Theo-Drama* IV, 320.

4. Ibid., 320.

5. Ibid., 321.

6. Rahner, *The Trinity*, 75–76, notes 28–30.

7. Balthasar, *Theo-Drama* IV, 321.

8. Ibid., 321.

9. Ibid., 321.

10. Moltmann, *The Trinity and the Kingdom*, 151.

writes, "God suffers with us—God suffers from us—God suffers for us; it is this experience of God that reveals the triune God."[11]

Balthasar shares Moltmann's concern to some extent and tries to avoid separating the immanent and economic Trinity in such a way that the events of the economy of salvation leave the immanent Trinity unaffected. Nevertheless, he is critical of Moltmann's view, because the God entangled in the world process in this way ends up becoming "a tragic, mythological God."[12] God's immutability and sovereignty must be preserved. God does not need the world for his self-fulfillment. God is love, but God does not *become* love just because he has the world as "Thou" to love. God is love already in himself. In Balthasar's words, "He does not *become* 'love' by having the world as his 'thou' and his 'partner': in himself, in lofty transcendence far above the world, he 'is love' already. Only in this way, in complete freedom, can he reveal himself and give himself to be loved."[13]

Therefore, Balthasar neither merely separates the immanent Trinity from the economic nor hastily concludes that the former remains unaffected by the latter. We must neither simply identify nor separate them. A way must be sought to let the immanent Trinity ground the economic Trinity so that the former remains the transcendent reality while relating to the latter more than just formally. In his own words, "We have to think of the immanent Trinity as that eternal and absolute self-giving, so that God in Godself is seen as being absolute love. This is the only thing that will explain God's free self-giving to the world as love, without God needing the cosmic process and the cross to become (and "mediate") Godself."[14] While avoiding both Rahner's and Moltmann's positions, Balthasar's own way of treating the immanent and economic Trinity is to *analogically* relate the "event" in the economic Trinity to the "event" of the divine processions within the immanent Trinity. For instance, he interprets that the *kenosis* of the Son in the paschal event is the economic form of the divine love of the Father and the Son, so it provides *an analogy* for the interpersonal relations within the immanent Trinity. Thus he maintains the distinction between the immanent and economic Trinity in a subtle way. It is significant to maintain such a nuanced relationship, for it is closely linked to both a proper understanding of God and a proper understanding of soteriology. What is at stake here is both God's sovereignty and the actuality of redemption. We would not want an unapproachable, sublime God who is not in living communication with the

---

11. Ibid., 4.

12. Balthasar, *Theo-Drama* IV, 322.

13. Balthasar, *Theo-Drama* III, 509.

14. Balthasar, *Theo-Drama* IV, 323.

world or a mere mythical character who is at the mercy of the events of history and in need of redemption himself. Carefully avoiding these extreme positions, Balthasar's approach to the relationship between the economic and immanent Trinity enables us to see God as both being independent from the world and as communicating with the world.

Further, the treatment of the relationship between the immanent and economic Trinity is closely linked to the problem of divine suffering, and ultimately, the problem of human suffering and God's response to it. Balthasar is careful not to attribute suffering to God, though he comes very close to doing so. He only attributes to God something *analogous* to suffering. According to Balthasar, since the immanent Trinity ontologically grounds the economic Trinity, the grounds for the possibility of what takes place in the economic Trinity are to be found in the immanent Trinity. Therefore, the God on the cross and in the descent into hell reveals only what God already is immanently, namely, kenotic love.

Moltmann, as one of the main advocates of "the suffering God" in the twentieth century, takes the position that God redeems the world through his suffering. However, for Balthasar, suffering merely has a secondary place next to kenotic love. He does speak about suffering as a possible result of the recklessness of his self-giving love, but he never directly ascribes suffering to God. In the following passage, we can see that he is extremely cautious about this point:

> If we ask whether there is suffering in God, the answer is this: *there is something in God that can develop into suffering.* This suffering occurs when the recklessness with which the Father gives away himself (and *all* that is his) encounters a freedom that, instead of responding in kind to his magnanimity, changes it into a calculating, cautious self-preservation. This contrasts with the essentially divine recklessness of the Son, who allows himself to be squandered, and of the Spirit who accompanies him.[15]

Thus, we can only affirm that there is something *analogous* to suffering in God that is the reckless self-giving of the inter-Trinitarian love, which "can develop into suffering." It is significant how to read this nuanced passage in order to evaluate Balthasar's position about divine suffering (we will come back to this point later). He tries to maintain both the view that God does not need to be involved in the world process and the view that the possibilities of drama in the world must be grounded in God. Balthasar himself admits that such an approach is "to walk on a knife edge"[16] and describes

15. Ibid., 327–28. The italics in the first sentence are added.

16. Ibid., 324.

his own approach as follows: "It avoids all the fashionable talk of 'the pain of God' and yet is bound to say that something happens in God that not only justifies the possibility and actual occurrence of all suffering in the world but also justifies God's sharing in the latter, in which he goes to the length of vicariously taking on man's God-lessness."[17] This "vicariously taking on man's Godlessness" refers to the Son's descent into hell. While criticizing "all the fashionable talk" of divine suffering, Balthasar tries to deal with the issue of human and divine suffering in his own way, and Christ's descent into hell can be placed at the center of this context.

In the last analysis, we have to seek not only the God who suffers for us, from us, and with us (as Moltmann does) but also the God who absolutely transcends suffering so that he can save us (as Rahner does). This issue requires a razor's edge kind of approach, which is made possible exactly by Balthasar's subtle and nuanced treatment of the relationship between the immanent and economic Trinity. We have seen *how* Balthasar treats the immanent and economic Trinity. Next, we turn to *what* he sees in the Trinity.

For Balthasar, the essential characteristic of the immanent Trinity is *kenosis*. He says that the generation of the Son by the Father is "an initial 'kenosis' within the Godhead that underpins all subsequent *kenosis*."[18] In this self-giving act, the Father gives all his divinity away to the Son without remainder. However, the Father does not exist prior to this *kenosis*, which would be an Arian mistake. Rather, this generation must be considered beyond the temporal sphere. Rather, "he *is* this movement of self-giving that holds nothing back."[19] Moreover, by giving all that is his, the Father does not lose himself at all. Though he does not keep back anything from the Son, he does not extinguish himself either by thus surrendering himself without reserve. Balthasar explains,

> For in this self-surrender, he *is* the whole divine essence; Here we see both God's infinite power and his powerlessness; he cannot be God in any other way but in this "*kenosis*" within the Godhead itself. (Yet what omnipotence is revealed here! He brings forth a God who is of equal substance and therefore uncreated, even if, in this self-surrender, he must go to the very extreme of self-lessness.)[20]

17. Ibid., 324.

18. Ibid., 323. He admits that he is following Sergei Bulgakov's idea on this point. For an examination of how Balthasar exactly adopts and modifies Bulgakov's kenotic Trinitarian theology, see Leamy, *The Holy Trinity*.

19. Balthasar, *Theo-Drama* IV, 323.

20. Ibid., 325.

Through this initial *kenosis*, the Son possesses divinity in a manner equal to the Father. This generation of the Son, who is "the second way of participating in (and of *being*) the identical Godhead,"[21] reveals both God's powerlessness and omnipotence at the same time. God lets go of his divinity, so it shows his powerlessness, but he is omnipotent because he does not lose himself even in letting go of himself. The paradoxical truth about God is already revealed here, as God's omnipotent power is shown in his very act of giving it up. According to Balthasar, God exists already in himself in no other way but this way of *kenosis*. He does not need the world as "Thou" in order to be kenotic love.

On the other hand, the Son's response to the gift of Godhead can only be "eternal thanksgiving" to the Father as the Source, which is "a thanksgiving as selfless and unreserved as the Father's original self-surrender."[22] Thus, there is a reciprocal self-giving relationship between the Father and the Son. It is the Holy Spirit that "as the essence of love" that "maintains the infinite difference between them, seals it, and since he is the one Spirit of them both, bridges it."[23] Here we have the basic model of the dynamic relationships between the divine persons within the immanent Trinity, which is reciprocal self-giving love.

As the Father generates the Son in the primal *kenosis*, also generated there is room for *Other*. In his words, "This Son is infinitely Other, but he is also the infinitely *Other of the Father*. Thus he both grounds and surpasses all we mean by separation, pain and alienation in the world and all we can envisage in terms of loving self-giving, interpersonal relationship and blessedness."[24] Along with such key words as "*kenosis*," "self-giving," and "self-surrender," another striking feature that permeates Balthasar's theology of the Trinity is this emphasis on the "otherness," "separation," and "distance" between the Father and the Son. The "infinite distance" between the Father and the Son is significant for us, because eventually it encompasses and surpasses even the utmost distance between God and us human beings, namely, between God and hell. That is because the finite distance between God and his creation is paradoxically smaller than the infinite distance between the Father and the Son. Balthasar writes, "It is the drama of the 'emptying' of the Father's heart, in the generation of the Son, that contains and surpasses all possible drama between God and a world. For any world only has its place within that distinction between Father and Son

21. Ibid., 323.

22. Ibid., 324.

23. Ibid., 324.

24. Ibid., 325.

that is maintained and bridged by the Holy Spirit."[25] Thus, the relationship between God and the world, which belongs to the limited temporal sphere, can only be contained in the eternal drama of the Trinity. The way the Father relates to the Son is reflected in the way God relates to the world. As the Father generates the Son in an act of *kenosis*, God the Father freely chooses to create the world out of love, not out of necessity in any way. Just as the Son responds to the love of the Father with love, the world is required to return God's love. However, God also gives his creation freedom, including the freedom to reject his love, thus binding himself in some sense. However, Balthasar reminds us that even this "No" from the creature's side is possible only because of God's limitless love:

> Man's refusal was possible because of the Trinitarian "reckless-ness" of divine love, which, in its self-giving, observed no limits and had no regard for itself. In this, it showed both its power and its powerlessness and fundamental vulnerability (the two are inseparable). So we must say both things at once: within God's own self—for where else is the creature to be found? —and in the defenselessness of absolute love, God endures the refusal of this love; and, on the other hand, in the omnipotence of the same love, he cannot and will not suffer it.[26]

Since God is limitlessly self-giving love, he unconditionally loves his creature even to the point of selflessness, which is what Balthasar calls "recklessness" (more or less similarly to the way the Greek Fathers boldly called God's love of humanity "foolish.") In this selflessness, God grants his creation genuine freedom, including even the freedom to reject his love. However, since God is omnipotent, God's freedom remains intact, whatever his creation does in the world he creates. Even when we reject God, we are still within God's love. First of all, as Balthasar says, creation can only be explained within the generation of the Son: "The world belongs to him and has him as its goal; only in the Son can the world be 'recapitulated.'"[27] Since the creature's freedom is analogous to the Son's autonomy received from the Father, even the creature's "No" "must be located within the Son's all-embracing Yes to the Father, in the Spirit."[28] Therefore, we can see that the Son, "the infinite Other of the Father," can encompass and surpass all possible human responses to God's love, which means even the possibilities of heaven and hell are contained within the Trinity. Thus, dismissing a

25. Ibid., 327.
26. Ibid., 329.
27. Ibid., 326.
28. Ibid., 329.

statement of a Hegelian process theology, "love is as strong as hell," Balthasar can declare, "no, it is stronger, for hell is only possible given the absolute and real separation of Father and Son."[29]

The Cross and the Descent into Hell as Trinitarian Events

Considering his description of divine and human freedom, it is not difficult to see that the ultimate point where these two freedoms meet cannot be anywhere else but hell. This is why we cannot fully comprehend the cost of redemption without considering the Son's descent into hell. However, before we examine the descent into hell as a Trinitarian event, we have to examine the cross as being revelatory of the Trinity.

As Rowan Williams writes, the question which motivates the entire theological vision of Balthasar, especially his thoughts on the Trinitarian life of God, is what it means to identify someone who declares himself abandoned by God as God.[30] The abandonment (*Verlassenheit* in German) of the Son by the Father, which is expressed most poignantly in the so-called "cry of dereliction" on the cross, "My God, my God, why have you forsaken me?" (Matt 27:46 and Mark 15:34), is the key to Balthasar's Trinitarian theology of the cross. The Son is forsaken by the Father. God is forsaken by God himself. Balthasar interprets the cross as abandonment of the Son by the Father (and this abandonment reaches the climax in his descent into hell). Balthasar argues that the Son's cry of dereliction on the cross is a cry of *obedience*, which can only be explained by God being Triune. To put it succinctly, the abandonment of the Son by the Father understood in the light of the Son's obedience is Balthasar's central interpretation of the cross.

The Son is forsaken both for the sake of the Father and the sinners. The Son loves the Father so much that in the ultimate form of obedience to the Father's plan for the redemption of the world he agrees to let go of his own intimacy with the Father. In other words, the Son chooses to be abandoned by the Father in order to experience the godforsakenness of the sinners to the fullest, because he wants to do everything he can do to renew the Father's fallen creation as a result of the foolish "recklessness" or "selflessness" of divine love as we have seen above. In Balthasar's words, "On Good Friday the Son's love renounces all sensible contact with the Father, so that he can experience in himself the sinner's distance from God. (No one can be more abandoned by the Father than the Son, because no one knows him

---

29. Ibid., 325.
30. Williams, "Balthasar and the Trinity," 37.

and depends on him as much as the Son."[31] Also, considering from the side of the Father, because the Father loves the Son and his creation so much, he wants the Son as a human being to experience the ultimate godforsakenness of his creation. No one has ever been so close to the Father as the Son, so the godforsakenness the Son experiences is paradoxically far greater than any sinner can ever experience. Therefore, surprisingly, Balthasar says that the abandonment on the cross is actually the ultimate form of mutual love between the Father and Son, which also involves the creation. In other words, such abandonment of the Son by the Father is made possible exactly because of the eternal mutual love between them, which is expressed as the Holy Spirit working as a bond. It is because of his salvific mission that the Son enters into solidarity with all who feel abandoned by God. Therefore, the cross reveals God's boundless love towards sinful humankind and God's intention to save the whole humanity. The cross also reveals the great love within the eternal Trinity. As Balthasar says, "only this *double* love gives the key to the understanding."[32]

If the cross reveals the Trinity, hence God as love, so does the Son's descent into hell. Moreover, this event is both inevitable and possible because of God being Triune. Let us examine the former point first.

First of all, hell, which is the supreme consequence of perverted human freedom, belongs to the Father. Balthasar explains as follows:

> If the Father must be considered as the Creator of human freedom—with all its foreseeable consequences—then judgment belongs primordially to him, and thereby Hell also; and when he sends the Son into the world to save it instead of judging it, and to equip him for this function, gives "all judgment to the Son" (John 5, 22), then he must also introduce the Son *made man* into "Hell" (as the supreme entailment of human liberty).[33]

God the Father creates the world out of love and gives it freedom, including the freedom to reject him, so hell ("the supreme entailment of human liberty") also belongs to him. We have already seen above that the possibilities of heaven and hell are all encompassed within the Trinity.[34] Therefore, as the Father sends the Son in order not to judge the world but to

31. Balthasar, *Our Task*, 65.

32. Balthasar, *The Glory of the Lord* VII, 207. Italics added.

33. Balthasar, *Mysterium Paschale*, 175.

34. Adrienne von Speyr also expresses hell as the "dark mystery" of the Father, which means the mystery of divine love. See Speyr, *Kreuz und Hölle* I, 91.

save it, the Son descends into hell as "the final consequence of the redemptive mission he has received from the Father."[35]

As we have seen above, God gives the world genuine freedom out of love, but this implies the risk of humanity choosing to reject God and so becoming lost. However, God can assume such a risk because he is able to gather such possible (or actual) lostness into himself. It is exactly through the Son's descent into hell that such gathering up of the lostness of humanity into God is accomplished. As Balthasar says, God gathers the abyss of lostness of humanity into "the abyss of absolute love."[36] This is not difficult to see, if we consider hell as the ultimate point where human and divine freedom meet.

By placing himself in solidarity with the sinners, the Son, a cadaver in hell, proves two things: God's utmost respect for human freedom to the point of allowing us to reject him completely and God's all-embracing love to the point of accompanying us even in hell. The Son descends there to be in solidarity with sinners. He is dead together with them "out of an ultimate love."[37] Thus, the sinner, who "wants to be 'damned' apart from God,"[38] ends up being with God after all. The sinner cannot escape from God's love even in hell. As Balthasar writes, the Son "disturbs the absolute loneliness striven for by the sinner."[39] (If one aspect of the traditional interpretation of the descent into hell was the belief that there is no place [even hell] where God's power does not reach, then Balthasar too stresses this point, even though he places more stress on the depth of God's love.) Therefore, while remaining a real possibility for the sinner, hell can also be placed in the limitless love of the triune God. The creation's freedom is not at all undermined, but God also freely chooses to be in solidarity with sinful humanity in hell.

Therefore, if we fully pursue the notion of God as Trinity, who is love itself, and also consider hell as "the supreme entailment of human liberty," which itself is a consequence of God's "reckless" love, we can clearly see that the Son's descent into hell is inevitable. Hell must be the final destination of his mission to save sinful humanity.

Further, the Son's descent into hell is possible only because God is Triune. Balthasar describes the mystery as follows:

> God can simultaneously remain in himself and step forth from himself. And, in thus stepping forth from himself, he descends

---

35. Balthasar, *Mysterium Paschale*, 174.

36. Balthasar, *Elucidations*, 52.

37. Balthasar, *The Von Balthasar Reader*, 153.

38. Ibid., 153.

39. Ibid., 153.

into the abyss of all that is anti-divine; God does nothing anti-divine—the sinner does—but he can experience it within his own reality. *This is Christ's descent into hell, into what God has utterly cast out of the world. This descent can take place in obedience* (the uttermost, absolute obedience, of which only the Son is capable) *because absolute obedience can become the economic form of the Son's absolute response to the Father.*[40]

Because of the immanent distance between the Father and the Son, God can even descend into hell, which is the abyss of all that is alien to God's nature, while remaining God. This is because even in this utmost separation between the Father and the Son, the Holy Spirit is working as a bridge between them to unite them. Without the Holy Spirit, the descent into hell would be impossible. Just as the Holy Spirit reveals the eternally unbreakable bond of communion between the Father and the Son on the cross, which is the very moment where the Son is abandoned by the Father, the Holy Spirit reveals the maximal possible intimacy between the Father and the Son in hell, where they seem to be the most separated from each other. The separation between the Father and the Son is only possible because of the Holy Spirit, who eternally accompanies them both. Balthasar states, "because he is triune, God can overcome even what is hostile to God within his eternal relations."[41] We have seen that the cross, interpreted as the abandonment of the Son by the Father, paradoxically reveals the eternal Trinitarian communion. In the same way, hell too paradoxically reveals the Trinity.

In sum, according to Balthasar, the descent into hell is both inevitable and possible because God is Triune. By emphasizing descent into hell as the climax of the Son's economic mission, Balthasar does not diminish the significance of the cross in any way. Rather, he believes that it is crucial to take the descent into hell with utmost seriousness in order to grasp fully the meaning of the cross, in other words, the cost of redemption. We can never appreciate the abyss of God's love without taking the Son's suffering in hell seriously.

The Question Concerning the Beatific Vision

By interpreting the cross and the descent into hell as the abandonment of the Son by the Father and stressing Christ's suffering in solidarity with sinful humanity, Balthasar departs from the traditional teaching, though we still

40. Balthasar, *Theo-Drama* III, 530. Italics added.

41. Ibid., 530.

have to stress that his position is *not* a complete reversal of it. The difference between the two becomes most notable in his discussion of the beatific vision. Pitstick strongly objects to Balthasar's treatment of this subject, and her objection is directly related to her concern that his theology threatens the unity of the Trinity and also of the consciousness of Christ.[42] This concern is worth considering, and we have to examine if his position could stand this criticism.

Traditionally speaking, St. Thomas Aquinas affirms (along with other scholastic authors) that even during his passion and descent into hell Jesus did not cease to enjoy the beatific vision of the Father, though he underwent the greatest suffering of all human sufferings.[43] St. Thomas balances these two points by referring to the different levels or ranges of experiences in Christ's human soul. In other words, while "Christ suffered in all his lower powers," his "superior reason" did not suffer.[44] The higher part of his soul kept on enjoying the beatific vision, which was prevented only by his human will to suffer for humankind from flowing into the lower part, where he was in utmost agony.[45]

Balthasar, however, refuses to accept this interpretation, mainly because he does not think it does full justice to the drama of redemption. Apparently, he wants to take with utmost seriousness the other notion of St. Thomas, namely that Christ suffered the most of all human beings. In his words,

> Any theology (including present-day echoes) which says that Christ on the Cross suffered only in the "lower" part of his soul, while the "peak of his [created] spirit" continued to enjoy the heavenly beatific vision, breaks the top off the drama of redemption. It does not see that the Son, as a whole takes on himself the situation of the sinful world that has turned away from God; indeed, by his absolute obedience he has "infiltrated" it and rendered it impotent. The Triune God is capable of more than pious theologians imagine.[46]

42. Pitstick, *Light in Darkness*, 166–190. This concern is also shared by Gavin D'Costa. See D'Costa, "The Descent into Hell as a Solution for the Problem of the Fate of the Unevangelized Non-Christians."

43. St. Thomas Aquinas, *Summa Theologiae*, III, q.46, a.6 and 8.

44. Ibid., III, q.46, a.7.

45. Ibid., III, q.46, a.8.

46. Balthasar, "Ist der Gekreuzugte 'selig'?," 108. The translation used here is the quotation from Saward, *The Mysteries of March*, 56–57.

On the other hand, St. John Paul II, for example, takes the position in the middle between St. Thomas and Balthasar. Consider the following catechetical address on the cry of dereliction:

> If Jesus felt abandoned by the Father, he knew however that that was not really so. He himself said, "I and the Father are one" (Jn 10:30). Speaking of his future passion he said, "I am not alone, for the Father is with me" (Jn 16:32). Jesus had the clear vision of God and the certainty of his union with the Father dominant in his mind. But in the sphere bordering on the senses, and therefore more subject to the impressions, emotions and influences of the internal and external experiences of pain, Jesus' human soul was reduced to a wasteland. He no longer felt the presence of the Father, but he underwent the tragic experience of the most complete desolation.[47]

Here St. John Paul II seems to go some way towards Balthasar's position without abandoning that of St. Thomas's. It should also be noted that St. Thomas understands the Father's "abandonment" as the Father's non-protection of the Son from his enemies rather than the abandonment purposefully done.

Placing Balthasar in contrast to these two authors, John Saward criticizes him for failing to distinguish between "the *feeling* of abandonment and its *reality*."[48] Saward cautiously suggests, "It is at least arguable that the greatest possible spiritual suffering is not so much the Godforsakenness of One who hitherto has enjoyed the vision of the Father but rather the feeling of God's absence in a soul that still, at some level, rests in his presence."[49] On the other hand, David Lauber opposes Saward's criticism by arguing that Balthasar is fully aware of the significant distinction between Jesus' feeling of abandonment and the objective relationship between the Father and the Son, which is unbroken love. He further says that it is rather Balthasar "who actually distinguishes between 'feeling' and 'reality,'" while Saward, St. John Paul II and the Scholastics fail to affirm "the profound gap between Christ's subjective experience and the reality of the unbroken relationship between the Father and the Son."[50]

Though these two scholars reach the seemingly opposing conclusions, they are actually referring to the same truth of the relationship between the Father and the Son. While Lauber is right to say that Balthasar is fully

---

47. John Paul II, "My God, My God, Why Have You Forsaken Me?," n.4.

48. Saward, *The Mysteries of March*, 55.

49. Ibid., 58.

50. Lauber, *Barth on the Descent into Hell*, 73.

aware of the distinction between the subjective experience of Jesus and the objective reality of the Father and the Son, his criticism of Saward is misplaced. What Saward refers to here is the distinction between the feeling of abandonment *and its* reality, not the distinction between the feeling of abandonment *and the reality of the unbroken love* between the Father and the Son. Nevertheless, Saward's criticism that Balthasar does not distinguish between the sentiment of abandonment and its reality is not necessarily fair. Rather, it is important that he does not make such distinction, because, after all, the abandonment too is a form of love, as Balthasar repeatedly says. In his words, "It is absolutely true that this "dereliction" between Father and Son (made possible through their common Spirit) is a most extreme form of their mutual love and of God's Triune love for the world."[51]

We cannot stress too much that in Balthasar's theology the abandonment of the Son by the Father is the most radical form of the mutual love between the two and that it is made possible exactly because of this unchanging love, though some critics of Balthasar including Pitstick seem to place a strong emphasis on the negative notion of abandonment. In the last analysis, as Aidan Nichols writes regarding this problem, though Balthasar denies the traditional teaching that the peak of Jesus' human soul continued to enjoy the beatific vision on the cross and in hell, it would "not amount to a complete reversal of the dogmatic intention of Aquinas's teaching to the contrary."[52] As Balthasar repeatedly says, after all, the abandonment of the Son by the Father is the ultimate form of their mutual love. Such abandonment itself is paradoxically made possible because of the eternal communion within the Trinity.

Since Balthasar himself does emphasize the unity of the Trinity, Pitstick's concern that Balthasar brings a rupture into the Trinity would not be so easily justified. Nevertheless, the way Balthasar puts together love and abandonment (and eventually joy and suffering) has been critiqued by other scholars too. It is actually one of the important questions concerning his theology that we discuss throughout this book, but let us discuss it below as far as it concerns his Trinitarian theology.

The Trinity and the Problem of Suffering

As we have seen so far, Balthasar's description of the Trinity is characterized by its dynamic liveliness and powerful vividness using such words as

51. Balthasar, "Ist der Gekreuzigte 'selig'?," 108. The translation used here is the quotation from Saward, *the Mysteries of March*, 57.

52. Nichols, *Divine Fruitfulness*, 183.

"distance," "difference," and "otherness." Partly because of the strong influence of Speyr, whose visions are strongly characterized by the Trinitarian drama, Balthasar's Trinitarian theology too is quite dramatic. This characteristic can be one of its strengths. Rowan Williams, for example, affirms that Balthasar gives "at least three novel and immensely suggestive insights"[53] to the schema involving the Father, the Son, the Holy Spirit, and the world. First of all, his Trinitarian theology defines the otherness between the Father and the Son in a new way, which leads to the second contribution, namely, his analogizing Trinitarian difference and sexual differentiation.[54] The first and second contribution lead to the third one that Trinitarian difference is effectively made "the basis of all analogy, all identity in difference, so that there truly is a metaphysic, an account of reality as such, that emerges from doctrine."[55] In other words, Balthasar's notion of infinite distance and radical otherness within the Trinity opens a new way of understanding about us, human beings, in terms of the relationship with God.

However, unsurprisingly, some theologians pose a question exactly because of this strength. *How can he know all this?* Is he not *too vivid?* In fact, *does he have a right to be so vivid?* This is one of the central questions raised against Balthasar by one of his critics Karen Kilby. She says that the problem "lies not in what Balthasar *says* about how one should reflect on the Trinity but in how he in fact *does* it."[56] According to Kilby, Balthasar contradicts himself about his own insistence on what she calls "epistemological humility" or "epistemic humility." Kilby argues that even though he does make "gestures of epistemic humility" at some points, Balthasar taken as a whole, writes confidently and fluently like a "novelist who, with a particular vision of the climactic scene (the cross) as starting point, freely fills out background, adds character details, and constructs prior scenes."[57]

---

53. Williams, "Balthasar and the Trinity," 49.

54. We also have to clarify that Williams does *not* approve of Balthasar's view of sexual differentiation itself. Williams clearly states that "what makes his analysis tantalizing is a central unclarity about how far sexual differentiation really can be said to partake of the differentiation of the Trinitarian persons, a differentiation in which there is no unilateral and fixed pattern of priority or derivation but a simultaneous, reciprocal conditioning, a pattern of identity *in* the other without remainder." (Williams, "Afterword," 177.) We will discuss Balthasar's view of sexual differentiation in chapter 3 as far as it is related to his Mariology.

55. Williams, "Balthasar and the Trinity," 50.

56. Kilby, "Hans Urs von Balthasar on the Trinity," 214. Also for Kilby's more extensive examination of Balthasar's Trinitarian theology, see Kilby, *Balthasar*, 94–122.

57. Kilby, "Hans Urs von Balthasar on the Trinity," 218. Also see Kilby, *Balthasar*, 114.

Ultimately, Kilby's criticism of Balthasar is aimed at his alleged "presumption of a God's eye view."[58]

This critique leads to another central issue she raises against Balthasar, which is directly related to the topic of this book, namely, how Balthasar's theology could deepen our understanding of Christian suffering. As we have seen, in Balthasar's theology distance can paradoxically reveal closeness and abandonment can reveal love. As we repeatedly mention, even hell can be located within the Trinity. However, this kind of integration is exactly what Kilby finds problematic. Though she is well aware that Balthasar does not attribute suffering directly to the Trinity, she still accuses Balthasar of "fundamentally blurring the distinction between love and loss, joy and suffering."[59] (Interestingly, this accusation sounds similar to Balthasar's criticism of Moltmann.) Kilby argues that because of *this tendency* in Balthasar's theology suffering and loss are ultimately given "a positive valuation" and "eternalized," which could eventually threaten Christianity being "good news."[60]

It would be helpful here to note that Kilby's critique sounds similar to Johann Baptist Metz's criticism of the so-called "Suffering God." He critically discusses the overall tendency of the twentieth century theology, which (according to his summary) tries to see the Trinitarian motifs to offer an interpretation of the human history of suffering. He says,

> Does it not indeed belong to the "specifically Christian" concern with the theodicy-question to see suffering "raised up" into God's self? Do the theologians not discuss with great seriousness—from Barth to Jüngel, from Bonhoeffer to Moltmann, and in the realm of Catholic theology most of all in Hans Urs von Balthasar—the suffering God, suffering between God and God and suffering in God? Certainly they do.[61]

58. Kilby, *Balthasar*, 161–67.

59. Kilby, "Hans Urs von Balthasar on the Trinity," 220. Also see Kilby, *Balthasar*, 120.

60. Ibid., 120.

61. Metz, "Suffering from God," 286. Interestingly, despite his critique against Balthasar on this point, Metz also argues for the importance of "Holy Saturday Christology" apparently under Balthasar's influence. Metz writes, "If I can put it this way, in Christology we have lost the way between Good Friday and Easter Sunday. We have too much Easter Sunday Christology. I feel that the atmosphere of Holy Saturday has to be narrated within Christology itself. For a long time now not everybody has experienced Easter Sunday as the third day after Good Friday." (Schuster and Bochert-Kimmig, *Hope Against Hope*, 45.) For a substantial comparison and contrast between Balthasar and Metz as two different styles of apocalyptic theology, see O'Regan, *The Anatomy of Misremembering*, 424–66.

While admitting that he listens respectfully to such discussions of divine suffering, Metz himself is hesitant and critical of it. One of the reasons he raises is that the talk of a suffering God actually seems to underestimate the negativity of suffering. In his words,

> How is it that the talk of the suffering God is not in the end merely a *sublime redoubling* of human suffering and of human powerlessness? How is it that the talk of suffering in God, especially of suffering between God and God, does not lead to *an eternalisation* of suffering? Do not God and humanity here fall under the quasi-mythical *universalisation* of suffering, which finally also breaks the upswing of opposition to injustice? . . . I have asked myself again and again whether or not in this talk of a suffering God there may operate a secret *aestheticisation* of suffering. But suffering, which causes us to cry out or finally to be pitifully silent is never something lofty, it is nothing great or exalted. In its roots it is completely different from a strong, compassionate solidarity. It is not even a sign of love, but far more frighteningly a symptom of not being able to love any more.[62]

These words warn us not to make sense of the negativity of human suffering too hastily in the name of God and love. Kilby too seems to share a similar sensitivity concerning the matter. In the context of criticizing Moltmann, she comments that "the insistence that God suffers, especially when presented as something new and important, is in danger of being a cheap move."[63] In short, Metz and Kilby argue that blurring the distinction between suffering and joy (or love) leads to the failure to maintain the perfect divinity of God and to the failure to take the negativity of human suffering seriously. Their moral concerns are obvious, so worth considering in depth.

Probably Moltmann can be more easily accused of blurring the distinction between suffering and love than Balthasar, as he unabashedly attributes suffering directly to God and blurs the economic and immanent Trinity. As we discussed in the beginning of this chapter, Balthasar himself is critical of Moltmann on this point. However, we have to pause before we use the same kind of criticism that Balthasar makes of Moltmann against Balthasar himself. While Metz's critique might be merely due to his misreading of Balthasar (as can be seen in the somewhat violent way he lumps together Balthasar and Moltmann), Kilby seems to be well aware of their difference. Nevertheless, referring to the extremely nuanced passage from

---

62. Metz, "Suffering from God," 286. Italics added. Also, see Metz, "Suffering Unto God."

63. Kilby, "Evil and the Limits of Theology," 21.

Theo-Drama where Balthasar says "*there is something in God that can de-velop into suffering,*"[64] she affirms that he does speak about something in the Trinity which can develop into suffering, of a "supra-suffering," and that he tries to "root the Cross firmly in the immanent Trinity."[65] Here Kilby seems to be saying that Balthasar is actually even more guilty of blurring the distinction between suffering and bliss than Moltmann. The problem probably lies in how to interpret the sentence, "*There is something in God that can develop into suffering,*" or more specifically, whether or not we appreciate the very careful way Balthasar puts it. If we read this statement more or less as an affirmation of suffering in God, even though remotely, then we may end up criticizing Balthasar on this point as Kilby and Metz do.

What does Balthasar's careful and nuanced position about suffering and love have to do with the issue of suffering? Regarding this topic, Kilby states that Christian theology ought *neither* to construct theodicies, *nor* ignore the kinds of problem theodicies try to address.[66] In the last analysis, this book entirely shares this position of Kilby's regarding systematized theodicy, and we believe Balthasar's own position about theodicy is not so different from Kilby's.

In terms of recent efforts to examine Balthasar's theology, especially his thoughts on the Trinity, as an answer to the problem of suffering, we should briefly mention Jacob Friesenhahn. He presents Balthasar's Trinitarian theology as an answer to the problem of evil. His argument is that since God manifests his utmost solidarity with sinful humanity through his own suffering on the cross and in the descent into hell, the suffering of the whole humanity can be transformed and taken up into the life of perfect love that is the Trinity, so there is hope for those who suffer. He concludes by saying, "All human suffering and death, conformed by God's grace to the Paschal Mystery of Christ, has ultimate meaning as grounded in the Triune God through the Incarnate Son."[67] However, if this conclusion is the whole answer to the problem of suffering we gain by studying Balthasar's Trinitarian theology, perhaps we cannot help feeling a little disappointed. Even though he is perfectly aware that Balthasar does not affirm divine suffering and that Balthasar seeks to occupy the middle ground between the impassibility and passibility of God, Friesenhahn's conclusion rather ends up indirectly supporting Kilby's criticism, because in the end it would not be too different from what she calls the "cheap move."

64. Balthasar, *Theo-Drama* IV, 328. Italics added.

65. Kilby, *Balthasar*, 120–21.

66. Kilby, "Evil and the Limits of Theology," 13.

67. Friesenhahn, *The Trinity and Theodicy*, 173–74.

It is true that Balthasar repeatedly stresses that Christ's suffering on the cross and in hell has been the greatest of all sufferings (as can be seen in his discussion of the beatific vision, for example). He states that the cross is a greater tragedy than Auschwitz.[68] He even writes, "Jesus Christ is the heir of all the tragedy of the world, that of the Greeks as well as that of the Jews, that of the so-called unbelievers as well as that of the so-called believers."[69] However, we should neither hastily conclude that Balthasar simply "explains away" human sufferings by including them in Christ's suffering nor easily "explain away" Balthasar's answer to the problem of suffering as such. Although his sensitivity toward human suffering is revealed in most of his writings, he does not propose a clear-cut "answer" to the problem of suffering, although he apparently thinks that the idea that Christ suffered the greatest suffering out of divine love certainly could entail hope for those who suffer. Rather, it should be noted that he actually refuses to give such an "answer." To do so would lead to the failure to take the cross and the descent into hell with utmost seriousness as well as human suffering. Metz suggests that the right attitude towards human suffering could be "passionate re-questioning that arises out of suffering, a requestioning of God, full of highly charged expectation" (and Kilby's statement seems to be in agreement with this attitude).[70] One should never settle down for a consoling answer to explain the negativity of suffering, but rather should keep on asking, "why, God, why?" without turning away from him. At least we can say that Balthasar's complex theology seems to respect this point, because, in his theology, we can find the possibility of giving hope for those who suffer while carefully refusing to explain away human suffering even in the name of God's love.

Consider the word "abyss (*Abgrund*)" he often uses. After all, both God's love and human suffering are all described as an "abyss," which defies human comprehension and imagination. He speaks about "the abyss of absolute love which embraces all abysses."[71] He says "every pain can, as such, without being denied its quality as pain, participate in the blessedness of the triune love."[72] However, before we can participate in such eternal bliss, the abyss of divine love already will have put to shame "our all too easy talk of

---

68. Balthasar, *Credo*, 97.

69. Balthasar, *Explorations in Theology* III, 400. We will discuss this particular statement in detail when we examine Balthasar's theological engagement with tragedy in chapter 4.

70. Metz, "Suffering Unto God," 621.

71. Balthasar, *Elucidations*, 52.

72. Ibid., 52.

the incomprehensibility of God."[73] Shown here is another significance of the descent into hell. There is no word to describe the depth of God's love. Even God sank into "silence" of hell in order to reveal his boundless love. His love is revealed by "a deed which sinks down into total darkness," no longer even a "word."[74] Balthasar seems to be well aware that an easy, clear-cut explanation about suffering does not justice to the abyss of human suffering or to the even greater abyss of divine love.

All these points are related to the very topic of this entire book. For the time being, let it suffice to say that in the end we will attempt to deal with the question by connecting the in-betweenness of Holy Saturday and the in-betweenness of Christian existence, which is located between suffering and victory. What we would like to do in the end is to reflect on the meaning of suffering in Christian life by emphasizing the fundamentally "in-between" state of the Christian represented by Christ himself in hell on Holy Saturday, and thus attempt to affirm the victory that is hidden but already present without explaining away the concrete reality of suffering.

For this purpose, we have been discussing the Trinitarian framework of the descent into hell so far. Now, let us go on to discuss its christological aspect, for Christology is deeply grounded in the Trinity.

The Christological Significance of the Descent into Hell

We will discuss below the descent into hell as a christological event, or rather, present the descent into hell as the very center of Balthasar's Christology.[75] For this purpose, we will focus on the following principal themes: *kenosis*, mission, and obedience. We characterize the main characteristic of his Christology as *kenosis* after the Trinity, so we will focus on the two concepts most relevant to *kenosis*, namely, mission and obedience (also the central concepts for Christian discipleship). After examining these concepts which are relevant for the descent into hell, we present this event as the center of Balthasar's kenotic Christology. In hell, where the economic mission of the Son reaches the last destination, in other words, where no further obedience is possible, the divine love is revealed in the supreme form.

73. Ibid., 52.

74. Ibid., 52.

75. From this perspective, Aidan Nichols's concise summary of Balthasar's Christology and the descent into hell is helpful. See Balthasar, *Mysterium Paschale*, 1–10.

Kenosis as the Essence of Balthasar's Christology Grounded in the Trinity

In this chapter we have seen that Balthasar's understanding of the Trinity is most strongly characterized by the concept of *kenosis*. This is also true of his Christology, which is anchored in the Trinity.[76] His theology pursues to the fullest what is stated in this pre-Pauline *kenosis* hymn:

> Christ Jesus,
> who, though he was in the *form of God*,
> did not regard equality with God as something to be exploited,
> but *emptied himself*, taking the *form of a slave*,
> being born in human likeness.
> And being found in *human form*,
> he humbled himself and became *obedient to the point of death*
> —even death on a cross (Phil 2:5–8).[77]

In this hymn, the incarnation is described as self-emptying of God into a human form. What Balthasar's insight adds to it is that this *kenosis* of the incarnation is made possible by the *kenosis* within the immanent Trinity itself. In his own words, "The ultimate presupposition of the Kenosis is the 'selflessness' of the Persons (when considered as pure relationships) in the inner-Trinitarian life of love."[78] However, we have to note that Balthasar applies the *kenosis* to the immanent Trinity only *analogically*. While the *kenosis* of the incarnation is the assumption of human nature by the Son, the Trinitarian *kenosis* refers to the giving and receiving among the divine persons within the immanent Trinity. As we have seen above, Balthasar stresses "the Trinitarian 'recklessness' of divine love, which, in its self-giving, observed no limits and had no regard for itself."[79] We have to bear it in mind that what Balthasar wants to stress by speaking of the *kenosis* within the Trinity is that God is absolute love, first and foremost, rather than absolute power.[80]

Also, the concept of *kenosis* enables Balthasar to argue that "the Incarnation is ordered to the Cross as its goal,"[81] as the incarnation as described as a *kenosis* "takes on the quality of the Passion from the very beginning."[82]

76. Regarding Balthasar's treatment of *kenosis*, see Oakes, "'He Descended into Hell'"; Ward, "*Kenosis*."

77. Italics added.

78. Balthasar, *Mysterium Paschale*, 35.

79. Balthasar, *Theo-Drama* IV, 329.

80. Balthasar, *Mysterium Paschale*, 28.

81. Ibid., 22.

82. Ibid., 12. Regarding the concept of *kenosis*, which connects the incarnation and

In the last analysis, the economic *kenosis* started in the incarnation, which is grounded in the *kenosis* within the immanent Trinity, reaches its climax on the cross followed by the descent into hell. Balthasar links the Jesus' literal "obedience of a corpse"[83] in hell to the Son's absolute response or thanksgiving to the Father's eternal generation. We always have to remember that Balthasar grounds the economic missions within the processions in the immanent Trinity. It is also important that he does not say that the Son's obedience in the economic mission *is identical with* the Son's absolute response to the Father within the immanent Trinity. As we saw above, Balthasar's nuanced and subtle treatment of the relationship between the immanent and economic Trinity must always be kept in mind. The immanent relationship between the Father and the Son united in the Holy Spirit grounds the Son's economic mission in the world. Since the immanent relationship can be characterized by its inter-personal kenotic love, the Son's mission in the world is also kenotic.

Working as a mediator between the Father and the world, everything the Son does is directed towards both the Father and humankind. By obeying the Father out of love, the Son loves and saves humankind out of love. There can be no conflict between the Son's love for the Father and love for the world, because the Father loves the world as Creator in the first place. The Father and the Son, united in the Holy Spirit, share the one and same will to save humankind. In order to complete the salvific work, the Son must experience the consequences of humankind's rejection of God's love, which is the extremity of creation's freedom, namely hell.

This is a rough sketch of Christ's descent into hell as a christological event which is strongly characterized by *kenosis*. In order to examine further how this event should be regarded as the center of Balthasar's kenotic Christology, we will see the two other significant concepts he relates to *kenosis*: mission and obedience.

Mission

In the third volume of *Theo-Drama*, Balthasar begins his Trinitarian theology by reflecting on the person of Jesus Christ, and he places his consciousness of *mission* at the very center of his existence. Balthasar identifies Jesus Christ with his mission. In other words, Jesus Christ *is* his mission itself. This statement underlies Balthasar's Christology, and by using the concept of mission Balthasar smoothly links Christology and the Trinity. To put it

---

the cross, especially see 12–36.

83. Ibid., 174.

more specifically, by using the concept of mission, Balthasar smoothly integrates the economic and immanent Trinity, or Christology and the Trinity, or even Christology and anthropology.

Balthasar develops the concept of mission (the "sending" and "coming" of the Son) on the basis of the New Testament, throughout which Jesus is portrayed as the eternal Son sent into the world by the Father. It is the Gospel of John which speaks the most frequently of the mission of the Son, so Balthasar's position is strongly Johannine in a sense, but nevertheless the idea is supported by the Synoptic Gospels and the Pauline letters as well.[84] As Balthasar says, "The Johannine *missio* Christology is only the logical development of implications already present in the Synoptics, which testify to a unique sense of mission on the part of Jesus."[85]

According to Balthasar, being a "person" is equal to being given a mission by God. This connection between person and mission can also be applied to the existence of Jesus, but there is a fundamental difference between him and other human beings. We ordinary human beings (sinners) may have a mission, but we have to go through a process in order to accept it. We can never be completely identified with our mission, while Jesus is fully his mission itself at all times. In Balthasar's own words, "We only receive our mission on the basis of our coming to faith, whereas Jesus always has and *is* his mission."[86]

By placing Jesus' mission-consciousness at the center of his self-consciousness, Balthasar smoothly integrates the immanent Trinity into Jesus' human life on earth, since his mission and person are identified as the Son eternally proceeding from the Father. As Balthasar points out, the concept of mission has two elements.[87] One is the relationship to the One who sent (the Father), and the other is the temporal and developmental aspect of a mission which must be implemented by the human energies of Jesus. For example, the latter point is related to the temptations (not only the temptation by Satan in the desert but also the temptation on the Mount of Olives as well as others which may have happened) and prayers of Jesus. Why does the Son of God have to go through temptations? The Son of God is plunged into this world, which offers him other possible ways to carry out his mission, but he rejects them all. Jesus sees the Father's presence behind his

---

84. For example, the verses in the New Testament Balthasar refers to are as follows: Mark 1:38; Matt 10:40; Luke 4:43, 9:48; John 5:43, 8:42, 13:16, 16:28; Gal 4:4; Rom 8:3–4. See Balthasar, *Theo-Drama* III, 150–54.

85. Balthasar, *Theo-Drama* III, 154.

86. Ibid., 171.

87. Ibid., 168.

mission, but it is not the Father but the mission itself that coincides with the freedom of Jesus as the Son. Citing from Matt 26:53–54 ("Do you think that I cannot appeal to my Father, and he will at once send me more than twelve legions of angels? But how then would the scriptures be fulfilled, which say it must happen in this way?"), Balthasar writes, "It is as if the mission's central position indicates the 'economic' revelation of a decision freely made in concert by the whole Trinity."[88] Why does the Son of God have to pray? The One who is sent must pray to the One who sends, because the mission is not open to the former in its entirety. The Son has to carry it out step by step by following the Father's instructions and it is in the Holy Spirit that he does so.

The divine consciousness and the human consciousness coincide in Jesus Christ in his entire awareness of his mission given by the Father. By placing his mission-consciousness at the center of his self-consciousness, we can solve the question of the relation between his human consciousness and divine consciousness. As we completely identify the person of Jesus with his mission, we can avoid turning Jesus into a docetic super-historical being or a mythical chimera of two distinctive natures. As Balthasar says,

> The task given him by the Father, that is, that of expressing God's Fatherhood through his entire being, through his life and death in and for the world, totally occupies his self-consciousness and fills it to the very brim. He sees himself so totally as "coming from the Father" to men, as "making known" the Father, as the "Word from the Father," that there is neither room nor time for any detached reflection of the "Who am I?" kind.[89]

Jesus' human consciousness is entirely aware of his divine self in relation to the Father. His mission, which is "to reconcile the whole world with God,"[90] is universal and has no temporal beginning. Such a mission is beyond any human capacity and "cannot be a secondary and accidental development of a human consciousness."[91] On the other hand, we should also remember that it is *only within the limits* of his mission that Jesus' divine consciousness and human consciousness coincide. This limitation enables us to see that Jesus' awareness of his filial relationship with the Father is not any innate theoretical knowledge but something progressively discovered in practice.

88. Ibid., 168.
89. Ibid., 172.
90. Ibid., 166.
91. Ibid., 166.

This point brings us to the question of Jesus' self-knowledge, but before we discuss the topic further, let us refer to the role of the Holy Spirit. Balthasar's theory of "Trinitarian inversion"[92] is worth noting here. His mission Christology allows us to pay great attention to the role of the Spirit. This theory of "Trinitarian inversion" is important not only because it emphasizes that the Son of God really took on human nature but also it is related to one of the central concepts in Balthasar's theology, namely, the obedience of the incarnate Son to the Father. In the eternal Trinitarian life, the Spirit proceeds from the Father and the Son. However, throughout the Son's life on earth, a certain "inversion" of the divine processions occurs, and the Spirit works as a guide *in* the Son as well as a "rule" *over* him. For example, Balthasar starts discussing this point by very strict reading of the Apostles' Creed, which states "He was conceived *by the power of the Holy Spirit* and born of the Virgin Mary."[93] Here the active role is taken by the Holy Spirit, and the Son is portrayed as passive. Therefore, Balthasar argues that "the Son's obedience does not come after an incarnation actively brought about by him: rather, his soteriological obedience starts with the Incarnation itself."[94] Certainly the Son's "passive" obedience is always a form of "action" freely chosen by him. Nevertheless, we can see that already in the incarnation process that the Son "becomes in one respect a product of the Spirit who brings him forth *ex Maria Virgine*, although within the Trinity itself the Spirit is the product of the united spiration of Father and Son."[95] Hence, it is called "inversion."

Moreover, as Balthasar argues, without the Holy Spirit working between the Father and the Son as "the objective witness to their difference-in-unity or unity-in-difference,"[96] the Son's obedience would not be possible. The difference between the Father and the Son means that while the Father is the one that sends the Son into the world, the Son is the one that chooses to carry out the mission at all costs. Therefore, the Holy Spirit has to operate between them to keep their unity. Throughout the Son's life on earth, the Spirit works "in" the Son to guide him to be aware of his mission step by step in order to complete it, working as the rule of the Father "over" him at the same time. For example, in the midst of the passion, it is the Spirit that presents the suffering Son with the Father's will, which seems rigid and

92. Ibid., 183–91.

93. *Catechism of the Catholic Church*, the Credo Chart. (Italics added.)

94. Balthasar, *Theo-Drama* III, 184. Also see Balthasar, *The Threefold Garland*, 27–34; *Theo-Logic* III, 48–51, 171–76.

95. Balthasar, *Theo-Drama* III, 186.

96. Ibid., 187.

pitiless. It is as if the Spirit is saying, "This is what you have wanted from all eternity; this is what, from all eternity, we have determined!"[97] Balthasar sees the presence of the Spirit within the incarnate Son as the economic form of the *filioque* that the Spirit proceeds from the Father and the Son. If we accept the *filioque*, then we have to conclude that there must be "a priori obedience" on the side of the eternal Son, which is determined within the immanent Trinity, prior to the incarnation. After all, what Balthasar calls the "inversion" is "ultimately only the projection of the immanent Trinity onto the 'economic' plane, whereby the Son's 'correspondence' to the Father is articulated as 'obedience.'"[98] Ultimately, it is the eternal love of the Son to the Father within the immanent Trinity that the Son's human obedience reveals.

After all these discussions, Balthasar goes back to the question of Jesus' knowledge.[99] On the one hand, there is the position taken by patristic and scholastic theologians which insists on the total omniscience of Jesus from his conception, and on the other hand the modern position which limits his knowledge to that of a prophet. Balthasar seeks a middle way between the opposing extremes. He not only affirms that the Son of God really took on human nature but also states that even the limitations of the human nature are the vehicles through which the Son of God reveals both the true humanity and divinity. Balthasar's whole Christology is permeated by the idea that Christ's divinity is revealed *exactly in* his humanity.[100] Again, Balthasar's argument is extremely Johannine. Balthasar points out that John emphasizes Jesus' obedience as well as his supramundane knowledge and that, because of this obedience, Jesus "laid up" the knowledge he could have had for the reasons of the economy of salvation. As Balthasar concisely summarizes, "He knows just as much and just as little as is necessary so that he can carry out his unique, all-embracing mission of world atonement."[101] Jesus knows of his unique mission as the redeemer of the world, who is portrayed as the Suffering Servant in the Book of Isaiah. Also, he knows that God's saving plan will triumph through him, whatever happens during the process. However, he is completely ignorant of "the hour" ("But about that day or hour no one knows, neither the angels in heaven, nor the Son, but only the Father"

---

97. Ibid., 188.

98. Ibid., 191.

99. Ibid., 191–97. Also see Balthasar, *You Crown the Year with Your Goodness*, 315–19.

100. Balthasar owes this idea to Maximus the Confessor. For his engagement with the patristic author, see Balthasar, *Cosmic Liturgy*.

101. Balthasar, *You Crown the Year with Your Goodness*, 318–19.

[Mark 13:32]), even though from the beginning Jesus is entirely aware that his whole life directs towards this coming "hour." Balthasar emphasizes this point and insists that we should take these words literally (unlike the scholastic position that Jesus merely *pretended* not to know). The Son of God is also God, so there is no doubt that he is omniscient. Therefore, his genuine ignorance is nothing but the result of his wish to become fully human. He could have known everything, but he chose not to know some things. It is only out of love for the world that the Son deposits his own divine attributes with the Father in heaven.

This interpretation is supported by the *kenosis* hymn in Philippians 2:6–8 we have seen above. This element of ignorance or unknowing of the incarnate Son is crucial and it is repeatedly stressed when Balthasar discusses the passion.[102] It is especially relevant for our discussion of suffering in Christian discipleship that Balthasar's so-called "high" Christology enables us to take seriously the authenticity and intensity of the extremely negative human experiences that the Son of God went through, namely, the suffering, unknowing, and godforsakenness on the cross and in the descent into hell. Interestingly, Balthasar refers to Christian mystical experience of God to gain the idea of the scope of Jesus' human knowledge and experience of God as follows: "The equally great variations found in Christian mystical experience of God—ranging from moments of illumination to the constrictions of dryness and forsakenness—can give us an inkling of the possible variety of forms of knowledge experienced by the earthly Jesus."[103]

Christ's full divinity is expressed in his full humanity. This thesis means that his divinity is paradoxically revealed in the very fact that Jesus suffered, died, and descended into hell as (and probably, more than) a finite human being. In Balthasar's own words, "The *paradox* must be allowed to stand: in the undiminished humanity of Jesus, the whole power and glory of God are made present to us."[104]

The Son's Obedience—the Economic Expression of the Eternal Love within the Immanent Trinity

Christ's full divinity is expressed in his full humanity. We need to consider this point by examining further the concept of obedience, the recurring theme in Balthasar's theology. The obedience of Jesus Christ is the supreme

---

102. In particular, Pitstick critically deals with this problem in detail. See Pitstick, *Light in Darkness*, 158–90.

103. Balthasar, *Theo-Drama* III, 197.

104. Balthasar, *Mysterium Paschale*, 33.

manifestation of his divinity.[105] Obedience (*Gehorsam*) permeates Jesus' whole life from the incarnation to the descent into hell. This idea is supported by the *kenosis* hymn as well as the whole narrative of the Gospel of John, which, as we have seen, supports the mission Christology. It is by the kenotic obedience of Jesus Christ that the disobedience of the whole creation is redeemed.

However, it should be noted that there can be no "obedience" within the Trinity in the sense of human obedience in the first place. The three divine persons are one, and the Son is equal to the Father, so they have only one divine will. On the other hand, the creation owes their being to the Creator forever, so human obedience is basically a result of necessary dependence on God. Nevertheless, since the incarnate Son of God is obedient, as testified by the Scripture, there must be a way in which obedience is not foreign to God. The concept of obedience is closely linked with the mission Christology, for the Son's mission to reconcile the world with God requires total obedience from him. Therefore, as his mission is the appearance in this world of his eternal procession from the Father, obedience can be considered as expressing the eternal love within the Trinity, which, as we have stressed, is most strongly characterized by *kenosis*.

In the last analysis, for Balthasar, obedience "is the revelation in human form of the eternal love of the divine Son for his eternal Father, who has eternally begotten him out of love."[106] In other words, the Son's eternal love for the Father is expressed as human obedience, in which the Son is conceived by the Holy Spirit in Virgin Mary and lives as a fully human being until the cross and the descent into hell. This insight is supported by the following words in John 14:31, for example: "I do as the Father has commanded me, so that the world may know that I love the Father." Here is *analogical* obedience. There is a primordial "obedience" within the immanent Trinity, which is explained as the filial way in which the Son responds to the Father, who eternally begets him. This archetype grounds the human obedience of the incarnate Son of God. Human obedience is basically rooted in the necessity on the side of the creation, who is dependent on the Creator, but when this concept is applied to God, it expresses perfectly self-less love without any hint of subordination. In other words, the concept of obedience, which has the element of subordination and necessity when described as a human experience, gains the positive element of freedom, when applied to God.

---

105. Further, for a discussion of Christ's obedience as well as the Christian's obedience based on the former, see Balthasar, *New Elucidations*, 228–55.

106. Balthasar, *First Glance at Adrienne von Speyr*, 59.

In his use of the word "obedience," Balthasar seems to be concretely working out St. Thomas Aquinas's analogical method of applying words to God.[107] As St. Thomas says, we cannot apply concepts or names to God either purely univocally or equivocally. On the one hand, there is a great dissimilarity between the Creator and the creation, as can be shown in the difference between the creation's ontological dependence on the Creator and the perfect freedom of God. On the other hand, we have to grant some kind of similarity between the two, so that "obedience" can actually be a form of expression of God's eternal love. As we will see later, Jesus Christ is called the concrete "analogy of being *(analogia entis)*." He is both "the unmediated unity of the divine and the human natures within the simplicity of his Person" and "the representation of the infinite distance between God and creature, exponentially raised and abysmally ruptured by sin."[108] We should also note that this double significance of Christ is possible only because of God being Triune, more specifically, because of the infinite distance between the Father and the Son, which encompasses the finite distance between God and the world. After all, "Christ's essence is itself Trinitarian."[109] In other words, the real analogy between God and the world is based on the eternal Trinitarian dissimilarity between the Father and the Son.

This framework enables Balthasar to discuss the possibility of *analogous* suffering in the divine nature.[110] In fact, the cross can be seen even as the highest revelation of the Father's *pathē* in the face of humanity's sinfulness. Balthasar writes, "We can even say that, in the cry of dereliction on the Cross, Jesus reveals how God is forsaken by sinners. Jesus' whole existence, including the aspect that the Greeks found so difficult, his *pathē*, is in the service of his proclamation of God."[111] As we have seen above, the Son's cry of dereliction should not be understood merely as a cry of despair or protest but an expression of obedience. Jesus is really abandoned by the Father, but only for the sake of his love for the Father and the creation. We should not think that there is any bitter resentment toward God in Jesus' cry of dereliction. The Son's love for the Father is complete and eternal. We should not think either that God "punishes" Jesus instead of the sinner or that Jesus feels "damned" by God. Rather, out of obedient love for the Father, the Son

107. Thomas Aquinas, *Summa Theologiae*, I, q.13, a.5.

108. Balthasar, *The Grain of Wheat*, 61–62.

109. Ibid., 62.

110. For example, see O'Hanlon, *The Immutability of God in the Theology of Hans Urs von Balthasar*, 44–46.

111. Balthasar, *Theo-Drama III*, 225. Also, this idea seems to be expressed in the beautiful poem "Twelfth Station" in Balthasar, *The Way of the Cross*, 26.

chooses to experience fully what the sinner deserves, namely, *separation from God*, which finally culminates in hell of godforsakeness.

Furthermore, as Balthasar repeatedly argues, because his whole life is unity with the Father, the Son suffers godforsakeness more profoundly than any other human being. Thus, this experience of godforsakeness is a result of the Son's complete obedience to the Father, expressed as complete solidarity with the sinner. This obedience is totally Trinitarian and engaging the three divine persons. As we have seen in our discussion of the Trinitarian inversion, the Son's obedience is directed to the Father but lived out in the Holy Spirit. In Balthasar's words, "in all 'economic' situations, there is no question of an 'I-thou' relationship between Son and Spirit. *The Son's only 'thou' is the Father; and he is this 'thou' in the Spirit.*"[112]

Further, as we will see in chapter 3, the Son's obedience not only is the "interpretation" of the Trinity's life of love but also the "epitome" of the creation's proper attitude towards God, especially of the church's proper attitude as his Body and Bride.[113] As Christ's obedience is the model and source of the obedience of the church, which begins with Virgin Mary's "Yes" to the annunciation, all of us are invited to follow his footsteps of obedience as his creation. We catch a glimpse of the real meaning of "personhood" in the mission of Christ, and this mission shows us that true freedom is attained in freely abandoning it. As Balthasar says, the Christian's required identification with their Christian mission "stands in an analogy to the identity that characterizes Jesus Christ. Thus, in the very discipleship in which the Christian 'loses his soul,' he can attain his true identity."[114]

Furthermore, this christological analogy of being, which is grounded in the Trinity and most explicitly expressed in his obedience on earth, helps us to see the way we can be included "in Christ." After all, Jesus Christ's is "the sum total of the world's reality," who embraces all that is possible in this world, from utmost bliss to Hell of godforsakenness.[115] Eventually, we might be able to found hope in Christ in the midst of suffering, because he is the one who knows all possible sufferings and griefs in the world. This is because no suffering has been as great as his suffering on the cross and in the descent into hell. As Balthasar says,

> we cannot know how much of humanity's endless suffering—
> the countless Auschwitz and Gulag Archipelagoes—has a direct

112. Balthasar, *Theo-Logic III*, 174. Italics added.

113. Balthasar, *First Glance at Adrienne von Speyr*, 59.

114. Balthasar, *Theo-Drama III*, 162. The relevant passages from the Scripture are Matt 16:25, Mark 8:35, and Luke 9:24.

115. Balthasar, *The Grain of Wheat*, 56.

relation to the Lord's expiatory suffering; if the latter were not in the background one would wonder how God could bear to behold it.[116]

The Descent into Hell as the Center of Kenotic Christology

So far we have examined the three principal themes in Balthasar's Christology (*kenosis*, mission, and obedience), which center around the cross and the descent into hell. Now we will put them together to describe the descent into hell as the center of his Christology. In short, it is in the descent into hell that the economic mission of the Son reaches its final point and his kenotic obedience reaches its climax.

We have seen above that Balthasar's Trinitarian framework explains that the Son's descent into hell is both possible and inevitable. The salvation of humankind planned by all the three persons of the Trinity would not be complete without the Son's entrance into hell. Since Jesus was fully human, it was only natural that he descended in hell (understood as *Sheol*, the abode of the dead[117]) after he died. Traditionally, this has been the first meaning of the doctrine of Christ's descent into hell; Jesus was really dead.[118] In his account of the descent, Balthasar too starts with this point. The crucified incarnate Son of God was as dead just as any human being. Balthasar expresses it as follows: "In the same way that, upon earth, he was in solidarity with the living, so, in the tomb, *he is in solidarity with the dead*."[119] The word "solidarity" here sounds paradoxical. Death is a state where there is no living communication, so this "solidarity" means that Jesus was "solitary like, and with, the others."[120] Balthasar describes death as "a situation which signifies in the first place the abandonment of all spontaneous activity and so a *passivity*, a state in which, perhaps, the vital activity now brought to its end is mysteriously summed up."[121] Jesus experienced death as a "passivity," just as any human being does. Therefore, Balthasar rejects all kinds of "activities" including Jesus' combat with the Devil in hell, which was traditionally ascribed to him. Holy Saturday is first and foremost characterized by this "passivity" of Christ, which is in contrast with his "active" self-surrender on

116. Balthasar, *Does Jesus Know Us—Do We Know Him?*, 38.

117. We will focus on the meaning of hell in chapter 2.

118. See *Catechism of the Catholic Church*, §632 and 636.

119. Balthasar, *Mysterium Paschale*, 148–49. Italics added.

120. Ibid., 165.

121. Ibid., 148. Italics added.

Good Friday. In other words, the descent into hell is a natural consequence of the incarnation. Christ had to go down to hell not because the cross was insufficient but because he assumed all the defects of a human being.[122] Since the penalty of sin was not only the death of the body but also the soul's descent into hell, the incarnate Son of God too had to descend into hell after death.[123] Therefore, hell is the last destination of the Son's economic mission in this rather literal sense.

However, not only did the Son experience death in the usual sense but also he went through "the second death" or "a vision of death (*visio mortis*).[124] Here Balthasar is following the insight of Nicholas of Cusa, who writes,

> The vision, *visio*, of death by the mode of immediate experience, *via cognoscentiae*, is the most complete punishment possible. And since the death of Christ was complete, since through his own experience he saw the death which he had freely chosen to undergo, the soul of Christ went down into the underworld, *ad inferna*, where the vision of death is . . . Christ's suffering, the greatest one could conceive, was like that of the damned who cannot be damned anymore . . . He alone through such a death entered into glory. He wanted to experience the *poena sensus* like the damned in Hell for the glorifying of his Father, and so as to show that one should obey the Father even to the utmost torture.[125]

122. Balthasar admits following Augustine and Thomas Aquinas on this point. See Balthasar, *Mysterium Paschale*, 164.

123. In relation to this point, we have to note that Balthasar's is an anthropology of "unity-in-duality" according to which corporeal and spiritual perception are inextricably intertwined with one another. In other words, his is a non-dualistic anthropology according to which the human being is understood as being fundamentally united in body and soul. This idea lies at the core of Balthasar's thanatology as well as his interpretation of the descent into hell. For him, it is not just the body that suffers death but the body-soul complex in its totality. Death is characterized by the loss of spiritual-corporeal integrity and consequently the loss of all relationality, rather than a simple "separation" of body and soul. That is why Balthasar criticizes the traditional, rather dualistic image of Christ's descent into hell as his soul seems "too active" or rather "too alive" (as can be seen in the image of his combat in hell with Satan) as if it were an entity completely separated from the dead body in the tomb. We will come back to this point again in the last chapter when we discuss the "bodiliness" of the Eucharist and the question of the body on Holy Saturday.

124. Balthasar, *Mysterium Paschale*, 50–52, 168–74.

125. Nicholas of Cusa, *Excitationes* 10, 659. Quoted by Balthasar in *Mysterium Paschale*, 170–71.

Jesus is not only truly human but also truly divine as the Son of God, so he goes through something only he can endure. The "vision of death" is beyond what any other human being can endure. In this "second death," the Son encounters "sin as such," or "sin in itself,"[126] which is a concept indebted to Speyr. It is "sheer sin as such, no longer sin as attaching to a particular human being, sin incarnate in living existences, but abstracted from that individuation, *contemplated in its bare reality as such* (for sin *is* a reality!)"[127] Balthasar goes on to say "the object of the *visio mortis* can only be the pure substantiality of 'Hell' which is 'sin in itself.'"[128] Thus, Balthasar integrates the insight of Nicholas of Cusa with Speyr's visions.

In this rather roundabout way, the Son's encounter of "sin as such" in *Sheol* becomes Balthasar's version of Christ's "triumphant" descent into hell. This vision of "sin as such" that Christ experiences is actually nothing other than a vision of his own triumph. On the cross, Jesus Christ bears the world's sin. The sin is separated from humankind and laid upon Christ on the cross, and through his death he takes it away from the world. Thus, the "sin as such" that he "contemplates" passively in the "second death" is exactly "the product of the active suffering of the Cross,"[129] hence a sign of his triumph. However, he does not yet *subjectively* recognize this "vision of death" as triumphant. There is no comfort for him yet. He still has to *wait* for the resurrection to recognize his triumph subjectively to the fullest. In chapter 2, by referring to the dark night of the soul, we will discuss this profound mixture of objective victory and subjective suffering, and eventually in chapter 4 we will explore its significance for the issue of Christian suffering. Here let us note the significance of Christ's *waiting* in hell for the victory the objective proof of which is already there in front of him.

Further, it is this "sin as such" that Balthasar and Speyr regard as the "substance of hell." Here we have to note that they are interpreting the following verse in 2 Corinthians in an almost literal sense: "For our sake *he [God] made him [Christ] to be sin who knew no sin*, so that in him we might become the righteousness of God." (2 Cor 5:21).[130] Putting this idea and the *kenosis* hymn together, we could say that the Son became *obedient to the point of becoming sin*. Therefore, Balthasar says, "Hell is a *product* of the Redemption, a product which henceforth must be 'contemplated' in its own

---

126. Balthasar, *Mysterium Paschale*, 172–74. We will discuss this concept in chapter 2.

127. Ibid., 173. Italics added.

128. Ibid., 173.

129. Ibid., 173.

130. Italics added.

'for itself' by the Redeemer, so as to become, in its state of sheer reprobation that which exists 'for him'; that over which, in his Resurrection, he receives the power and the keys."[131]

Thus, we can see the descent into hell is not only the center of Balthasar's Christology but also the very center of his soteriology. Balthasar quotes Irenaeus's principle that "only what has been endured is healed and saved," and uses it as his own grounding principle.[132] The very "passive" presence of Christ in hell is salvific, for the presence of Christ, who is also "the Form of God," can shape the formless chaos of hell into a new order. Speyr describes the mass of sin in hell as "formless."[133] The image of the form of God in the midst of formless sin is metaphorically important, because for Balthasar and Speyr hell is "the second chaos," which is "a chaos of sins, a kind of reflection of the chaos at the beginning of Creation."[134] Therefore, it makes perfect sense that the Son in the economic mission descends into hell so that he can save humankind and re-form the creation. In *the Heart of the World*, his early work, Balthasar poetically expresses this idea:

> The magic of Holy Saturday. The chaotic fountain remains directionless. Could this be the residue of the Son's love which, poured out to the last when every vessel cracked and the old world perished, is now making a path for itself to the Father through glooms of nought? . . . Is it a protoplasm producing itself in the beginning, the first seed of the New Heaven and the New Earth?[135]

We have to pause to consider further the full significance of the concept of the second chaos. Balthasar and Speyr describe the hell into which Christ descended and where he waited for victory in a subjective sense as the chaos similar to the beginning of the creation. It means, for them, it is in hell that the new creation started. Therefore, as Speyr reminds us, it is not from the cross but from hell the Son is resurrected. Hell is the starting point of the Son's glorious resurrection. As a result of the Son's descent into hell, a way is paved towards heaven. Purgatory too comes into being. Now, *Sheol*, the realm of the dead, makes a transition into hell in the New Testament

---

131. Balthasar, *Mysterium Paschale*, 174.

132. Ibid., 165. Quoting from Irenaeus, *Adversus Haereses*, III. 23, 2.

133. See Balthasar, "Adrienne von Speyr über das Geheimnis des Karsamstags," 34.

134. Speyr, *Kreuz und Hölle* I, 175: "das ein Chaos der Sünde ist, ist wie ein Spiegelbild zum Chaos bei Schöpfungsbeginn."

135. Balthasar, *Heart of the World*, 152.

sense (*Gehenna*, hell for the damned). Therefore, for Balthasar and Speyr, hell, purgatory, and heaven are all christological concepts.[136]

The emphasis on hell as the second chaos and as the starting point of the new creation is significant for our stance concerning Balthasar's interpretation of Christ's descent into hell, because, in this way, we can see that hell represents "the turning point of the old and new Eons." Hell was not only the last destination of the Son's economic mission but also the starting point of the new creation. Holy Saturday is the day Christ the Savior himself went through this transition from the old to the new aeon. This is why the aspect of waiting is significant. This point eventually enables us to connect Christ's waiting in hell to the long "waiting" of the Christian in this world. Balthasar clearly affirms this point:

> When does the old change into the new? We must recall one of the things Paul said that we cited earlier: "Therefore if anyone is in Christ, he is a new creation; the old has gone, the new has come! (2 Cor 5:17) The turning point lies in Christ, or, more exactly, in the drama of the Paschal transition from Good Friday to Easter Sunday. Christians exist in this event.[137]

We have already suggested the way Christ's own obedience in following his mission shows the perfect role model for Christian discipleship, but now we start to see that the Christian's "life in transition" between the old and new aeon itself has already been assumed by Christ himself. (We will discuss this point further in chapter 4.)

Lastly, how is all this related to *kenosis*? Hell, where the obedience of the Son is described as the "obedience of the corpse," is the point where no further obedience is possible. Therefore, the descent into hell is the climax of the Son's economic kenosis. The Son identified himself with the sinner to such an extreme point, in other words, the point of becoming sin. This is all because of the economic mission to save humankind out of love. Further, as the economic mission is grounded in the immanent Trinity, we can conclude that the passive, obedient, disfigured Christ in hell reveals what the Triune God really is in himself: kenotic love. In Balthasar's words, "God's splendor . . . reveals and authenticates itself definitively precisely in its own apparent antithesis (in the *kenosis* of the descent into hell) as love selflessly serving out of love."[138]

---

136. We will discuss this point in chapter 2.

137. Balthasar, *Explorations in Theology* IV, 463.

138. Balthasar, *My Work*, 81.

The Importance of "Analogy" in Balthasar's Theology

On the one hand, the appealing points of his Christology (as well as his entire theology) are not difficult to see. Balthasar presents Jesus Christ on Holy Saturday as the embodiment of the divine, kenotic love. As his readers often admit, it is all very vivid and powerful.

Donald MacKinnon, for example, hugely appreciates his Christology as "one of the profoundest contributions to Christology made by any theologian since the second world war."[139] By referring to John 3:16 ("God so loved the world that he gave his only Son"), he commends Balthasar as one of "those very few theologians who have devoted superlative scholarship and talent to constrain their readers to attend to the height and to the depth of that love."[140] He also reads Balthasar as a theologian who considers the horrors of Holocaust with utmost seriousness, even though his sensitivity to evil and human suffering is not overtly expressed in his writings. In MacKinnon's own words,

> In the pages of his work with which we are here concerned [*Theo-drama*] there is comparatively little that treats directly of these horrors; but the nervous tension of the whole argument bears witness to the author's *passionate concern to present the engagement of God with his world in a way that refuses to turn aside from the overwhelming, pervasive reality of evil.* It is not that Balthasar indulges in any facile cult of pessimism; for one thing he is too well schooled in the great traditions of European literature for such triviality. It is rather that he insists on a vision that can only be won through the most strenuous acknowledgement of the cost of human redemption.[141]

MacKinnon is not the only one that senses Balthasar's sensitivity to the overwhelming reality of evil as well as his "passionate concern to present the engagement of God with his world." While admitting he feels somewhat puzzled by Balthasar's (and von Speyr's) account of the descent into hell, John Saward also recognizes its theological and apologetical importance. He writes,

> Hell is an exact description of the life on earth of many human beings today. . .There is nowhere God has not been, no depth of Godforsakenness which he has not explored in person, no

---

139. MacKinnon, "Some Reflections on Hans Urs von Balthasar's Christology," 173.

140. Ibid., 173.

141. Ibid., 165. Italics added.

darkness into which he has not poured light. However deep we may feel we have descended, God made man has descended more deeply.[142]

In other words, it is implied that Balthasar's account of Holy Saturday has significant implications for the problem of evil and suffering, because it explains that God himself descended into hell of godforsakeness. There is no place at all where God's love and power does not reach. Aidan Nichols concisely summarizes this point, "For Balthasar, the descent 'solves' the problem of theodicy, by showing us the conditions on which God accepted our foreknown abuse of freedom; namely, his own plan to take to himself our self-damnation in Hell."[143]

On the other hand, this strength in his theology can cause uneasiness among his critics. For example, Pitstick, among many other things, is extremely critical of the way that the image of divine glory is "perverted in the image of mankind's sins."[144] Pitstick's main concern is expressed as follows: "It [the traditional doctrine of the ("triumphant") descent] is essential to preserving and preaching the full truth of Christ and His redeeming work on our behalf—and this also specifically in the oh-so-mature and demythologized contemporary age."[145] Apparently, for Pitstick, Balthasar's theology is categorized as "tragic Christianity," and "it would be the worst betrayal of this age . . . to offer it elaborate theological platitudes suggesting its wounds are its life, thereby remaking God in its image."[146] This perspective is more or less shared by Kilby. In particular, she criticizes the way Balthasar "moves us towards a high perspective where resolution begins to seem possible: sin and suffering find a place, and can be made sense of, in the context of the eternal distance between Father and Son."[147] Even if we leave aside the question of whether it is actually a bad thing that "resolution begins to seem possible," Kilby's accusation that Balthasar has the tendency to take a "high" perspective (in other words, an overarching perspective) must be seriously considered.

Perhaps it would be helpful to note here that the criticisms expressed by Pitstick and Kilby are partly reminiscent of Karl Rahner's criticism of Balthasar. When asked by an interviewer to respond to the criticism that his own Christology lacked a sufficient *theologia crucis*, (which is an accusation

142. Saward, *The Mysteries of March*, 132.

143. Nichols, "Introduction," 7.

144. Pitstick, *Light in Darkness*, 348.

145. Ibid., 347.

146. Ibid., 347.

147. Kilby, *Balthasar*, 167.

famously made by Balthasar against Rahner),[148] Rahner said, "there is a modern tendency . . . to develop a theology of the death of God that, in the last analysis, seems to me to be gnostic. One can find this in Hans Urs von Balthasar and in Adrienn von Speyr."[149] Then, after critically referring to Moltmann and the Patripassianism found in others as well, he said,

> first of all: what do we know then so precisely about God? And second, I would ask: What use would that be to me as consolation in the true sense of the word? . . .Perhaps it is possible to be an orthodox Nestorian or an orthodox Monophysite. If this were the case, then I would prefer to be an orthodox Nestorian.[150]

What Rahner means here is that he himself values the distinction between the two natures in Christ so as not to threaten the impassibility of God or to deprive the inner-Trinitarian life of its mystery, but a theology of the cross seems to overstress the kenotic meaning of the cross and thus claims to *know too much* about the inner life of God. We have to note that this criticism is also closely connected to the difference between Rahner and Balthasar concerning their treatments of the immanent and economic Trinity, which we have seen earlier in this chapter. Let us repeat here what we emphasized then. Balthasar's method is strongly characterized by *analogy*. As we have noted at several points in this chapter, his use of words and concepts is almost always analogical.

We need to say a few more words about Balthasar's treatment of the relation between the divinity and humanity of Jesus Christ, though we have to continue with this issue in the next chapter when we discuss hell as a christological concept. (As we mentioned in Introduction, Pitstick shows the concern that Balthasar fails to distinguish the divinity and humanity of Christ.) Just as the way he maintains a nuanced position about the relation between the immanent and economic Trinity, he goes beyond the traditional Chalecedonian Christology, which affirms both the divinity and humanity of Jesus Christ, while trying to walk "the knife-edge between Nestorianism and Monophysitism."[151] While distinguishing the two different natures and simultaneously maintaining the unity in Christ, Balthasar refuses to limit the human experiences of Jesus to his human nature alone.[152] After all, if the human nature of Christ does not affect his divine nature in any way, it

---

148. Balthasar, *The Moment of Christian Witness*, 108–9.

149. Rahner, *Karl Rahner in Dialogue*, 126.

150. Ibid., 127.

151. Balthasar, *Theo-Drama* III, 221.

152. Balthasar, *Mysterium Paschale*, 23–41.

merely ends up being Nestorianism. Balthasar takes seriously the Theopaschist formula: "One of the Trinity suffered." On the other hand, Balthasar refuses to attribute suffering to the immanent Trinity directly. Likewise, he refuses to attribute suffering directly to the divine nature of Christ. He does so only analogically.

Further, in relation to this, let us see what Balthasar says about Jesus Christ as the concrete "analogy of being." He writes that

> the person of the Logos in whom the hypostatic union takes place cannot function, in any way, as the ("higher") unity between God and man; this person, as such, is God. Since the person of the Logos is the ultimate union of divine and created being, it must constitute the final proportion [Mass] between the two and hence must be the "concrete *analogia entis*" itself. However, it must not in any way overstep this analogy in the direction of identity.[153]

The analogy between the Creator and his creation, which is established in the incarnation, does not abolish the great abyss between the two. Analogy is not equal to identity. However, still there must be a real analogy between the two in some way. Similarity must be sought within dissimilarity, and vice versa. In other words, analogy makes sense only when there is both similarity and dissimilarity.

We have to bear in mind that Balthasar locates the finite difference and distance between the Creator and his creation within the infinite difference and distance between the divine persons of the Trinity. Therefore, already at the outset, there is room for linking humanity to divinity in a somewhat positive light. The difference of the creaturely being should not be merely negatively construed or completely eliminated in their reconciliation with the Creator. There is some goodness in the world, so this goodness has to be preserved in its very difference from God. After all, there is an analogy between the Father's eternal generation of the Son and his creation of the world. In relation to this point, it is also significant that Jesus Christ simultaneously reveals the true nature of the human being and the true nature of the Triune God. Furthermore, as Balthasar repeatedly suggests, Christ's divinity is expressed exactly in his humanity. If there were not any analogy between God and human beings, it would be impossible for Christ's divinity to be expressed in his humanity.

All these points are crucial, especially for our discussion of suffering in Christian discipleship, for Balthasar's nuanced treatment of the relation between the divinity and humanity of Christ, along with his discussion of the

153. Balthasar, *Theo-Drama* III, 221–22.

christological analogy of being, enables us to see that eventually all human beings can be "included" in the person of Jesus Christ and the whole human history can be defined by reference to him, without collapsing the necessary "distance" between God and human beings. Therefore, as an answer to respond to the critique that Balthasar blurs the distinction between the divinity and humanity of Christ, we emphasize the significance of analogy for his entire theological style.

Conclusion

We have started this chapter by discussing the Trinitarian framework of Christ's descent into hell. Because God is Triune, in other words, completely self-giving love, the Son can descend into hell, which is everything anti-divine, for the sake of sinful humanity. We have also examined the concern about whether Balthasar brings a rupture into the unity of the Trinity, which is most explicitly shown in the problem concerning the beatific vision. We have stressed that for Balthasar separation or abandonment is a paradoxical form of love and unity. In relation to this point, we have further discussed the critique that he blurs the distinction between love and suffering and eventually ends up divinizing and elevating the negativity of suffering. Concerning these points, we have attempted to argue that Balthasar takes a subtle and nuanced approach to divine and human suffering so he could escape the critique. (After all, we have to note that even Kilby only accuses of *the tendency* of his theology.)

Then we have attempted to present the christological significance of the descent into hell by narrating it as the center of kenotic Christology. In particular, we have highlighted the three principal themes: *kenosis*, mission, and obedience. The Son of God descended into hell, which is the last destination of his salvific mission, in the literal obedience of a corpse. The kenotic love of the Triune God for humanity is revealed in this self-giving "act" of the Son. Further, we have mentioned how Christ's perfect obedience to the point of becoming sin in hell is supposed to be the role model for the Christian's obedience in carrying out their mission from God. Furthermore, we have pointed out that hell is not only the last destination of the Son's economic mission but also the place where the Son *waited* until the new creation started. (We will come back to these points in chapter 4.) On the other hand, as a main critique raised against Balthasar's Christology, we have examined his treatment of the divinity and humanity of Christ. We have argued that Balthasar's way of treating this subject is also cautious and analogical, but we cannot fully discuss the question concerning Balthasar's treatment of the divinity and humanity of Christ without considering his concept of hell, which is itself christological. Therefore, we will discuss it in the next chapter.

2

Hell as the Dark Night of the Soul

Introduction

IN THE PREVIOUS CHAPTER, WE HAVE SUMMARIZED THE TRINITARIAN AND christological bases of Christ's descent into hell presented by Balthasar. As we have seen, hell, which is considered as being encompassed within the infinite distance between the Father and Son, hence the ultimate destination of the economic mission of the obedient Son, is the place their inseparable unity and their limitless love for the world is most vividly revealed.

Now in this chapter we will focus on hell itself. First, we will see the mystical visions of Adrienne von Speyr, which provide an abundance of material for Balthasar to reflect on the state of hell. According to Balthasar's summary, the hell which Speyr experienced is

> actually more horrible than the hell depicted for us by medieval imagination; it is the knowledge of having lost God forever; it is being engulfed in the chaotic mire of the anti-divine; the absence of faith, hope and love; the loss as well, therefore, of any human communication. It is the metamorphosis of thought into a meaningless prattle of lifeless logic.[1]

Also, as we will see in her accounts in *Kreuz und Hölle*, such words as "loneliness," "hopelessness," and "emptiness" are repeatedly used to describe the state of hell.

Most importantly, they consider hell as a christological concept first and last, and this point can be explained in the following four senses: 1) only Christ has fully suffered separation from God, by virtue of his *kenosis*; 2) his abandonment to death by the Father is a unique one which is made

---

1. Balthasar, *First Glance at Adrienne von Speyr*, 66–67.

possible only by the Trinity; 3) he experiences what Nicholas of Cusa calls *visio mortis*, and faces the whole fruit of the cross, "sin-in-itself," in hell; and 4) only after going through all this, he becomes the "judge" and thus the true possessor of hell.[2] In the previous chapter, we have already mentioned these four points. In this chapter, we will endeavor to examine the third and fourth points further on the basis of the first and second.

After examining Speyr's mystical visions of hell, we will go on to discuss the problematic but central concept of "sin-in-itself." We will then discuss the distinction between *Sheol* and *Gehenna*, and go on to explore hell as the absolute loneliness of the sinner. We will also examine the christological significance of hell, as both Balthasar and Speyr argue that no human being has ever suffered the horror of hell as fully as Christ, because no one can be more abandoned by the Father than the Son, because no one is as close to him. This is actually a working out of the idea that the infinite distance between the Father and the Son encompasses the finite distance between God and creation, including hell. As we have seen in the previous chapter, this notion permeates both Balthasar's (and Speyr's) thoughts. However, how can anyone who is in perfectly intimate union with God actually *be* or *feel* abandoned by him? This christological paradox is one of the questions we have to explore further in this chapter. It is not only on Speyr's mystical experiences that Balthasar bases his thoughts. In order to gain insights into the inner mystery of Christ's suffering in hell, he also turns to the writings of the saints in history, such as St. John of the Cross and St. Thérèse of Lisieux, who wrote about their own versions of "descent into hell." These experiences are described as "the dark night of the soul." We will examine the impacts which these saints have on Balthasar's theology. In relation to this point, we will continue to discuss the christological problem we have briefly seen in chapter 1, namely, Balthasar's treatment of the divinity and humanity of Jesus Christ.

Further, we have to explore where all these ideas lead to. By arguing that Christ descended into hell more deeply than any human being, Balthasar seems to suggest universalism (at least to some extent). We will briefly refer to his famous (or notorious) notion of "hope" for universal salvation, and then go on to discuss how his theology can actually take the encounter between human freedom and divine love with utmost seriousness. Then, we will reflect on how Balthasar's thoughts on hell are still helpful for the Christian life today.

At the end of this chapter, we will conclude our examination of Balthasar's interpretation of Christ's descent into hell, which we started

---

2. Balthasar, *The Glory of the Lord* VII, 233.

in chapter 1, by briefly reflecting on what we could learn about Christian discipleship and suffering from Balthasar and Speyr on the basis of these chapters. In particular, the concept of the dark night of faith is significant for understanding Christ's suffering as well as the Christian's. In the end, even hell (the seemingly exact opposite of love and communion) could be explained only because of the divine self-giving love. Now we can see that the Triune God's love is deeper than hell and that God is actually with us even when he seems to be absent or dead in the midst of our suffering. We will also point out that his theology is very sensitive to the paradoxical mystery of love and faith instead of simply blurring the distinction between love and loss or between joy and suffering in an overarching way as some of his critics argue.

The section titles of this chapter are as follows: 1) Adrienne von Speyr's mystical visions of hell, 2) "sin-in-itself," 3) hell as the absolute loneliness of the sinner, 4) hell as the dark night of the soul, 5) a christological problem concerning the divinity and humanity of Jesus Christ, 6) "hope" for universal salvation, 7) how should we reflect on the questions concerning hell?, and 8) conclusion: love alone can descend into hell.

Adrienne von Speyr's Mystical Visions of Hell

Let us take a look at Adrienne von Speyr's mystical visions. Whenever Balthasar's theology of Holy Saturday is discussed, it is usually mentioned (even if just briefly) that he was greatly inspired by her mystical experiences. However, it is surprisingly rare that the actual contents of those mystical experiences are discussed.[3] Speyr had these visions each Holy Week from

---

3. This point is certainly related to the fact that the spiritual relationship between Balthasar and Speyr has been one of the most controversial subjects in the Balthasarian scholarship. For example, Karen Kilby finds it problematic that Balthasar appeals to the experiences "of someone in whose house he lived and with whom he himself was closely involved" (Kilby, *Balthasar*, 30.) Fergus Kerr also questions the way Balthasar relies on Speyr's visions to "revise" the traditional interpretation of Christ's descent into hell, saying, "It is not a very traditional way in which to develop Catholic doctrine." (Kerr, "Adrienne von Speyr and Hans Urs von Balthasar," 32.) Let us clarify our position concerning this matter. There are mainly two reasons why we believe it is important to include Speyr's writings in our examination of Balthasar's theology of Holy Saturday. They are directly related to the main two points we maintain throughout this thesis: to be respectful to the combination of theology and spirituality valued by Balthasar, and to argue that Balthasar remains faithful to the Catholic tradition even in his innovative interpretation of Christ's descent into hell. Regarding the first point, Speyr is definitely one of the main spiritual sources for Balthasar, so it is important for us to examine her writings in order to pay full respect to the genre within which he is

1941 to 1965. We can read the whole accounts of these visions in *Kreuz und Hölle*.[4] Some images (for example, the stream made of human sins running in hell) were more or less the same every year, while there were different sub-themes running through these visions from year to year.[5] Balthasar himself witnessed her going through the extremely painful and disturbing visions about the entire passion of Christ. Those visions were fragmentary, but vivid and powerful, and deeply affected him. Let us see below the fragments of these visions by mainly turning to the account of 1941 (the first vision), which was recorded by Balthasar himself.[6] We believe that the 1941 account is particularly important as it shows us most vividly Balthasar's own surprise and struggle to understand what is happening in front of him.[7] We

---

working. Also, we have to point out that at least he carefully supports her ideas by appealing to various sources within the Catholic tradition, including Scripture, and other mystics', saints', and patristic authors' writings. As a proof of this point, for example, we should note that in his major work on the paschal mystery, *Mysterium Paschale*, he hardly refers to Speyr. In this book, he is mostly concerned with how to construct a theological interpretation on the basis of the spiritual material provided by her. For example, as we will see below, Balthasar combines Speyr's concept of "sin-in-itself" with the notion of *visio mortis* presented by Nicholas of Cusa, and compares Speyr's vision of hell with the dark night of the soul experienced by St. John of the Cross. In short, while Speyr could be considered as one of the main sources of inspiration for Balthasar, she certainly is not the only source for constructing his theology. It is important to take her writings into consideration in order to have a balanced view of Balthasar's sources and to see how he actually uses Speyr's unique concepts by supporting them with various traditional writings. Therefore, in order to see how Balthasar remains faithful to the traditional teaching, it is necessary to examine Speyr's visions as his inspirational source. Nevertheless, we also have to note that the focus of this whole book is on Balthasar's theology of Holy Saturday, not on the comparison or contrast between Balthasar and Speyr. Therefore, throughout this book, we will make reference to her only when it is relevant.

4. Also we can read some fragments from these visions in Speyr, *The Passion from Within*.

5. Balthasar himself gives a list of these subthemes: Hell and Confession (1944), Hell and the Trinity (1945), Hell and Confession with a Marian theme (1946), Hell and Choice (1948), Hell and Co-redemption (1949), the Wood (1951), Anxiety (1953), Searching (1955), Patience (1956), the Truth and Importance (1957), Excessive Demand (1958), Fatigue (1959), Futility (1960), the Seamless Dress (1961), Time (1963), the Cross and the Church today (1964), and Prayer (1965). (Balthasar, "Einleitung," 8.)

6. See Balthasar, "Einleitung," 12.

7. In the later years (after around 1945), they established their system of dictation, which means Balthasar's perspective and voice increasingly fades into the background (more as an interviewer) in these accounts as the years went by. Shelly Rambo, for instance, implies that something unique and vivid was lost after they "theologized" these visions into a theology of Holy Saturday. She writes, "Holy Saturday, as it is developed in their thought, loses the traces of a more textured and entangled witness to the hiatus

also make reference to the accounts of the other years on the basis of his own summary[8] accordingly.

Speyr's first experience of hell started on Good Friday of April 11, 1941. Balthasar records this beginning as follows:

> In the Friday afternoon, the suffering ended exactly at 3 pm, as I had suspected. I had expected that only a strong relief would follow; I was not able to imagine anything for Holy Saturday for sure, but there came something totally different.[9]

Balthasar goes on to describe how at half past 3 pm Speyr started to feel the odor of death coming out of her body. Then at 5 pm the visions of hell began. She did not see anyone or any soul in hell. She was not sure if anyone was there or not. Speyr described the state of hell as "incalculable emptiness and desertedness."[10] In hell she saw a slowly flowing river of mud. There were no "flames" of hell in her sight.

It was impossible for her to pray or confess on Holy Saturday, because "everything is distant. She is like without any soul, like 'misplaced.'"[11] She described her feeling on Holy Saturday as "enormous loneliness. Separation from all men."[12] She could hardly talk with people on that day. There seemed to be an infinite distance even between her and the person nearest to her. On the other hand, she felt "the burning need to communicate and express herself and to explain everything," as intensely as she had never felt before.[13]

Further, her unwillingness to pray and confess on Holy Saturday was closely connected to the strange sense of isolation or "indifference" she experienced towards sin on the day. Balthasar writes, "The complete isolation from sins, both her own and strangers', increasingly became the central

---

of Holy Saturday." Rambo, *Spirit and Trauma*, 62.

8. For his own summary of Speyr's visions, see Balthasar, "Adrienne von Speyr über das Geheimnis des Karsamstags." For a more analyitical summary of these visions, see Balthasar, "Theologie des Abstiegs zur Hölle."

9. Speyr, *Kreuz und Hölle* I, 27–28: "Am Nachmittag des Freitags war, wie ich vemutet hatte, das Leiden ziemlich genau um deri Uhr zu Ende. Ich hatte erwartet, daß nun eine starke Erleichterung eintreten würde; ich konnte mir unter dem Karsamstag nichts genaues vorstellen. Doch es kam ganz anders."

10. Ibid., 28: "Unabsehbare Leere und Verlassenheit."

11. Ibid., 30: "Alles ist fern. Sie ist wie ohne Seele, wie 'verlegt.'"

12. Ibid., 29: "Eine ungeheure Einsamkeit. Trennung von allen Menschen."

13. Ibid.,. 29: "das bernnende Bedürfnis, sich mitzuteilen, auszusprechen, alles zu erzählen."

mystery of Holy Saturday for her."[14] Speyr described sin as "a rock," before which one stands powerless and helpless. The sense of loneliness one feels before the rock of sin is so strong that, as she described, "it seems to be a sort of happiness to have sins themselves" though such an idea seems to be "a completely paradoxical and probably a wrong sort."[15] However, such is the kind of loneliness a sinner feels in hell. As she described, it is a kind of loneliness "which really had nothing human in itself."[16]

To some extent, Speyr's descriptions of these visions themselves already are theological interpretations. The Son on the cross atones for all the sins of the world (including the sins which have not yet occurred). Speyr says, "One cannot suffer unless they are really faced with sins."[17] The burden of these sins is unimaginable, "but still the Lord suffers what must be suffered for the sins of the world."[18] The Son must experience from inside the absurdity of sins and their remoteness from God, which takes the form of absolute anxiety, in which "nothing makes sense anymore."[19] The Son is "crushed" and "suffocated" by the sins.[20] In the cry of derelection, "the Son cannot see any longer that He is doing the will of the Father."[21]

Speyr's sharing in the passion, which lasted till the afternoon of Good Friday, was not only physical but also (or rather) spiritual torture, because she had to go through the inner state of Jesus, namely, anxiety, shame, horror, sense of futility, and "the inner night he had to suffer,"[22] (which is similar to "the dark night" of St. John of the Cross.) Speyr's experience could be characterized by curious two-foldness. On the one hand, her self was completely lost in these visions, but on the other hand, she experienced the deep fear about her own sinfulness. Also it is interesting that Speyr did not

14. Ibid., 30: "Das völlige Getrenntsein von den Sünden, den eigenen und den fremden, wird ihr immer mehr zum zentralen Geheimnis des Tages."

15. Ibid., 30: "scheint es eine Art von Glück zu sein, selber Sünden zu haben—der Satz erscheint ihr als völlig paradox und vielleicht als falsche Art."

16. Ibid., 31: "eine Einsamkeit, die eigentlich nichts Menschiches mehr an sich hatte."

17. Quoted by Balthasar in "Adrienne von Speyr über das Geheimnis des Karsamstags," 32: "Leiden kan man nicht, ohne wirklich von der Sünde getroffen zu sein."

18. Ibid., 32: "Dennoch leidet der Herr mehr, als was für die Sünde der Welt gelitten warden müßte."

19. Ibid., 32: "in der 'nichts mehr entspricht,' und alles 'umsonst' scheint."

20. Ibid., 32: "erdrckt," "erstickt."

21. Ibid., 32: "sieht der Herr in keiner Weise mehr, daß er den Willen des Vaters tut."

22. Ibid., 33: "innere Nacht zu erleiden."

distinguish between her own personal sins and those of all the other human beings.

In her experience of the descent into hell, which began in the afternoon of Good Friday, she had no more physical pain, but there was "another, even deeper form of timelessness," because in hell "duration is standing still"[23] and "everything is only the "now.""[24] The cross itself is "atemporal," because all the sins of the world from the past and future are gathered on the Son, who is "made sin." In this sense, the cross is the zero hour. However, hell is atemporal in a completely different way. The timelessness of hell is characterized by the sense that nothing can last, the crushing weight of sins, and the finality of meaninglessness, so it is in stark contrast to heaven, where "all time is fulfilled in the eternity of God."[25]

On Holy Saturday, every contact with human beings is shut out. Speyr's behaviours on Holy Saturdays were mechanical and she was "like a puppet, or better, like someone with catatonia, who adopts any position that another person gives her."[26] According to her, the human beings in hell "have nothing infinite any more, but they are *pure finitude*."[27] Speyr herself was in hell not as one of "the damned" but as someone in a paradoxical state. Further, she tried to find the traces of Christ in hell but she found it impossible. On earth, the traces of the grace of Christ can be found everywhere, but not in hell, where "the dead Christ is no longer active."[28]

In short, "loneliness," "hopelessness," and "emptiness" are the examples of the words that she uses to describe the state of hell.[29] These images seem to be quite different from the more popular image of the medieval "fiery" hell, but as we will argue later, these images help us to see the relevance of hell for our postmodern mindset. The hell in Speyr's visions is characterized by the separation from God and from fellow human beings as well as a complete loss of communication. Since these negative experiences of alienation have been so commonly shared in our postmodern world, Speyr's visions

---

23. Speyr, *Kreuz und Hölle* I, 273: "Die Dauer is Stillstand."

24. Ibid., 276: "In der Hölle ist alles nur Jetzt."

25. Ibid., 365: "es in der Ewigkeit Gottes die Erfüllung aller Zeit gibt."

26. Ibid., 49: "wie eine Puppe, oder besser, wie ein Katatoniker, der jede Stellung annnimt, die ihm ein anderer gibt."

27. Quoted by Balthasar in "Adrienne von Speyr über das Geheimnis des Karsamstags," 33: "hat nichts Unendliches mehr, er ist reine Endlichkeit." Italics added.

28. Ibid., 34: "Der tote Christus ist in der Hölle nicht mehr aktiv."

29. Respectively, "die Einsamkeit," "die Hoffnungslosigkeit," and "die Leere" in German. See, for example, Speyr, *Kreuz und Hölle* I, 28-31, 38, 48, 50, 86, etc.

of the hell of loneliness help us to argue for the relevance of the doctrine of Christ's descent into hell for human suffering today.

"Sin-in-itself"

Probably the theologically most problematic image in Speyr's visions is the one concerning "the substance of hell." She says that hell is made of human sins. The Son descends into hell before he returns to the Father in order to see "the result of his passion," which is "the removal of sin from the sinners."[30] Speyr says, "hell is the reality of the sins removed from the world."[31] In her visions, sins actually look like a river of stinking mud. It is "an immense, brown, stinking river, whose movement is dead and mechanical" and every Holy Saturday Speyr saw "the totally slow river of the sin becoming formless."[32] She says, "In hell, human beings will confront their own sins: in this stinking mud must they recognize themselves."[33]

Further, in hell, the Son also encounters what Speyr calls "effigies."[34] The effigies are hollow impressions made from individual sinners, because each sinner is supposed to give something from their own substance to a sin they commit. Balthasar explains as follows:

> They [The effigies] are what in each sinner God has condemned and cast out, hence what he had to throw into Hell in order to save the living person and make him through Christ into a child of God. The effigies are not unreal, because the sinful person has given away some of their own reality to sin. So each redeemed sinner has a kind of their own reproduction in Hell.[35]

---

30. Quoted by Balthasar in "Adrienne von Speyr über das Geheimnis des Karsamstags," 34: "was das Ergebnis seiner Passion ist; die Trennung der Sünde von den Sünden. "

31. Ibid., 34: "Die Hölle ist die Wirklichkeit der von der Welt getrennten Sünde."

32. Ibid., 34: "Ein unermeßlicher, brauner, stinkender Strom, der sich tot und mechanisch bewegt"; "Ganz langsamen Fluß der formlos gewordenen Sünden."

33. Ibid., 34: "In der Hölle wird der Mensch mit seiner Sünde konfrontiert: in diesem stinkenden Schlamm muß er sich erkennen."

34. Ibid., 35. Also see Balthasar, *Theo-Logic* II, 355–56.

35. Balthasar, "Theologie des Abstiegs zur Hölle," 143: "Sie sind das, was Gott von jedem Sünder von sich weg verdammen, also in die Hölle werfen mußte, um ihm als den lebendigen Menschen zu retten, aus ihm durch Christus ein Kind Gottes zu machen. Die Effigien sind nicht unreal, weil der sündige Mensch der Sünde etwas von seiner lebendigen Wirklichkeit weggeschenkt hat. So hat jeder erlöste Sünder etwas wie ein Abbild seiner selbst in der Hölle."

Therefore, what human beings have lost of their own substance due to their sins is replaced by the grace of Christ. The concepts of "sins removed from sinners" and "effigies" are inseparably connected.

However, as we consider their meanings, we have to refer to the fundamental question of what sin is, or rather, what it really means for a human being to sin. John Saward, for instance, tries to see the image of the effigies as "a way of saying that sin depersonalizes."[36] For example, Satan, ontologically a real personal entity, can be seen as an "unperson." Of Speyr's description of the effigies, Saward writes, "Here is the 'unadmirable exchange' of human iniquity: the impersonal and insubstantial becomes personal; the personal becomes impersonal."[37] If we believe that human beings can only be fully human through union with Christ, we can say that to sin, or to turn away from God, is to lose one's true humanity. Interestingly enough, Balthasar himself does not develop the notion of the effigies very much. (Basically, he mentions this notion only in the context where he presents Speyr's visions.)[38]

Setting aside the effigies, we have to examine "sin without sinners" or "sin removed from sinners." Balthasar develops it as "sin-in-itself" in his own theology, but it seems to stand in tension with the traditional understanding of sin, because traditionally sin has been regarded not as substance but as an event.[39] St. Thomas Aquinas, for example, writes that "sin is nothing else but a bad human act. A human act is human because it is voluntary, whether it is internal, e.g. to will or to choose; or external, e.g. to speak or to act. A human act is evil because it does not meet the standard for human behaviour. Standards are nothing other than rules."[40] In other words, sin is an act that "does not meet the standard for human behavior." Citing from St. Augustine, St. Thomas goes on to write that sin is a word, deed, or desire contrary to the eternal law.[41] Also the Catechism of the Catholic Church cites this sentence in its definition of sin:

> Sin is an offense against reason, truth, and right conscience; it is failure in genuine love for God and neighbor caused by a perverse attachment to certain goods. It wounds the nature of

36. Saward, *The Mysteries of March*, 131.

37. Ibid., 131–32.

38. For a few places he mentions this concept, see, for example, Balthasar, *Theo-Logic* II, 355–56; "Adrienne von Speyr über das Geheimnis des Karsamstags," 35.

39. See "Sin" in *The Catholic Encyclopedia*.

40. Thomas Aquinas, *Summa Theologiae*, I-II, q.71, a.6.

41. Ibid., I-II, q.71, a.6.

man and injures human solidarity. It has been defined as "an utterance, a deed, or a desire contrary to the eternal law."[42]

Again, such words as "failure" and "wound" here suggest that sin, in so far as it is evil, is the privation of the good just as sickness or a wound is the privation of health. However, we must also note that sin as an act is still understood as a "reality." In short, the difference between the traditional teachings and the Speyr-Balthasar theology concerns how to express the reality of sin. Traditionally evil has not been understood to have any ontological existence. What could we gain from describing the reality of sin as "sin-in-itself" or even as a kind of substance?

For one thing, it has been pointed out that such reification of sin allows for clear distinction between the sinner and their act so both the God's abhorrence of sin and God's deep love for the sinner can be powerfully expressed.[43] Also such distinction enables us to see the enormity of evil in a somewhat symbolic way, so such an image of sin could help us consider corporate or institutionalized sin in which the human being is not only an agent but also a victim. Also, in such a concrete image of sin, we can see the stark contrast between God's infinite love and the finitude of sin. On this matter Anne Hunt writes, "While the horror and reality of sin is powerfully acknowledged, in reifying it von Balthasar effectively diminishes it in contrast to the infinity of God's love."[44] Therefore, some merits can be found in such a graphic description of sin separated from sinners. As Hunt suggests, such separation of sin from sinners and concrete visualization of sin allows for an abstract argument about evil per se.

Further, we should add that this concept could act as a significant bridge between Speyr-Balthasar's version of the descent into hell and the traditional interpretations of this doctrine. In the traditional interpretations, Christ is believed to have descended into hell as the conqueror of sin and death, and some sort of combat between Christ and Satan, the personified evil, is often depicted. In Balthasar's and Speyr's theology of the descent, Christ's vision of sin-in-itself in hell is *objectively* a vision of his victory over sin and death, though he must wait for the resurrection to appreciate his triumph *subjectively*. Thus, this notion of sin-in-itself enables us to regard Christ's descent into hell as the victory over sin and death, even if in a roundabout way. Therefore, we can say that while the traditional interpretations are characterized by the glory of Easter rather than the suffering of Good Friday, Balthasar's and Speyr's version of Holy Saturday presents

42. See *Catechism of the Catholic Church*, §1849.

43. See Hunt, *The Trinity and the Paschal Mystery*, 73.

44. Ibid., 74.

a real middle-point between the cross and the resurrection. The victory of Easter is objectively already there, but its subjective sentiment is not there yet. Sin-in-itself is thus a crucial concept for us to see how they take the in-betweenness of Holy Saturday seriously while staying within the traditional interpretations.

Hell as the Absolute Loneliness of the Sinner

We have been simply using the word, "hell," so far (rather intentionally), but technically speaking the place Christ entered after he died should be called *Sheol* or Hades.[45] This point is also shared by the traditional inter-pretations.[46] The word "hell" used in the Apostles' Creed does not mean the hell of eternal damnation as we imagine today. In Latin, the word translated as hell in English is *inferna*. In the ancient world, this word had the generic meaning of "underworld," which is translated as *Sheol* in Hebrew and *Hades* in Greek. In the Old Testament,[47] *Sheol* is described the abode of the dead, a place of darkness cut off from God, which includes the good and the bad alike, though it "does not mean that their lot is identical."[48]

It is only as a consequence of Christ's descent there that the "hell" of eternal damnation, in other words, *Gehenna*, came to exist. *Gehenna* is the name used in the New Testament to refer to the hell of the damned.[49] It is a Greek adaptation of a Hebrew name, *ge'hinnom*, the valley of Hinnon, which is an area to the south-west of the city of Jerusalem used for casting rubbish. This image is also relevant when we consider the sin-in-itself, as it is the "residue" of human sin and the whole fruit of Christ's redemptive work. This point helps us to see how the theological "transition" from hell as *Sheol* to hell as *Gehenna* took place.

In *Summa Theologiae*, St. Thomas Aquinas poses the question of whether Christ descended into the hell of the damned and responds that the soul of Christ had *an effect* on all the inhabitants of the underworld, includ-ing the damned, those in the purgatory, and the holy fathers in Abraham's

---

45. For an extensive study of the concept of *Sheol*, see Johnston, *Shades of Sheol*.

46. See *Catechism of the Catholic Church*, §633.

47. For instance, Job 10:21–22, 17:13, 26:5; and Psalms 89:48, 88:6.

48. *Catechism of the Catholic Church*, §633. For example, there is "Abraham's bo-som" into which the poor man Lazarus was received (Luke 16:22).

49. It appears 11 times in the Synoptic Gospels, typically accompanied by the im-agery of fire, darkness, worms, howling and gnashing of teeth. See Matt 5:22, 29, 30, 10:28, 18:9, 23:15, 33; Mark 9:43, 45, 47; Luke 12:5; and Jas 3:6.

bosom, but *in its essence* the soul of Christ visited only the holy fathers.[50] Balthasar argues that this question is wrongly posed in the first place because there was neither hell as *Gehenna* nor purgatory nor heaven before Christ's descent into *Sheol*. Rather, these three states are its results, hence *christological* concepts.

First of all, *Sheol* is a place where there is no vision of God. Balthasar summarizes that in *Sheol* "all that reigns is the darkness of perfect loneliness."[51] For Balthasar, loneliness is an important concept that connects sin and salvation. In his own words,

And exactly in this Christian, eventually *Christological loneliness* lies a hope for the one who condemns himself, rejecting all love. Will the one, who wants to be completely alone, eventually not find someone even lonelier, the Son abandoned by the Father, who will prevent him from experiencing his self-chosen Hell to the end?[52]

The loneliness of the sinner who locks themselves up in their own shell and rejects God's love is redeemed by the deeper loneliness of Christ, who descended into hell fully forsaken by God and humankind. (Balthasar further argues that the foundation of the community of love, which is the church, has its foundation on this "Christological" loneliness.[53])

Theologically speaking, the concept of hell as absolute loneliness makes perfect sense, since loneliness can be considered as a product of sin, as long as it is understood as the inability to step outside of oneself or as the state of being that one lives only for oneself. This view seems to be shared by other theologians. Piet Schoonenberg, for example, writes that "sin always and necessarily makes for loneliness."[54] He even writes that "the whole punishment of sin in Genesis iii may be conceived as loneliness and may be summarized in that concept" and that "Hell, too, the final consequence of sin, may totally be summarized as extreme loneliness which man has chosen for ever and to which God delivers him."[55] Similarly, Pope Emeritus Benedict XVI, too, once wrote (long before he became Pope) that Christ's descent into hell means that he "strode through the gate of our final loneli-

50. Thomas Aquinas, *Summa Theologiae*, III, q. 52, a.2.

51. Balthasar, *Explorations in Theology* IV, 408.

52. Balthasar, "Theologie des Abstiegs zur Hölle," 145–46.

53. See Balthasar, *The Moment of Christian Witness*, 30–38; Balthasar, *Explorations in Theology* IV, 261–98.

54. Schoonenberg, *Man and Sin*, 91.

55. Ibid., 91.

ness, that in his passion he went down into the abyss of our abandonment."[56] He also reminds us that death (the consequence of sin) and hell were identical before Christ and actually that is what the word *Sheol* conveys.[57] Only after Christ's descent into *Sheol*, death can mean either a path for heaven (as communion with God), hell (as *Gehenna*), or purgatory.

We should note that not only *Sheol* but also *Gehenna* is eventually characterized by such loneliness caused by separation from God, while the difference between the two is that the former is a "pre-Christ," temporal state and the latter "post-Christ," self-chosen eternal punishment. This point is confirmed by the Catechism itself:

> To die in mortal sin without repenting and accepting God's merciful love means remaining separated from him for ever by our own free choice. This state of definitive self-exclusion from communion with God and the blessed is called "Hell."[58]

If the essence of hell (whether it is as *Sheol* or *Gehenna*) is understood as the absolute loneliness of the sinner caused by separation from God, there is no human being that has suffered it as fully as Christ. Balthasar stresses that because he is closest to God, he can be more abandoned than any sinful human being. We will explore below this christological paradox by examining Balthasar's reading of two Carmelite saints, namely, St. John of the Cross and St. Thérèse of Lisieux.

Hell as "the Dark Night of the Soul"

Speyr herself often compares the descent into hell she has gone through to the "dark night of the soul" explored by St. John of the Cross (1542–1591),[59] and Balthasar follows her on this point.[60] If we read both mystics' accounts together,[61] we cannot help noticing the similarities between them even on

56. Ratzinger, *Introduction to Christianity*, 301.

57. Ibid., 301.

58. *Catechism of the Catholic Church*, §1033.

59. Speyr, *Kreuz und Hölle* I, 201–2, 204, 210, 237, 265; and *Kreuz und Hölle* II, 58, 396, 406, 407, 439, 449, 450, 459. It would be worthwhile to compare and contrast these two mystics further in detail. Especially, it might be interesting to examine the "influence" of Martin Luther on both (one is a mystic in the counter-reformation context, and the other is a convert from the Lutheran faith).

60. Balthasar, "Adrienne von Speyr über das Geheimnis des Karsamstags," 33; "Theologie des Abstiegs zur Hölle," 142.

61. For the writings by St. John of the Cross, see *The Complete Works of St. John of the Cross* (All the following quotations from St. John are from this version of translation).

a superficial level, even though Balthasar and Speyr are critical of St. John's "neo-platonic representation of the purification of the soul"[62] and they are well aware that St. John himself does not directly connect his dark night to Christ's descent into hell (he only connects it to the cross).

First of all, the mysticism of both St. John and Speyr is deeply Trinitarian.[63] The structure of *The Ascent to Mount Carmel* of St. John as "the active night" and *The Dark Night of the Soul* as the "passive night" is also reminiscent of Speyr's interpretation of the Cross as the active suffering and the descent into hell as the passive one. Most of all, the dark night of the soul is a sign that the soul is right on the way to the intimate union with God (hence "the midnight before the dawn"), while the Son's descent into hell is "the shortest way back to the Father" and it itself is already the victory against sin. In short, "objectively" speaking, the suffering of the dark night of the soul itself is already a gift of grace, even though it is still unbearably painful in a "subjective" sense. It is exactly due to this distinction between "objectivity" and "subjectivity" that Speyr regards the dark night of St. John as "the night of Holy Saturday," rather than that of the cross.[64]

With their similarities in mind we can examine Balthasar's reading of St. John of the Cross[65] to explore the hell into which Jesus descended. In short, the hell Jesus entered in full solidarity with the sinful humanity is considered as being similar to the dark night of the soul on the way to its union with God. This point is directly related to the mystery of separation of sin from sinners, which itself is a blessing in an "objective" sense, but it is still felt for the soul as hell "subjectively."

If light and darkness are the two poles of all Christian mysticism, St. John is obviously classified as "a mystic of the dark," and he has the tendency to seek light *within* darkness.[66] This characteristic seems to be true

---

As a summary of St. John of the Cross, the following books are helpful: Brenan, *St. John of the Cross*; Williams, *The Wound of Knowledge*, 159–79; O'Donoghue, *Mystics for Our Time*, 53–109.

62. Balthasar, "Theologie des Abstiegs zur Hölle," 142. Balthasar distinguishes the kind of Christian mysticism which is rooted in the paschal mystery and the kind which is not free from the neoplatonic inheritance. In short, he appreciates the former but criticizes the latter, because it is the kind of mysticism in which the soul tries to transcend itself to be united with the Absolute One but tends to be self-preoccupied with analyses of its own states. (See Balthasar, *Explorations in Theology* IV, 309–35.)

63. Balthasar, *Theo-Drama* V, 429–33. Also, regarding St. John's insights into the mystery of the Trinity, see Hunt, *The Trinity*, 144–67.

64. Speyr, *Kreuz und Hölle* I, 265.

65. Balthasar, *The Glory of the Lord* III, 105–71.

66. See O'Donoghue, *Mystics for Our Time*, 68–69.

of Balthasar's theology in general as well, so it is not difficult to see why the mysticism of St. John of the Cross appeals to him. In short, for both of them (and Speyr), the way to heaven is paved through hell.

According to St. John's account of the spiritual journey, before the soul enters into intimate union with God, there is a stage where God seems to be hostile and even absent. This is what Balthasar interprets as St. John's version of the descent into hell. In Balthasar's words, St. John "must enter the night of Hell, for only in the absolute distinction between the sinful creature and the absolute God in his total purity can the divine in its truth be perceived."[67] Since there is an insurmountable disparity between God and his creation, the deeper the soul experiences God, the more it is bound to feel its own death and the "absence" of God. St. John expresses this condition of the soul as follows:

> What the sorrowful soul feels most in this condition is its clear perception, as it thinks, that God has abandoned it, and, in His abhorrence of it, has flung it into darkness; it is a grave and piteous grief for it to believe that God has forsaken it . . .the soul feels very keenly the shadow of death and the lamentations of death and the pains of hell, which consist in its feeling itself to be without God, and chastised and cast out, and unworthy of Him.[68]

Moreover, the soul feels that this "absence" of God will last forever and consequently it loses all hope. At this stage, even a prayer becomes impossible for the soul.[69] However, this dark night of the soul is in reality a way to the union with God. This sense of "absence" is actually a form of God's brightest "presence," which only feels as a dark night for the soul, for God's light is too blinding for it. In the following passage, Balthasar summarizes St. John's dark night using the distinction between "subjectivity" and "objectivity" which we have mentioned above[70]:

67. Balthasar, *The Glory of the Lord* III, 110.

68. John of the Cross, *The Dark Night of the Soul*, II. 6, 2. Quoted by Balthasar in *The Glory of the Lord* III, 110.

69. As we saw above, Speyr too said she cannot bring herself to pray on Holy Saturday.

70. In relation of this mixture of objectivity and subjectivity, let us briefly note that it also plays a significant role in Balthasar's interpretation of 1 Peter 3:19 and 4:6, which say that the gospel was preached to the dead. This text has traditionally been the *locus classicus* for the doctrine of Christ's descent into hell. As Balthasar denies any kind of activity in death, he explains that the preaching described here cannot be a subjective kind of preaching which is meant to move the audience to conversion. Rather, it is "an objective announcement of the fact." It is the fact of God's reconciliation with

At first the night is *subjectively* death, although *objectively* it is already resurrection; but as the way of the soul's dying, it has its twilight, midnight, and dawn that ushers in eternal life, when the veil that separates her from the vision of God is stretched to the breaking point. And yet the midnight is already *objectively* the brightest of light.[71]

Further, Balthasar points out that St. John of the Cross himself connects this dark night to the paschal mystery. In his words,

One must rather consider that . . . John has entirely in view the living, elective God of the Bible, who "descended into Hell and leads back out again"; even the Cross, upon which the Son is abandoned by the Father, as seen by the Father, is purest light, the light that is glorified even *in extremis*.[72]

Thus, in St. John's account of the dark night of the soul of the sinner, Balthasar finds the link to the paschal mystery. This point is significant for us to understand Balthasar's Christology, as he argues that the Son, by virtue of his *kenosis*, suffered the full fate of the sinful humanity to the point of hell. Therefore, the abandonment of the Son by the Father, which is expressed in the cry of dereliction and in the descent into hell, is understood in terms of what the *presence* of God feels like for the soul of the sinner.[73]

Further, such an account of the dark night of the soul seems to explain how the closer the soul is to God, the possibility for the soul to feel his absence increases, or even how abandonment could actually be a form of union. Therefore, we might start to think that the dark night of the soul gives us a clue to the christological mystery that the Son could be abandoned by the Father more fully than any human being. However, we have to consider another Carmelite saint's contribution to Balthasar's Christology before we reach such a conclusion.

---

humanity, which was accomplished on the cross. This point is important, because Balthasar never says that the descent into hell completed something which the cross had not. Christ has already defeated sin, death, and evil by his death on the cross. It is in the descent into hell that this fact of victory is proclaimed first. In this sense, Balthasar is trying to stay in the tradition that Christ's descent into hell is a victorious event. (For Balthasar's interpretation of 1 Peter 3:19, see *Mysterium Paschale*, 156–60, and 180–81.)

71. Balthasar, *The Glory of the Lord* III, 136–37.

72. Ibid., 137.

73. See McIntosh, *Christology from Within*, 99–101.

The saint in question is St. Thérèse of Lisieux (1873–1897), a French discalced Carmelite nun, who is also known as "the little flower."[74] (She was a great reader of St. John of the Cross too.[75]) Her spirituality, which is characterized by what she called the "little way," greatly inspired Balthasar, especially on the topic of hell. Her influence should not be underestimated.

St. Thérèse is relevant for our discussion here, because she also experienced her own version of the dark night (even though it was "a half-night," according to Balthasar.) Towards the end of her life, she experienced the condition of what she herself calls *La nuit du néant*, the night of nothingness. This is the state of being, which (interestingly enough) might have been used by Martin Heideggar or Jean Paul Sartre about thirty years later.[76] During the Easter of 1896, after the Good Friday when she first spat up blood (which is the symptom of tuberculosis, which led her to death eighteen months later), God showed her "that there really are souls without faith who, by misusing graces, lose these precious gifts, the only source of true and pure joy."[77] St. Thérèse wished to suffer vicariously for the sake of these damned souls, and God granted her wish. In her words, God allowed "my little soul to be darkened by the thickest gloom, so that the thought of heaven, so sweet to me up until then, becomes an occasion of torment and agony."[78] This condition (the condition she herself calls "my dark night"[79])

---

74. Balthasar, *Two Sisters in the Spirit*. The following books on St. Thérèse are relevant and helpful for reflection on the topic of this chapter: O'Donoghue, *Mystics for Our Time*, 113–51; Bro, *The Little Way*.

75. Especially, Balthasar points out that his manner of interpreting Scripture had an impact on her. See Balthasar, *Two Sisters in the Spirit*, 82, and 91–92.

76. Regarding the profound connection between St. Thérèse's night of nothingness and the existential hell, see O'Donoghue, *Mystics for Our Time*, 122–23; Bro, *The Little Way*, 5. For example, the following words of Sartre seem to share the same sentiment of godforsakenness experienced by St. Thérèse, "I prayed, I pleaded for a sign, I sent Heaven messages: no reply. Heaven doesn't even know my name. I kept wondering what I was in God's eyes. Now I know the answer: nothing. God doesn't see me, God doesn't hear me, God doesn't know me. You see the void above our heads? That is God. You see this hole in the ground? That's what God is. You see this crack in the door? That's God too. Silence is God. Absence is God. God is human loneliness." (Quoted by Bro in *The Little Way*, 5.)

77. Thérèse of Lisieux, *Story of a Soul*, 211. Quoted by Balthasar in *Two Sisters in the Spirit*, 339.

78. Thérèse of Lisieux, *Story of a Soul*, 212. Quoted by Balthasar in *Two Sisters in the Spirit*, 339.

79. Thérèse of Lisieux, *Story of a Soul*, 214. Quoted by Balthasar in *Two Sisters in the Spirit*, 339.

lasted until her death, and she declared that she herself was ready to remain in this night. St. Thérèse herself writes about this condition as follows:

> When I want to rest my heart, weary of the surrounding darkness, by the memory of the luminous country after which I aspire, my anguish only increases. It seems as if the darkness, echoing the voices of sinners is mocking me, saying, "You dream of light, of a fragrant homeland, you dream that you will possess the Creator of these wonders for all eternity, you believe that you will one day emerge from this gloom . . . Go on! Look forward to death, which will give you—not what you hope—but a still darker night, the night of nothingness!"[80]

This experience of "the night of nothingness," which she herself wanted to suffer vicariously out of love for God and for sinners, appears to be St. Thérèse's version of the dark night of the soul. However, Balthasar critically analyzes her experience and declares her "night of nothingness" does *not* reach the same depth as the dark night of the soul explored by St. John of the Cross (let alone Christ's descent of hell).[81] According to Balthasar, this is partly because St. Thérèse was able to keep faith itself even in the midst of this "night." He also points out that she was able to sense a higher kind of joy in this suffering. In St. Thérèse's own words, "the road I follow is one that affords me no consolation, yet it brings every consolation."[82] Balthasar further argues that even her seemingly most extreme statement ("I no longer believe in eternal life; it seems to me there is nothing beyond this mortal life. Everything is brought to an end. *Love alone remains.*"[83]) would only serve to show that hers was not a complete dark night, for if she knew *love alone remains*, that would not be the dark night of the soul (in other words, that would not be hell).[84] Balthasar calls her night "a sort of 'half-night,'" because

> *The complete night involves complete solidarity with the sinners and the damned; it means identifying oneself with their lot and sharing their fate utterly.* But how could Thérèse, knowing herself to be a saint, abandon herself unconditionally to the community

---

80. Thérèse of Lisieux, *Story of a Soul*, 213. Quoted by Balthasar in *Two Sisters in the Spirit*, 340.

81. Balthasar, *Two Sisters in Spirit*, 340.

82. Thérèse of Lisieux, *Collected Letters*, 139. Quoted by Balthasar in *Two Sisters in the Spirit*, 341.

83. Quotation from Ida Frederike Görres, *The Hidden Face: A Study of St. Thérèse of Lisieux* (Pantheon, 1959), 358, 360. Quoted by Balthasar in *Two Sisters in the Spirit*, 342. Italics added.

84. Balthasar, *Two Sisters in the Spirit*, 342.

of sinners? She would have to relinquish all her truth. She would have to give up the meaning of her theological existence.[85]

In other words, St. Thérèse's "night" cannot be a complete dark night of the soul, because she cannot be "in complete solidarity with the sinners and the damned." This is partly due to her peculiar relationship to sin, which is regarded as her "self-conscious sanctity"[86] at some point. It is important to consider Balthasar's critical analysis of her "night" in the context of his Christology. In the first place, as a saint, St. Thérèse lacks the normal self-awareness of a sinner, so she lacks the real understanding of the cross and hell as well. As Balthasar writes, "Preserved from sin, she stands outside all relationship with hell."[87] Also, "Hell only shows up in her vision of the world when *others* seem in danger of going there. It is simply that *from which* souls must be saved"[88] Because of her peculiar relationship to sin, as Balthasar analyzes, her theology significantly lacks some of the central mysteries, such as the mystery of bearing sins and of solidarity in sin, the mystery of how love may be coupled with an awareness of sin, and above all the mystery of confession.[89] In other words, she cannot fully understand the mystery of the cross and the descent into hell because of her lack of awareness as a sinner. As Balthasar writes,

> Thérèse's world remains immune from the effects of elemental evil—a fact that confirms our opinion that her night of the soul never reached the dimensions of the night of the Cross, that point where the Son is brought face to face with the sinner's absolute abandonment by God.[90]

This logic is significant to appreciate the paradox in Balthasar's Christology. A saint like St. Thérèse, who lacks self-awareness as a sinner, cannot reach the full dimensions of the inner night suffered by the absolutely

85. Ibid., 342–43. Italics added.

86. Ibid., 343.

87. Ibid., 354. This was originally caused by two peculiar experiences during her childhood. She experienced a miracle, and she was declared sinless. See Balthasar, *Two Sisters in the Spirit*, 97–114.

88. Ibid., 355. This perspective is also relevant for Balthasar's hope for universal salvation.

89. Ibid., 108. Speyr also notes St. Thérèse's "peculiar knowledge of sin." See Speyr, *Confession*, 259–60.

90. Balthasar, *Two Sisters in the Spirit*, 356.

sinless man Jesus Christ. As Balthasar writes, "Thérèse's little way leaves her at the beginning of the Passion; it confines her to the Mount of Olives."[91]

Further, along with Balthasar, we have to note the way St. Thérèse can never fully identify herself with the sinners and the damned, even though that is what she wishes to do as she proudly declares, "At last I have found my vocation! My final vocation is love."[92] It is impossible for her to carry it out because she can never let her own sainthood be completely lost. As Balthasar says, for St. Thérèse, the community of sinners "would be the self-destruction of her being, and, in her eyes, the abandonment of her mission to holiness. God might ask it, perhaps, of other saints who are not always meditating on their own sanctity. But not from Thérèse."[93] This is her limitation as a human being in terms of the identification of one's mission and person,[94] even though she is a saint. As Balthasar says, "her Carmelite mission demands that *she should identify herself with the community of sinners*, but her self-conscious sanctity makes such solidarity impossible."[95] This is also the limitation of her self-giving love, even though as Balthasar appreciates, "she lives out of love, through love, for love; a love that is not her own but God's within her."[96] As we saw in Balthasar's Christology, these two elements (identification of mission with person and self-giving love) are fully realized only in Jesus Christ.

While Balthasar's reading of St. John and St. Thérèse helps us to have a glimpse into Christ's wish for vicarious suffering on behalf of the sinner and his full experience of hell as the sinner's absolute separation from God, a significant question arises naturally. The dark night of the soul is after all the spiritual journey of a sinner, even if a saint. If the hell experienced by the Son is considered as being similar to such a night, is the Christ presented by Balthasar not too human? Moreover, is Balthasar not significantly blurring his divinity and humanity? As we mentioned in the introduction and chapter 1, this is one of the criticisms presented by Pitstick against Balthasar.[97] We will discuss it further below.

91. Ibid., 356.

92. Thérèse of Lisieux, *Story of a Soul*, 194. Quoted by Balthasar in *Two Sisters in the Spirit*, 203.

93. Balthasar, *Two Sisters in the Spirit*, 343.

94. We discussed this point in chapter 1.

95. Balthasar, *Two Sisters in the Spirit*, 343. Italics added.

96. Ibid., 72. Here reference is made to Thérèse of Lisieux, *Story of a Soul*, 256.

97. Pitstick, *Light in Darkness*, 293–302. For a response to Pitstick's criticism concerning Balthasar's Christology, see Oakes, "The Internal Logic of Holy Saturday."

A Christological Problem—Concerning the Divinity and Humanity of Jesus Christ

First of all, we have to clarify one point concerning union with God and abandonment by him. On the basis of St. John's account of the dark night of the soul which is supposed to happen on the way to its intimate union with God, we seem to be able to explain how the closer the soul is to God, the possibility for the soul to feel his absence increases, at least to some extent, or even how abandonment could actually be a form of union. However, this kind of abandonment on the way to union cannot be the case for Jesus Christ, even if Balthasar's reading of St. John of the Cross seems to suggest it in some way. This is because such abandonment is a form of ascent for the sinful soul, while Jesus, being sinless, never needs such a purification process, even as a full human being. His unique abandonment by God can only be a form of descent for him, because he chooses to be abandoned by God *exactly because he is already with God.* Therefore, Balthasar writes,

> Only the person who has truly "possessed" God in the Covenant, knows what it means to be truly abandoned by him. But all the experiences of night in both Old and New Testaments are at best approaches, distant allusions to the inaccessible mystery of the Cross—so unique is the Son of God, so unique is his abandonment by the Father.[98]

Thus, when Balthasar says that no one can be more abandoned by the Father than the Son, what he means is rather that only the Son *can afford to be fully abandoned* because of his perfect union with the Father. When we think about the case of St. Thérèse, this point becomes clearer. She shows that the closer the soul becomes to God, the more it becomes love itself even to the point of wishing to be abandoned. We ordinary sinners can only try to ascend to be united with God, and as we are already far from him, we cannot be abandoned further than we already are. This way of explanation also clarifies the other definitive expression made by Balthasar, namely, that the infinite distance between the Father and the Son encompasses the finite distance between God and the sinner. As we saw in chapter 1, only the two-fold love directed both at the Father and at the world could explain the paschal mystery.

Further, as we also saw in chapter 1, Balthasar's main christological thesis is that Christ's full divinity is expressed exactly in his full humanity.[99]

---

98. Balthasar, *Mysterium Paschale*, 78–79.

99. This thesis is based on his reading of Maximus the Confessor.

This is how he both maintains the Chalcedonian formula and departs from it, but at the same time this paradoxical idea can make sense only in terms of *kenosis*. At least Balthasar is consistent in following the logic of self-giving love to the fullest. That is why his reference to St. Thérèse's example is important (though Pitstick curiously omits it from her discussion). Why could the sinless Son of God experience the dark night of the sinner to the fullest? Why could he feel the "absence" of God most strongly (even though it is not despair)? This is a paradoxical mystery, but at least Balthasar presents a clue to solve it by referring to the actual example of St. Thérèse's self-giving love. If a human being (though a saint) could wish out of love to be in hell but fails to do so perfectly, because of her limitations as a human being, it is not illogical at all to say that the Son of God wished for it even more strongly and succeeded in doing so. St. Thérèse's wish for vicarious suffering and her actual experience did really happen, so it would not be too far-fetched to speculate that something similar happened in the case of Christ as well.

Balthasar turns to the writings of various saints and mystics in history, because they present the best examples of those who were actually drawn into the inner life of Jesus Christ. For Balthasar, they can give us not only the insights into the inner mystery of Jesus Christ's suffering, death, and descent into hell but also the concrete examples of how to live as hs followers.[100] We should bear this point in mind, as it is one of our goals to pay full respect to the genre in which he is working, which we understand to be a combination of theology and spirituality.

"Hope" for Universal Salvation

St. Thérèse is again a source of inspiration for Balthasar along with many others[101] when it comes to his famous "hope" for universal salvation. It is well known that towards the end of his life he was harshly criticized by conservative Catholic circles for this "hope." It is true that he was inclined to hope that hell might be empty, but that "hope" itself was based on a strong fear of hell, a glimpse into which he gained by witnessing Speyr's mystical suffering year after year. In his own words,

> Her [Speyr's] experience of it [hell] was so real that, *in view of it, it would be ridiculous and blasphemous* to speak of the

---

100. See McIntosh, *Christology from Within*, 89–113; *Mystical Theology*, 101–14.

101. Another major influence on this point is Karl Barth, as we mentioned in the Introduction to this book.

nonexistence of hell or even just of *apokatastasis* in the "systematic" sense.[102]

Balthasar and Speyr remind us that the true answer cannot be a simple Either/Or of Origen and Augustine. As Speyr says, "Both are part of an expression of the whole truth."[103] Along with Speyr, Balthasar takes a nuanced position in the issue of universal salvation. While denying the universalism in the systematic sense, he proposes that we have a right and even a duty to "hope" for the salvation of the whole humanity, as it may be possible that even the worst sinners are moved by God's grace to repent before they die. He also points out the opposite possibility. Since we are able to resist the grace of God, none of us is really "safe." We must therefore leave the question speculatively open, thinking primarily of the danger in which we ourselves stand. Balthasar writes, "'Hell' here is something that falls to me personally—not hypothetically but by full rights—which, without any side glances at others, I have to withstand in utmost seriousness."[104] After all, it is not our business to brood on who is or will be in hell "objectively" as if we ourselves were just curious onlookers. Our first priority is to take personally the profound depth of the love of God, who even descended into hell to save us from damnation. There is a popular idea that the only people in hell are those who would like other people to be in it, but there is something profound to the idea.

In *A Short Discourse on Hell*, Balthasar somberly refers to St. Paul's poignant willingness to be accursed and cut off from Christ himself for the sake of his brethren,[105] which Paul states in the Epistle to the Romans 9:3. In the preceding passage, Paul declares rather proudly that nothing in the world could ever separate him from the love of God, but then, right after it, he expresses his sorrow on account of his own people, saying, "I could wish that I myself were accursed and cut off from Christ for the sake of my own people, my kindred according to the flesh" (Rom 9:3). Balthasar refers to this statement of Paul as an example of extreme love. He further points out that in the history of the saints there have been many other similar wishes made to sacrifice one's own salvation for the sake of salvation of others (as we have seen in the case of St. Thérèse).

Contemplation of such examples of love makes us think that the ultimate faith in God cannot simply be about believing that one has secured a

---

102. Balthasar, *First Glance at Adrienne von Speyr*, 67. Italics added.

103. Speyr, *Kreuz und Hölle* II, 85: "Beides ist ein Teilausdruck der totalen Wahrheit."

104. Balthasar, *Dare We Hope "That all Men be Saved"?*, 189.

105. Ibid., 204–6.

place in heaven. Certainly, such a wish cannot be, and in fact must not be, made lightly. As Paul's example suggests, only the one that has no doubt about their love for God or only the one that is living in perfect union with God could have such a wish. And Jesus is the only one that fully satisfies the condition. After all, "Only One has descended into Hell," as C. S. Lewis says in *The Great Divorce*, because "Only the Greatest of all can make Himself small enough to enter Hell."[106] We can see that the saints' loving willingness to be in hell for the sake of others is actually encompassed within Jesus Christ's obedient love towards the Father and the world, which was revealed in the abandonment on the Cross and in the descent into hell.

The abyss of divine love encompasses that of hell, but the reality of hell along with the human freedom to commit sin is not at all undermined. Hell still remains a possibility for those who reject the love of God, for it is considered as a christological concept or a result of Christ's descent into *Sheol*. However, Pitstick has argued that despite the fact Balthasar presents universal salvation merely as a "hope," this structure necessarily leads to universal salvation in a systematic sense.[107] As this point is also related to the question concerning whether Balthasar's theology stays within the tradition or not, let us discuss this point below further.

For example, the following passage from *Love Alone is Credible* is quite suggestive for our discussion:

> The ultimate abysses of man's freedom to oppose God open up at the place where God, in the freedom of his love, makes the decision to descend kenotically all the way into the forsakenness of the world. With his descent, he reveals this forsakenness: to himself, insofar as he wants to experience abandonment by God, and to the world, which only now measures the entire breadth of its own freedom to oppose God against the dimensions of God's love . . . *From this point on, true, deliberate atheism becomes possible for the very first time, since, prior to this, without a genuine concept of God, there could be no true atheism.*[108]

What Balthasar presents as "true atheism" here is no mere unbelief or doubts about the existence of God. It is rather a real, deliberate rejection of God based on the full understanding of the cost of redemption. Pitstick argues that such a complete rejection of God is impossible before death so Balthasar's theology *necessarily* leads to universal salvation, despite the fact

---

106. Lewis, *The Great Divorce*, 139.

107. See Pitstick, *Light in Darkness*, 263–74.

108. Balthasar, *Love Alone is Credible*, 91–92.

that he only presents it as a "hope."[109] However, is such a total rejection really impossible? We can put the question in another way: can we not know God's existence and his love and still reject him? If not, we are left with the classic problem of hell.[110] In fact, Balthasar is among many who take the self-choice of hell with utmost seriousness. For example, the following passage written by C. S. Lewis is quite insistent on this matter:

> There are only two kinds of people in the end: those who say to God, "Thy will be done," and those to whom God says, in the end, "*Thy* will be done." All that are in Hell, choose it. Without that self-choice there could be no Hell.[111]

In the last analysis, Balthasar's hope for universal salvation seems to balance well this kind of self-choice for eternal damnation and the universal scope of salvation, which seems to be attested by Scripture itself. Balthasar's theology has the potential to take the human freedom to commit sins and the depth of God's love far more seriously than any other. Hell is the place where the human freedom and divine freedom ultimately meet, but Balthasar tries to present the love of God as being deeper than the sinner's refusal. Balthasar's thesis is that the love of God is deeper than hell, but at the same time he tries to maintain the human freedom to the fullest. In

---

109. Pitstick, *Light in the Darkness*, 268–69.

110. For further examination of the problem of hell, see Adams, *Horrendous Evils and the Goodness of God*; Kvanvig, *The Problem of Hell*; Seymour, *A Theodicy of Hell*; and Walls, *Hell*. Thanks to these scholars, the doctrine of hell has been seeing renewed interest for the past few decades, but the problem of hell remains one of the most difficult problems facing Christianity. Why does an all-loving and all-powerful God punish anyone eternally? Traditionally, hell was justified as a matter of retributive justice which God imposes on sinners who deserve it (For example, St. Augustine, St. Thomas Aquinas, St. Anselm, and Jonathan Edwards take this position). Though once a very popular idea, today it has very few defenders. Many scholars who take up the issue of hell seriously today argue that the punishment model of hell is not the best way to defend the doctrine, mainly because "infinite" punishment cannot be proportional to any sins that "finite" beings can ever commit. Instead, now the most common way of explaining hell is to appeal to human freedom which includes the freedom to reject God eternally (see Seymour and Walls). Some people actually choose hell themselves. The freedom theory of hell could give a convincing alternative to the problematic punishment model of hell, but still is not free from criticism. For instance, strong criticisms come from those who advocate universalism (see Adams). Therefore, we still have to seek a way to solve the conflict between the freedom model of hell and universalism. This is the context where Balthasar's treatment of hell and hope for universal salvation should be evaluated.

111. Lewis, *The Great Divorce*, 75.

this sense, Balthasar's description of the lonely sinner with the even lonelier Savior beside them makes perfect sense. In his own words,

> There can be no more talk of doing violence to freedom if God appears in the loneliness of the one who has chosen the total loneliness of living only for himself (or perhaps one should say: who thinks that is how he has chosen) and shows himself to be as the One who is still lonelier than the sinner.[112]

How Should We Reflect on the Questions Concerning Hell?

let us pause here to briefly reflect on why the discussion of hell (and consequently heaven too) is important. These days hell seems to be far from being a "popular" topic among theologians and lay Christians alike, while the belief in hell itself still seems to be common.[113] Hannah Arendt once said that "the most significant consequence of the secularization of the modern age may well be the elimination from public life, along with religion, of the only political element in traditional religion, the fear of hell."[114] However, this "elimination of the fear of hell" could have serious consequences. Anthony Kelly, for example, discusses the alarming consequences of evading the issue of hell and makes a point that hell can reemerge "in a secular guise." He writes, "When the topic of hell cannot be mentioned, the destructive force of evil is unacknowledged. Talking only of the goodness of God be-

112. Balthasar, *Explorations in Theology* IV, 456–57.

113. For example, according to a survey conducted by Gallup in 2011, 75 percent of the Americans surveyed said "yes" to the question, "Do you believe in Hell?" (whereas 85 percent said "yes" to the question, "Do you believe in Heaven?") Considering that in the same survey, 92 percent answered that they believe in God, it would be safe to say that the belief in heaven and hell is still an important aspect of religious faith (See Gallup.com: http://www.gallup.com/poll/1690/religion.aspx). If we turn to Catholics, there is one online survey reporting that 83 percent of the Catholics surveyed believe in hell, but interestingly, very few of them (0.4 percent in this survey) actually believe they will go to hell after they die themselves. Further, this tendency not to believe in hell for oneself but for others seems to be found more or less in any denomination. This point should be taken rather seriously, for it is one thing to believe in heaven and hell, but it is entirely another to believe that there are actually some specific people suffering in there. Is there not something even selfish or unethical about such a belief? We should rather take a nuanced and sophisticated approach when we consider the questions about hell and heaven (See Beliefnet.com: http://www.beliefnet.com/Faiths/2007/01/What-Catholics-Believe-About-Hell.aspx).

114. Arendt, *Between Past and Future*, 133.

comes nauseatingly unreal and so fuels an angry despair over the evils of the world."[115] As a consequence, we end up with the situations too often described as "hell on earth." The "hellish" situations can be socially or politically determined ones, but not always.

In the beginning of his interpretation of the article of the descent into hell in the Apostles' Creed, Benedict XVI writes, "possibly no article of the Creed is so far from present-day attitudes of mind of this one."[116] Then he goes on to "demythologize" the article and points out that this article, which at first seems so outdated, is in reality "particularly close to our day and is to a particular degree the experience of our century."[117] Balthasar himself often mentions the impact of Holy Saturday on the modern "death-of-God" philosophy.[118] He locates this "modern" image of hell as "the condition of the self-enclosed 'I,' the 'I' unliberated by God"[119] in his theology of Holy Saturday. Balthasar certainly has the nineteenth-twentieth century philosophy and literature in the scope of his theology of Holy Saturday, and he even writes that the world probably had to wait for the modern experience of the "death of God" in order to appreciate Speyr's mystical visions of hell,[120] which is characterized by such "modern" words as loneliness, emptiness, futility. (It is in this context that, for example, Matthew Lewis Sutton argues that "to comfort, to redeem, to heal, the theology of Holy Saturday as the descent of God into hell is the only compelling belief in God for us in this postmodern age."[121])

If we turn to the area of literature, we still find a variety of authors portraying the hellish realities in an existential sense, which are characterized by anxiety, despair, loneliness, and other negative sentiments[122] and Balthasar himself refers to a variety of authors who wrote on this topic.[123] There are two well-known definitions of hell written in the twentieth century. T. S. Eliot, in *The Cocktail Party*, has one character saying, "What is

---

115. Kelly, *Eschatology and Hope*, 139.

116. Ratzinger, *Introduction to Christianity*, 293.

117. Ibid., 294.

118. For example, Balthasar, *Mysterium Paschale*, 51–52.

119. Ibid., 77.

120. Balthasar, "Einleitung," 10.

121. Sutton, "Does God Suffer?," 179.

122. For example, Wilhelm Maas refers to Rimbaud, Baudelaire, Claudel, Sartre, etc. as those who have experienced their own "hell." (See Maas, *Gott und die Hölle*). For a survey of more contemporary approaches to hell, see Falconer, *Hell in Contemporary Literature*.

123. For example, Balthasar, *Glory of the Lord* III; *Theo-Drama* V, 300–21.

hell? Hell is oneself, hell is alone, the other figures in it merely projections. There is nothing to escape from and nothing to escape to. One is always alone."[124] On the other hand, the seemingly opposite expression of hell is given by Jean Paul Sartre in his play, *No Exit*. One character, who is locked up with two despicable women forever in hell shouts at the end of the play, "Hell is other people!"[125] These two expressions seem to describe the opposite states of being on the surface, but in fact they could be understood to describe hell as absolute loneliness in different ways, because it is the state of being where one is separated from God and isolated from other human beings, whether one is in a crowded room or literally by oneself. In short, the reality of "hell" as loneliness caused by separation from God or from other people cannot be emphasized too much. Therefore, it is crucial for serious Christian theologians to deal with the issue of hell and seek to provide some "hope" for an answer. For this purpose, Balthasar's and Speyr's contributions are still worthy of our recognition.

In this chapter, on the basis of their writings, we have explored hell as the state of absolute loneliness of the sinner and as a christological concept. Let us pause here to reflect on why such an approach is important. In the last analysis, it is significant to think about hell, purgatory, and heaven as christological concepts, in other words, as direct results of Christ's redemptive work, because it means that these states are determined entirely by *our relationship with Jesus Christ*. To put it differently, these states cannot be merely about our afterlife, but should be directly related to our present, current states of being in this world. St. John Paul II once said that hell, purgatory, and heaven should be understood as "states of being" in relation to God rather than actual places. He described heaven as "a living, personal relationship with the Holy Trinity"[126] and likewise hell as "the state of those who freely and definitively separate themselves from God, the source of all life and joy."[127] We also have to note that we should consider these states in terms of the divine-human relationship because the language of place is inadequate to describe the realities of these states, not because they only have symbolic meanings. Further, this point is directly related to the quality of faith.

As we mentioned briefly when we discussed the hope for universal salvation, faith in God cannot just mean reservation of a place in heaven. Rather, it should be the transformation in our present life based on our

---

124. Eliot, *The Cocktail Party*, 87.

125. Sartre, *No Exit and Three Other Plays*, 45.

126. John Paul II, "Hell is the State of Those who Reject God," n.p.

127. John Paul II, "Purgatory is Necessary Purification," n.p.

living, dynamic relationship with God. Likewise, damnation cannot merely be a bad fate which falls on us only after we die. If we choose to reject the love of God, then our present life leads to loneliness caused by separation from God. After all, God is the living God for the living, so our belief in heaven, purgatory, and hell should be exactly reflected in our present way of life. Heaven should not be sought as a reward for faith, even though heaven is unquestionably is a place for those who seek God lovingly. Balthasar, who combines theology and spirituality by turning to the examples of saints in history such as St. John and St. Thérèse, clarifies this point. Apparently, his concern does not lie so much in shaping the Catholic doctrine of hell as in exploring aspects of hell for the sake of the life of Christian faith.[128] His insistence (inspired by Speyr) that we should overcome the Either/Or between Origen and Augustine shows this point well (for if we try to systematize the doctrine, we would have no choice but to accept either Origen or Augustine). Rather, he tries to show a way of contemplating the state of heaven and hell with a healthy sense of fear and hope understood in terms of our relationship with God. He does so by following the examples of the saints like St. John and St. Thérèse. In the last analysis, Balthasar proposes that we should seek God himself alone, who is revealed in Jesus Christ, as these saints do. In his words,

> God is the "last thing" of the creature. Gained, he is heaven; lost, he is hell; examining, he is judgment; purifying, he is purgatory. To him finite being dies, and through and to and in him it rises. But this is God as he presents himself to the world, that is, in his Son, *Jesus Christ*, who is the revelation of God and therefore the whole essence of the last things.[129]

It is also worth noting that, with such a focus on God himself, Balthasar is countering a neo-scholastic treatment of the traditional four last things (death, judgment, heaven, and hell), which was essentially concerned with the afterlife, in other words, what happens to the soul after death.

In short, we consider it one of the contributions made by Balthasar's theology of Holy Saturday that he has given a clue to how we should reflect on the matter of hell in our age where the topic of hell is not popular anymore in Christian life but still highly relevant. We should not exclude discussion of hell and heaven from our life of faith as something obsolete or even unpleasant, for, as Balthasar and Speyr have shown, it is directly related to the quality of our faith.

---

128. Balthasar, "Theologie des Abstiegs zur Hölle," 146.
129. Balthasar, *Explorations in Theology* I, 260–61.

Conclusion: Love Alone Can Descend into Hell

In this chapter, we have examined hell as a christological concept. We started this chapter by examining Speyr's mystical visions of hell. Then we went on to discuss "sin-in-itself" as a significant concept for appreciating the in-betweenness of Holy Saturday captured by Balthasar and Speyr. We have also described the hell into which Christ descended as the absolute loneliness of the sinner, which is also called the dark night of the soul. On the basis of Balthasar's reading of St. John of the Cross and St. Thérèse of Lisieux, we have explored the christological paradox that Jesus Christ the incarnate Son of God has experienced godforsakenness more deeply than any human being. We have taken up the issue of Balthasar's treatment of the divinity and humanity of Christ again, and have argued that at least Balthasar is consistent with his logic of kenotic love. We could even say that his christological thesis that Christ's divinity is expressed in his humanity would make sense only in the name of kenotic love. Balthasar values the logic of love in his "hope" for universal salvation as well. Despite the critique that his theology of Holy Saturday inevitably leads to affirming universal salvation in a systematic sense, we have attempted to argue that Balthasar actually seems to balance well the human freedom to reject God and God's universal love for humanity.

In addition, we have pointed out how the concept of hell is still relevant for the Christian life today, and argued that the hell described as the loneliness of the sinner separated from God and from fellow human beings makes it easier for us to see the relevance of the doctrine of Christ's descent into hell for our postmodern world, where many people seem to suffer from the sense of isolation or alienation in various forms. Therefore, one implication that Balthasar's theology of Holy Saturday can provide for Christian suffering is related to the concept of hell as the dark night of the soul.

Thus, in chapters 1 and 2, we have discussed Balthasar's interpretation of Christ's descent into hell. We have highlighted two points in particular; first, Balthasar attempts to appreciate the "in-between" state of Christ in *Sheol* on Holy Saturday instead of departing far from the "traditional" interpretation; and secondly Balthasar apparently shows a deep interest in the reality of human suffering. Both points will be discussed further in detail as we connect them to the "tragic" in-between state of Christian existence in chapter 4. As a conclusion of this chapter, let us discuss below what we can learn to deepen our understanding of Christian suffering and discipleship on the basis of what we have examined so far.

We would like to stress again the significance of the dark night of the soul for Balthasar's theology of Holy Saturday. The concept is significant because it helps us to locate clearly the genre within which Balthasar is working and to understand the spiritual aspect of Christ's suffering as well as the Christian's. In particular, we have focused on St. John of the Cross and St. Thérèse of Lisieux as the main influences on Balthasar and Speyr concerning this matter. These two Carmelites show one distinctive form of suffering in Christian discipleship. Their examples tell us that God is in fact with us even when he seems to be absent or dead in the midst of our suffering. They also show us one Christian way to persevere in the seeming absence of God for the sake of love for our brethren.

These points are significant for examination of Balthasar's treatments of the Trinity, Christology, and universal salvation as well. After all, throughout his theological writings, he is not so much concerned with presenting a systematic view of theological concepts as with contemplatively exploring the abyss of kenotic divine love to the fullest. This attitude permeates his entire theological corpus, so something will be missed if we seek to systematize his thoughts in a strictly scholastic way. At least he seems to be aware of the potential issues and endeavors to avoid them subtly, so even his critics can only accuse of the "tendency" of his theology. At least he is consistent with his logic of kenotic love, and he explains even hell (the exact opposite of love and communion) on the basis of the divine love, which is perfectly self-giving to the point of sheer recklessness. On the other hand, this kind of exploration has invited a criticism that his style is presumptuously overarching and has the potential danger of blurring the distinction between love and loss or between suffering and joy.[130] Regarding this point, we would rather suggest that he may be only sensitive to the paradoxical mystery of love and faith.

In order to clarify this point, let us discuss one of the recent examples of the dark night of the soul persevered for the sake of others: St. Mother Teresa. She is probably the most unexpected person in our age that has confessed to having experienced a dark night of the soul.[131] Certainly, Balthasar himself did not know that St. Mother Teresa was going through the dark night but this connection seems to be relevant for our discussion. She said, "In my soul I feel just that terrible pain of loss, of God not wanting me—of God not being God—of God not existing."[132] She also confessed, "when I open my mouth to speak to the sisters and to people about God and God's

130. See chapter 1.

131. For examination of St. Mother Teresa's dark night of the soul, see, for example, Murray, *I Loved Jesus in the Night*.

132. Mother Teresa, quoted in *The New York Times*, 23 August, 2007. Quoted by Hart in *Knowing Darkness*, 1.

work, it brings them light, joy and courage. But I get nothing out of it. Inside it is all dark and feeling that I am totally cut off from God."[133] She is known to have undergone the dark night to the end of her life. While she used to feel ashamed of herself having lost faith in God, eventually she reached the stage that she was able to accept it with joy because she realized that this experience could unite her even more closely with the poorest and the loneliest. As she said, "The physical situation of my poor left in the streets unwanted, unloved, unclaimed—are the true picture of my own spiritual life."[134] Further, in the following words of hers we can see a certain sense of joy paradoxically coexisting with the suffering of the dark night:

> Thank God all went well yesterday, sisters, children, the lepers, the sick and our poor families have all been so happy and contented this year. A real Christmas. —Yet within me—nothing but darkness, conflict, loneliness so terrible. I am perfectly happy to be like this to the end of life.[135]

This is certainly one exemplary form of Christian suffering in the sense that the suffering from a loss of faith or the apparent absence of God was patiently persevered out of love for brethren.[136] One important merit of examining such an experience is that now we can see that our suffering of loss of faith can be of service for God and for our brethren instead of merely causing embarrassment or a sense of guilt within us. In Balthasar's words, "where tangible joy is withdrawn from us, we are right to hope that other hearts may light up because of our darkness,"[137] though it does not mean at all that we should actively seek to go through the dark night of the soul ourselves. Certainly this kind of suffering is *not* accessible for everyone. Nevertheless this is one of the insights Balthasar's theology of Holy Saturday can provide for Christian suffering and discipleship.

As ultimately shown in the case of Christ's suffering in the hell of god-forsakenness, Balthasar's theology dramatically presents the paradoxical mystery of love. The more intimate our relationship with God is, the more

---

133. Mother Teresa to Bishop Picachy, 21 September, 1962. See *Come Be My Light*, 238. Quoted by Murray in *I Loved Jesus in the Night*, 63.

134. Mother Teresa to Father Neuner, 12 May, 1962. See *Come Be My Light*, 232. Quoted by Murray in *I Loved Jesus in the Night*, 68.

135. Mother Teresa to Bishop Picachy, 26 December, 1959. See *Come Be My Light*, 198. Quoted by Murray in *I Loved Jesus in the Night*, 66.

136. Speyr's mystical experience of Christ's passion too can be placed within this context. After all, she accepted this mystical suffering for the sake of other brethren and Balthasar presented it as a great charismatic gift for the whole church.

137. Balthasar, *You Crown the Year with Your Goodness*, 30–31.

likely we are to experience godforsakenness. Therefore, we can even argue that love alone can descend into hell, which is nothing less than the exact opposite of love. This is not a contradiction or a mere theological word play. The actual examples of St. John, St. Thérèse, St. Mother Teresa, and many other saints and mystics in history show us that there is some profound truth in this paradox appreciated by Balthasar.

Thus, we would like to suggest that his approach to the relationship between love and loss or between suffering and joy should be described as "paradoxical" rather than "overarching" as some critics may say. However, this point cannot be fully justified until the end of chapter 4, where we will discuss the in-between state of the Christian, whose paradoxical existence can be characterized by the long waiting between the times.

Holy Saturday and Mary

Introduction

IN THE PREVIOUS CHAPTERS, WE HAVE EXAMINED BALTHASAR'S THEOLOGY of Holy Saturday by focusing on its three principal aspects, its Trinitarian framework, its christological significance, and its soteriological effects. As the conclusion of this examination, we discussed that, paradoxically, love alone can descend into hell (the opposite of love) and that God is in fact with us even when he seems to be absent or dead in the midst of our suffering. We also pointed out how Balthasar's theology is rooted in the tradition of the dark night of the soul, which reveals one Christian way to bear suffering out of love for brethren. In addition, we have highlighted two points: first, that Balthasar does not try to present a radical reinterpretation of the doctrine of the descent into hell in contrast to the traditional teachings, but rather endeavors to appreciate the "in-between" state of Christ in *Sheol* on Holy Saturday more seriously than any other theologian has ever done; and secondly, that Balthasar shows a deep interest in the reality of human suffering throughout his theological corpus.

Now, in the following chapters, we will discuss these two points in greater depth and try to present some implications of Balthasar's theology of Holy Saturday for Christian suffering and discipleship. The specific question we will explore further in the following chapters is: How does Balthasar's theology of Holy Saturday help us understand the role of suffering in Christian discipleship and help Christians deal with their suffering? This question is worth exploring for the following two reasons.

First, even if Christians have the means to find salvific meaning in their suffering by regarding it as a participation in the paschal mystery in theory,[1] suffering still remains an immense challenge for many Christians. Therefore, it has always been an open topic and it would be helpful if we could add some insights into this problem by focusing on the specific position of Holy Saturday as the day between the cross and the resurrection. As we will discuss in chapter 4, in many ways, the Christian life seems to be best characterized by the in-betweenness of Holy Saturday. In short, *our* Holy Saturday can be meaningful and bearable because of Christ's Holy Saturday.

Secondly, scholars' opinions actually divide concerning Balthasar's treatment of human suffering. For some, Balthasar's theology provides an ideal approach (even an answer) to the problem of suffering and evil. Balthasar roughly belongs to the one tradition in the church which "tends to" align love with suffering and faith with dying to self, and which even regards some form of suffering as a necessary part of Christian discipleship.[2] Some scholars seem to be critical of this tendency or "genre" itself.[3] However, some of the critiques raised against him seem to arise from something more than a mere genre difference. We could largely summarize such critiques into two points: first, that Balthasar does not engage with concrete social and historical contexts despite his deep concerns for human suffering, and secondly, that he presents too positive a view of human suffering. In the following chapters, we will deal with these critiques and examine whether or not Balthasar's theology of Holy Saturday can stand them. In the last analysis, we will conclude that his theology of Holy Saturday can provide a hopeful message for those who are suffering, but we will do so with some reserve.

In the previous chapters, our focus was on Christ's Holy Saturday. As we have seen, Balthasar's theology of Holy Saturday provides profound material for us to contemplate Christ in *Sheol* on Holy Saturday, so we have examined them from Trinitarian, christological, and soteriological perspectives. Most of the discussions on this subject usually terminate here. Many commentators have discussed the abyss of God's kenotic love, which descends as deep as hell. However, we believe that it does not do full justice to the wide scope that Balthasar's theology of Holy Saturday potentially has, if we limit our examination to Christ's descent into hell alone. As we mentioned in the introduction, Balthasar himself has preferred this liturgical phrase "Holy Saturday" to the more doctrinal phrase "Christ's descent

1. One exemplary Christian response to the problem of suffering is St. John Paul II's *Salvifici Doloris.*

2. We have already discussed the dark night of the soul as a significant concept for Balthasar's theology.

3. For example, we can say that Pitstick and Kilby belong to this group. See Kilby, *Balthasar*, 118–19.

into hell." It is not merely about the activity or passivity of Christ in hell. It is not only about what Christ did, or where he was on this particular day, or in what condition, but it has in its scope the whole "Holy Saturday" experience, which is characterized by silent waiting. We also believe that this aspect of waiting is important to understand the way Balthasar remains faithful to the Catholic tradition. Throughout this book we attempt to read him as the one who fully appreciates the strange silent pause between death and life, and between suffering and victory. For example, in his meditation on the fourteenth station of the cross ("Jesus is laid in the tomb") he writes as follows:

> So already his unquiet image haunts heads and hearts.
> Already the spirit is freed.
> Already the Easter question takes shape . . .
> But silently.
> For tomorrow is only Holy Saturday.
> The day when God is dead,
> and the Church holds her breath.
> The strange day that separates life and death
> in order to join them in a marriage beyond all human thought.[4]

As we have noted, once we pay attention to Balthasar's emphasis on the "in-betweenness" of Holy Saturday, hence, on the aspect of waiting, we start to discern the possibility of widening its scope to explore its implications for Christian life. On Holy Saturday, Christ waited in hell for the resurrection, while Mary (and other women) waited at the tomb in faith and trust to God. Liturgically, we relive this waiting every year on Holy Saturday.

For Balthasar, Mary's *fiat* is the perfect role model of Christian discipleship, which has originated in Christ's own kenotic obedience. In chapter 3, we will discuss how Mary obediently participated in her son's mission from the beginning to the end. However, Balthasar's Mariology also has a serious problem because of his departure from Vatican II's Mariology. He attempts to incorporate his outdated view of sexual differentiation into Mariology and as a consequence his Mariology becomes fragile and indefensible against critiques. In relation to this point and also as a preparation for chapter 4, we will discuss his critics' concern that Balthasar's theology does not really serve the cause of social justice, including gender equality.

Chapter 3 is divided into the following sections: 1) the Marian principle and the significance of Mary in Balthasar's theology, 2) Mary's *fiat* from the Annunciation to the foot of the cross, 3) Mary on Holy Saturday, 4)

---

4. Balthasar, *The Way of the Cross*, 30.

Balthasar's view of childlikeness, and 5) conclusion: Balthasar's problematic view of sexual differentiation.

The Marian Principle and the Significance of Mary in Balthasar's Theology

First, let us start discussing the place and significance of Our Lady in Balthasar's theology and clarify why it is relevant for us to discuss her here. For Balthasar, Mariology is clearly located within both Christology and ecclesiology.[5] However, this position does not in the least mean that Mariology is a minor subject which would not affect our understanding of his theology even if we skip it. Rather, as John Saward states, for Balthasar "there can be no Christology without Trinitarian doctrine, but there can likewise be no Christology without Mariology, neither Incarnation nor Cross without the Virgin who said Yes."[6] In the Apostles' Creed the name of Mary appears in the context of the incarnation, and this point indicates that Mariology is first of all located in Christology. The inseparable link between Christology and Mariology can be traced back to the patristic writings, and Balthasar unquestionably endeavors to work within this long tradition. As has been pointed out by some,[7] he evidently believed himself to be living in the era where Mariology was neglected and tried to return Our Lady back in the position she deserves within the church and theology. Balthasar also warns about how "inhuman," "soulless," and "boring" the church would be without the presence of Mary:

> Without Mariology Christianity threatens imperceptibly to become *inhuman*. The Church becomes functionalistic, *soulless*, a hectic enterprise without any point of rest, estranged from its true nature by the planners. And because, in this *manly-masculine* world, all that we have is one ideology replacing another, everything becomes polemical, critical, bitter, humourless and

---

5. For example, see Balthasar, *Elucidations*, 65–66. As to the secondary sources on Balthasar's Mariology, see Murphy, "Immaculate Mary"; Gardner, "Balthasar and the Figure of Mary"; Leahy, *The Marian Profile*; Nichols, "Marian Co-redemption."

6. Saward, *The Mysteries of March*, 61.

7. For example, Aidan Nichols explains how Balthasar tried to overcome the false dichotomy between the maximalistic and minimalistic understandings of the role of Mary existent in the Catholic Mariology of his time. Nichols, *Divine Fruitfulness*, 235–36.

ultimately *boring*, and people in their masses run away from such a Church.[8]

As can be detected from this quote, the Marian principle is believed to add distinctively "feminine" characteristics to the church. The question of what is meant by the word "feminine" underlies this whole chapter, and in order to fully understand it, we must first refer to Balthasar's concept of "the Christological constellation" as the foundation of the structure of the church.

Like all areas in his theological corpus, Balthasar does not offer a systematic ecclesiology. Rather, his ecclesiology is composed of his reflections on a constellation of the following three figures who embody the church: the Virgin Mary, St. Peter, and St. John, who respectively represent the Marian, the Petrine, and the Johannine principles. This emphasis on the subjective principles derived from these three figures who were closest to Christ is based on Balthasar's strong conviction that the church is first of all the primordial subject of believing. (On this point, he follows his mentor Henri de Lubac and goes further.[9]) Therefore, for Balthasar, the question concerning the identity of the church should be addressed as "*Who* is the church?" instead of "*What* is the church?"[10]

Who, then, is the church? He explores this question throughout his theological corpus, but perhaps the most concise answer is the following one:

> The Church in her deepest reality is the unity of those who, gathered and formed by the immaculate and therefore limitless assent of Mary, which through grace has the form of Christ, are prepared to let the saving will of God take place in themselves and for all their brothers.[11]

As can be seen in this quote, the Marian principle derived from Our Lady, which is mostly characterized by her obedient faith and loving consent (as we will discuss in detail below), is considered as the most comprehensive principle of the church, which embraces all others (the Petrine and the Johannine).[12] The Petrine principle represents the "male" official hierar-

8. Balthasar, *Elucidations*, 72. Italics added.

9. See Nichols, *Divine Fruitfulness*, 200.

10. See for example, his essay "Who is the Church?" in Balthasar, *Explorations in Theology* II, 143–91.

11. Balthasar, *My Work*, 63.

12. To be accurate, Balthasar also mentions the Pauline principle, which is characterized by charismatic and visionary graces, but due to the fact that those who are

chy of the church which succeeds the apostolic preaching and ministering of sacraments, and which has the Pope as its apex.[13] The principle which combines the Marian principle (feminine/lay) and the Petrine (masculine/official) is the Johannine principle derived from St. John (the Beloved Disciple), which is the principle of love. This structure is most symbolically represented by the scene at the foot of the cross, where, as Balthasar explains, the church is born. While Peter is absent, John represents the official side of the church, and Christ hands over his Mother to John's care. These three principles together constitute the archetypes of Christian experiences, but the Marian principle is the most central of these three. Mary, as the immaculately conceived one, realizes in advance what the church is supposed to be (*Ecclesia Immaculata*) in her own person. In Balthasar's words, "Mary is the womb and archetype of the Church, she is the fruitfulness of the Church herself, she is the internal form of the Church, since she is the Bride of Christ . . .Mary is the virginal-nuptial vessel of all obedience, out of which flows not only the Christian's obedience but Peter's demands as well."[14]

There is probably nothing particularly wrong with such a typology and categorization itself, but the inherent problem starts to appear when Balthasar uses this typological ecclesiology to explain the current structure of the Catholic Church. This point becomes most apparent in the logic Balthasar uses to deny the possibility of the ordination of women.[15] With his typological ecclesiology he attempts to explain that it is because of the comprehensive "feminine" Marian principle that the complete "maleness" of the priesthood can be justified without calling into question the equality between men and women. Balthasar stresses that the Marian or feminine principle precedes the Petrine or masculine principle. In contrast to the Apostles, who "begin as failures . . . and can never match the quality of the primordial Church, the 'perfect Bride,' the *Immaculata*,"[16] the Virgin Mary is the first to believe in Christ and the one who gives perfect consent to the incarnation, hence to God's salvific plan for the whole humanity. The church existed in her even before any of the men were called to be an Apostle. Therefore, the Petrine office is "a partial share in the total

---

gifted with such graces are limited, it does not enter into the description of the "basic" structure of the church. See Nichols, *Divine Fruitfulness*, 200–1.

13. In other words, "objective" holiness.

14. Balthasar, *Razing the Bastions*, 40.

15. Balthasar, *New Elucidations*, 187–98.

16. Ibid., 192.

flawlessness of the feminine, marian Church,"[17] while Mary as "the Queen of Apostles" has a unique and all-encompassing role, even though it represents the lay position. Therefore, Balthasar argues that a woman who would aspire to be ordained is actually asking for something *less* than what they have now. Balthasar further says, "Because of her unique structure, the Catholic Church is perhaps humanity's last bulwark of genuine appreciation of the difference between the sexes."[18] However, as we will discuss later, this kind of logic contains the danger of being merely utilized to silence the voices of women.

In relation to this point, we have to mention Balthasar's reaction to Vatican II's Mariology, for his attempt to link Mariology to the sexual differences is where Balthasar departs from the Council's position.[19] While Balthasar appreciates Vatican II's acknowledgement that Mary is the archetype of the church, he also finds the Council's position deficient as it does not include a number of relevant issues, such as sexual difference, in its treatment of Mary. For Balthasar, Mary does not just happen to be a woman. She is *the Woman*, and she can represent the whole creation in front of God precisely because she is a woman. This is related to the fact that Balthasar applies the analogy of the man-woman difference to the Creator-creation relationship. For Balthasar, essentially, to be a man is to give and to be a woman is to receive. The following passage inserted in his discussion of the Marian principle is a good summary of his view of sexual difference. After affirming the fact that the woman is as active as the man in the act of generation, he declares as follows:

> It is undeniable, however, that *the woman is the one who receives and that it is the man who gives*. Conclusion: to receive, to consent, to accept, to let things be is perhaps a no less active and creative attitude than that of giving, forming, imposing. And if in the Incarnation the part of man is taken by God, who is essentially the one who gives, indeed, who imposes, the part of the woman, who, as creature, accepts the divine gift, is far from being passive. Let us say, rather, that this acquiescence is the highest and most fruitful of human activities; in Pauline terms: faith is more fundamentally required than any works.[20]

17. Ibid., 193.

18. Ibid., 195.

19. For Balthasar's reaction to Vatican II, see Balthasar, *Theo-Drama* III, 316–18. For a critical summary and analysis of Balthasar's response to Vatican II's treatment of Mary, for example, see Imperatori-Lee, "The Use of Marian Imagery in Catholic Ecclesiology since Vatican II," 59–92.

20. Balthasar and Speyr, *To the Heart of the Mystery of Redemption*, 50. Italics

Consequently, the Marian feminine principle is characterized by a receptive attitude to God, in other words, obedience, the notion which permeates Balthasar's whole theology. As we discussed the notion of obedience in Balthasar's Christology in chapter 1, it does not mean something passive but rather "active" in the sense that the Son *actively* agrees to suffer the godforsakenness of the sinner in utter passivity. Nevertheless, it is highly important to note that for Balthasar the "feminine" basically means "receptive," "obedient," and "open." Unsurprisingly, such an essentialist kind of categorization has invited many critiques. (We will come back to this point later.)

So far, we have summarized the significance of the Marian principle in Balthasar's theology. Last but not least, we cannot overlook the influence of Adrienne von Speyr. Mariology is one of the areas where her influence on Balthasar is the strongest.[21] This point alone might justify our inclusion of the Marian principle in our examination of his theology of Holy Saturday, which has Speyr's visions as one of its main inspirational sources. Not only the presence of Our Lady shaped the spiritual and ecclesial relationship between them (along with St Ignatius of Loyola), but also Speyr is the one that really drove home to Balthasar the significance of the role of Mary in the economy of salvation and in the church.[22] It has also been pointed out that many leit-motifs in Balthasar's Mariology were already present in Speyr's major work on this topic, *Handmaid of the Lord*, in 1948.[23] As we will discuss later, Speyr's mystical visions of the paschal mystery were permeated by the presence of Mary. The following account of her vision in 1942 is symbolically a clear example of Speyr's understanding of Mary, which is also shared by Balthasar:

> In the afternoon, a vision of the Mother of God, on a meadow near the stream [stream made of human sin]. She holds her child tightly. Then she comprehends what is demanded: she should let the Child go up to the stream. She is horrified. Then she says Yes. In infinite inner greatness and goodness. The Child stands before her at the bottom, and takes a few steps. The Mother follows him a little. He, meanwhile, has grown to manhood and

---

added.

21. This fact may sound ironical, considering Speyr's Lutheran origin, but perhaps it was precisely because of her Lutheran past she understood how the church tends to be "inhuman" or "masculine" without the presence of Mary.

22. See Roten, "The Two Halves of the Moon."

23. See Nichols, "Marian Co-redemption," 252.

stands by the stream. Mary has disappeared. Where is she? Praying somewhere, completely separated from Him.[24]

Speyr sees Mary's entire life as being characterized by a perfect consent to the will of God,[25] which is most notably seen in the annunciation and at the foot of the cross. Further, in this vision we can see Speyr's (and eventually Balthasar's) view of the poignant relationship between Jesus and Mary; Mary participates in his salvific mission by consenting to be abandoned by him in a similar way that he agrees to be abandoned by the Father (though on a much smaller scale). She follows him, but only *at a distance*. Exactly because she is the closest to the Son, she has to experience abandonment as a form of perfect love.

Now, let us see below how Balthasar and Speyr actually present the figure of Mary as the role model of Christian faith. Through their portrayal of Mary, we can see their ideas on Christian discipleship as well as their approach to Christian suffering.

Mary's *Fiat* from the Annunciation to the Foot of the Cross

Mary's whole life is characterized by her consent to God's will. As the immaculately conceived one, her consent represents the perfect form of human consent to God's salvific plan. This is the basic stance of Balthasar's and Speyr's Mariology. Aidan Nichols concisely summarizes it as follows: "Balthasar's Mariology has at its heart the question, What of the human consent to all God has done for us in the saving drama found in the Trinitarian revelation, and climaxing in the Paschal Triduum, with the victorious humiliation of the Death and Descent into Hell?"[26]

For Balthasar and Speyr, the role model of the Christian's obedience to the will of God can be most clearly seen in Our Lady's *fiat* at the

24. Speyr, *Kreuz und Hölle* I, 49: "Nachmittag eine Vision der Mutter Gottes, auf einer Wiese in der Nähe des Stromes. Sie hält fest ihr Kind. Dann begreift sie, was gefordert wird: sie soll das Kind gehen lassen, bis zum Strom hin. Sie erschrickt. Dann sagt sie Ja. In unendlicher innerer Größe und Güte. Das Kind steht vor ihr auf dem Boden, macht einige Schritte. Die Mutter folgt ihm ein wenig. Er ist unterdessen zum Mann gewachsen und steht beim Strom. Maria ist verschwunden. Wo ist sie? Irgend wo betend, völlig von ihm getrennt."

25. Speyr writes, "As a sheaf of grain is tied together in the middle and spreads out at either end, so Mary's life is bound together by her assent. From this assent her life receives its meaning and form and unfolds toward past and future." (Speyr, *Handmaid of the Lord*, 7.)

26. Nichols, *Divine Fruitfulness*, 229.

annunciation: "Here am I, the servant of the Lord; let it be with me according to your word" (Luke 1:38). Mary consented not only to the incarnation but also to everything that subsequently happened, including the sorrow, the grief, and the state of godforsakenness that she had to go through all because of her son's salvific mission. Let us discuss below the series of her consents, as Christians are required to imitate the Marian consent at every occasion in their everyday lives. In Balthasar's own words, "If Christ, in Luke, commands us to carry our cross every day, he implies very precisely that this dull, ordinary cross consists in persevering at every moment in the Marian Yes, which transforms everyday mishaps as much as possible into situations that are fruitful in Christian terms."[27]

First of all, at the annunciation, Mary gave a full consent to the incarnation. In many ways, Mary at the annunciation is considered as the best representation of her whole life, which was lived in perfectly prayerful obedience to God (as the "Handmaid of the Lord"). Also, importantly for us, the whole setting where Mary uttered her full consent shows the way that divine and human freedom, in other words infinite and finite freedom, meet in perfect harmony. Balthasar says that Mary's freedom (as the immaculately conceived one) is unique in a different sense from Christ's, as "the figure of Mary exhibits an utterly exuberant form of creaturely freedom . . . the finite freedom that hands itself over and entrusts itself to the sphere of infinite freedom, which, through grace, stands wide open."[28] The perfect form of creaturely freedom is represented by Mary, as "no finite freedom can be freer from restrictions than when giving its consent to infinite freedom."[29] It is important to note here that God does not simply impose his Son on his creation. He waits for Mary's *response* (in other words, his creation's reply, as here Mary represents not only Israel but also the whole human race). Further, as *Lumen Gentium* of Vatican II states (by following many of the patristic authors), Mary, by this consent, is "freely cooperating in the work of human salvation through faith and obedience."[30] (As Christ's obedience is the counterpart to Adam's disobedience in Eden, Mary's obedience is the counterpart to Eve's.[31]) We can follow the perfect harmony between the infinite and finite freedom further by recognizing the nuptial image traditionally used and shared by Balthasar to describe the mystery of hypostatic union. For example, St. Augustine says, "the nuptial union is

27. Balthasar and Speyr, *To the Heart of the Mystery of Redemption*, 58.

28. Balthasar, *Theo-Drama* III, 299.

29. Ibid., 300.

30. Vatican II Council, *Lumen Gentium*, n. 56.

31. Ibid., n. 56.

effected between the Word and human flesh, and the place where the union is consummated is the Virgin's womb,"[32] and St. Thomas Aquinas writes that "a kind of spiritual marriage is taking place between the Son of God and human nature. The Virgin's consent, then, which was petitioned during the course of the announcement stood for the consent of all men."[33] We have to note here again that Balthasar develops the idea that Mary represents the whole human race in response to God the Creator to the notion that the whole creation is "feminine" in terms of its "obedient," "receptive," and "open" relationship to God. Since the Creator-creation relationship is in no way an equal one, to characterize the receptive and dependent attitude of creation as "feminine" eventually leads to affirming the fixed notion that women are supposed to be receptive and dependent. No wonder, then, Balthasar has received more criticism on what he says about women than on any other area of his theology.[34]

Mary also consented to Christ's public ministry, and her faithful attitude throughout his ministry (and eventually at the cross) is regarded as the role model for Christian faith, for even though she did not fully comprehend the mystery surrounding her son she never hesitated to believe and consent. Also, she was destined to suffer enormously as the Mother of God, as Simeon predicted to Mary herself, "a sword will pierce your own soul too" (Luke 2:35), but she was obedient and faithful to the end.

For example, the Gospel of Luke tells us the anecdote of Mary and Joseph searching for the twelve-year-old boy Jesus for three days. When they finally found him in the temple, they did not understand the meaning of Jesus's words, "I must be in my Father's house"[35] (Luke 2:49), but still the Mother "treasured all these things in her heart" (Luke 2:51). Further, Balthasar's interpretation of this small anecdote in Jesus's childhood is worth noting as he sees a typological relationship between this event and the paschal mystery.[36] He writes, "It is there, in the mystery of the Three Days, that he will have to be sought, just as his Mother and his foster father find him after three days of fruitless seeking. He will have to be sought where

---

32. Augustine, *Expositions of the Psalms 33–50* III/16, 282.

33. Thomas Aquinas, *Summa Theologiae*, III, q.30, a.1.

34. For example, Kilby says, "there is little in his thought that is such a flashpoint for controversy as what he has to say about women." *Balthasar*, 123.

35. Alternatively, this verse is translated as "I must be about my Father's interests."

36. Also, it should be noted that Pitstick too pays attention to this event in Jesus' childhood as a prefiguration of the paschal mystery and argues that this typological relationship shows that Christ's descent into hell was accomplished *gloriously* as "one of authority and wisdom recognized" as the boy Jesus was among the teachers in the temple and thus "going about the Father's business." Pitstick, *Light in Darkness*, 39.

he is not: in sinners, in those alienated from God, in his solidarity with his enemies, with those who are lost, in those places where on the third day he makes himself known."[37] As Mary says to Jesus, "Why have you treated us like this? Look, your father and I have been searching for you in great anxiety" (Luke 2:48), searching for Jesus for three days naturally caused Mary and Joseph much emotional pain. It is worth noting here the way Balthasar says that Jesus "cannot spare them this pain,"[38] because Balthasar often presents such an emotionally distressing experience of the absence of Jesus as one significant way of experiencing his presence or of sharing his suffering. Balthasar even writes, "the measure of inner fellowship with Jesus is the measure of our experience of absence."[39] As we frequently noted in the previous chapters, in Balthasar's theology those who are the closest to God are believed to be the ones that are most likely to experience the dark night of his absence.[40] As a natural outcome of this reasoning, his Mother is considered as the one that has experienced the darkest night ever (surpassed only by Jesus himself).

It is certainly in the Catholic tradition to contemplate Mary's unique sorrow as the Mother of God,[41] but Balthasar's Mariology is quite radical in the sense that it characterizes her relationship with the Son by his distancing himself from her, which increases in terms of scale and intensity, and culminates at the cross.[42] Balthasar interprets the "sword" predicted by Simeon

37. Balthasar, *The Threefold Garland*, 61.

38. Ibid., 61.

39. Balthasar, *Truth is Symphonic*, 131.

40. For example, in addition to Mary, the sisters of Lazarus (Mary and Martha) and Mary Magdalene are also presented as the ones who had to go through the painful absence of Jesus exactly because of their closeness with the Lord. See Balthasar, *Truth is Symphonic*, 130–34. Unsurprisingly, Balthasar's critics find this kind of interpretation problematic (as Jesus seems to "intentionally" inflict such an emotional pain of separation on his closest ones). For example, see Kilby, *Balthasar*, 117–19.

41. For example, the devotion to the Seven Sorrows of Mary. Further, St. John Paul II also says that Mary experienced "a particular heaviness of heart, linked with a sort of night of faith," as the one that "lived in intimacy with the mystery of her Son," referring to the dark night of the soul of St. John of the Cross. John Paul II, *Redemptoris Mater*, n.17.

42. Pope Emeritus Benedict XVI echoes him on this point: "She must complete the Yes to God's will that made her a mother by withdrawing into the background and letting Jesus enter upon his mission. Jesus' rebuffs during his public life and her withdrawal are an important step that will reach its goal on the Cross with the words 'behold, your son.' . . . To accept and to be available is the first step required of her; to let go and to release is the second. Only in this way does her motherhood become complete." (Ratzinger and Balthasar, *Mary*, 76.)

to pierce her heart as "a sword of separation."[43] Three days of absence of Jesus in his childhood is extended into three years of absence due to his public ministry, during which he seems to reject her on several occasions; at the wedding in Cana, Jesus says to Mary, "Woman, what concern is that to you and to me?" (John 2:4); in the middle of Jesus' public ministry, when Mary and his brothers visit him, they are left standing at the door while he is saying to the crowds, "Who is my mother, and who are my brothers? . . .whoever does the will of my Father in heaven is my brother and sister and mother." (Matt 12:48–50); when a woman acclaimed the womb that bore him, Jesus replied, "Blessed rather are those who hear the word of God and obey it!" (Luke 11:28); and finally, all these rejections and humiliations culminate at the foot of the cross, where Jesus withdraws his sonship from Mary and gives her a new son, in other words, a 'substitute': "Woman, behold your son" (John 19:26). What is striking about Balthasar's Mariology is that all these texts, which are commonly used to justify a low Mariology, are interpreted to present Mary as the most important suffering participant in the Son's salvific mission, for as Balthasar explains it is precisely through all these rejections and humiliations of Mary by Christ that "the perfect union between the two is accomplished: just as the Father abandons his Son, the Son separates himself from his Mother."[44] As the Son's abandonment by the Father is based on their perfect union by the Holy Spirit in love, the Mother's abandonment by the Son is a sign of their loving union. In other words, Jesus is inviting his Mother to share his own suffering of godforsakenness precisely because he loves her. In Balthasar's own words, here we see "the community of love and forsakenness that unites Jesus and his Mother."[45]

Moreover, it is significant that Mary herself consented to participate in this horrible godforsakenness, though this consent is done *in silence.*[46] This is her second major *fiat*, the first one having been uttered at the annunciation. Like her first *fiat*, her second *fiat* also has a soteriological significance. Her consent to share in her son's godforsakenness makes both his death and her participation in it fruitful. The "fruit" born at the foot of the cross is the church. Balthasar writes,

> This form of union[the union accomplished by the Son being abandoned by the Father and the Mother being abandoned by

---

43. Balthasar, *Truth is Symphonic*, 130.

44. Balthasar, *To the Heart of the Mystery of Redemption*, 56. Also, see Balthasar, *Truth is Symphonic*, 130–31.

45. Balthasar, *Theo-Drama IV*, 501.

46. How we should interpret this silence is itself a complex question. We will discuss this point at the end of this chapter.

the Son] was necessary so that Mary—who henceforth would have to form the center of the Church—might know from experience the mystery of the redemption and might be able to transmit it to her new children.[47]

Mary's *fiat* at the foot of the cross is the archetype of faith of the church, which was born at this very scene of double abandonment, as well as of the individual Christian. It is relevant here to note the typological relationship between Mary and Abraham, the Father of Faith. In Mary's case, however, no angels intervene. She had to go through the sacrifice of her child to the end. In this sense, her faith was more complete than Abraham's. As Balthasar says, hers was "a faith that, in a certain sense, collaborates with the redemption and could well be called a co-redemptive faith,"[48]though Balthasar himself cautiously uses the word "co-redemption." (In Mary's case, as Speyr points out, co-redemption is made possible by pre-redemption.[49])

It is exactly here at the foot of the cross, where this double abandonment in union happened, that the church, the Bride of Christ, was born. In Balthasar's words, "Mary begins by being the Mother, but at the Cross she ends by becoming the Bride, the quintessence of the Church."[50] The church is born from the pierced wound of the obedient Son and the pierced heart of the obedient Mother. Therefore, the church and the individual Christian are required to imitate this profound obedience shown by the Son and the Mother (now the Bride), and that is how they are supposed to participate in the redemption.

Mary on Holy Saturday: The Church Waiting in Silent Faith

Now, let us turn to Mary on Holy Saturday. Traditionally, Our Lady's sorrow on this particular day has been most poignantly expressed in the image of the *Pietà*, the Mother grieving for her dead Son. Who would deny

47. Balthasar, *To the Heart of the Mystery of Redemption*, 56.

48. Ibid., 57.

49. Speyr, *Mary in the Redemption*, 80: "She does not become the one who is pre-redeemed through the co-redemption, but rather she becomes Co-Redemption through the pre-redemption." Also, see Speyr, *Handmaid of the Lord*, 116–17: "He had redeemed her also, by preserving her from sin. That gives her the capacity to suffer with him, vicariously for all, as an embodiment of the meaning of the redemption, in the perfect unity of human nature and divine grace."

50. Balthasar, *To the Heart of the Mystery of Redemption*, 53.

the heart-wrenching power of this image? Pope Emeritus Benedict XVI, for example, once wrote of the importance of this image for Christianity as follows:

> In her, God's maternal affliction [*Leiden*] is open to view. In her we can behold it and touch it. She is the *compassio* of God, displayed in a human being who has let herself be drawn wholly into God's mystery. It is because human life is at all times suffering that the image of the suffering Mother, the image of *rahmim* of God, is of such importance for Christianity. The *Pietà* completes the picture of the Cross, because Mary is the accepted Cross, the Cross communicating itself in love, the Cross that now allows us to experience in her compassion the compassion of God. In this way the Mother's affliction is Easter affliction, which already inaugurates the transformation of death into the redemptive being-with of love.[51]

The image of the *Pietà* is particularly relevant for our discussion because it is related to the question underlying this whole thesis: whether or not Balthasar's and Speyr's interpretation of Holy Saturday radically departs from the traditional teachings. As we mentioned in the introduction to this book, what their innovative interpretation of Christ's descent into hell has in fact sought to achieve was to reconcile this tradition of mourning, most poignantly expressed in the image of *Pietà*, on the one hand and the tradition of the image of Christ as victor over death on the other. They see the close connection between the image of the *Pietà* and the church's liturgical silence on Holy Saturday. In other words, on Holy Saturday, *we wait for Easter with Mary at the tomb.*[52] This point also shows that examination of their interpretation of Christ's descent into hell would not actually be complete without reflection on Mary's Holy Saturday (and consequently *our* Holy Saturday), because it is included in its scope from the beginning.

This point is further confirmed when we look at Speyr's mystical visions of the paschal mystery, which are permeated with the presence of Our Lady, as we mentioned at the beginning of this chapter. Further, in terms of the theological relation between Mary and Holy Saturday, she often talks about the close connection between the incarnation and the descent into hell. For Speyr, Mary and hell are the two poles which respectively mark the beginning and the end of the life of Jesus Christ. In her words, "The earthly life of the Lord is indeed in the middle between the Mother and hell," in other words, from the womb of the Virgin to the womb of hell, both

---

51. Ratzinger and Balthasar, *Mary*, 78–79.
52. See Balthasar, "Theologie des Abstiegs zur Hölle," 142, 146.

of which were forever transformed because of his entrance.[53] Hence, there is clearly a parallel between the expectation in the Mother's womb and the waiting in hell on Holy Saturday, hence between Christmas and Easter.[54] To see a parallel between the incarnation and the descent into hell, however, is not so original. This parallel can be traced back to the patristic authors.[55] For example, St Ephrem the Syrian often compares the womb of the Virgin and the "womb" of *Sheol*:

> The womb and Sheol shouted with joy and cried out
>
> about Your resurrection. The womb that was sealed,
>
> conceived You. Sheol that was secured,
>
> brought You forth. Against nature
>
> the womb conceived and Sheol yielded.
>
> Sealed was the grave which they entrusted
>
> with keeping the dead man. Virginal was the womb
>
> that no man knew. The virginal womb
>
> and the sealed grave like trumpets
>
> for a deaf people, shouted in its ear.[56]

This typology in itself has nothing to do with Mary on Holy Saturday but it is still worth noting as it helps to strengthen our claim that Balthasar's and Speyr's emphasis on the "passive" waiting of Christ in hell (which is seemingly in contrast to the patristic image of Christ the "active" conqueror of hell) is not a radical departure from the tradition.

Now let us return to the grief and sorrow of Our Lady on Holy Saturday. There have been many prayers, meditations, and reflections on the Mother's suffering and faith on this day with the aim of nurturing piety,[57] but the theological questions we should ask in our study of Balthasar's theology of Holy Saturday are as follows: how does he describe Mary's participation in the godforsakenness of the Son on Holy Saturday? And how different is that from his description of her abandonment at the foot of the cross

---

53. Speyr, *Kreuz und Hölle* II, 107.

54. Ibid., 100.

55. See Saward, *The Mysteries of March*, 105–6.

56. Ephrem the Syrian, *Hymns on the Nativity*, n.10, 7–9, quoted by José Granados in "Mary and the Truth about Life," 31. Also see Buchan, *Blessed is He who has Brought Adam from Sheol*, 99–106.

57. For example, see Martini, *Our Lady of Holy Saturday*; Faber, *At the Foot of the Cross*, 397–444.

on Good Friday? These questions ultimately concern Christian discipleship too, for how can we participate in the mystery of Holy Saturday while we are living in this world?

One important thing to note concerning this point is that a naïve use of the word "participation" fails on Holy Saturday, even if applied to Our Lady. Regarding the question of "participation" in the mystery of Holy Saturday, Balthasar himself actually seems to leave it unresolved. For example, in *Mysterium Paschale*, he concludes the chapter on Holy Saturday as follows:

> On Holy Saturday the Church is invited rather to follow *at a distance.* . . .It remains to ask how such *an accompanying* is theologically possible—granted that the Redeemer placed himself, by substitution, in the supreme solitude—and how, moreover, that accompanying can be characterized if not by way of a genuine, that is, a Christianly imposed, sharing in such solitude: being dead with the dead God.[58]

A few interpreters have tried to speculate further on the possibility of participation in Christ's descent into hell. John Saward, for example, suggests two practical answers (by referring to the meditations of St. Thomas Aquinas).[59] First of all, we can regularly meditate on hell, and Balthasar definitely follows the idea (especially when he uses the spiritual exercises of St Ignatius). Secondly, we can pray for the souls in purgatory. Saward further suggests that Balthasar and Speyr offer more than these practical answers. He writes, "They envisage the possibility of certain souls in this life being given the grace to taste something of the Lord's experience in Sheol, not as an end in itself, but in order, in and through Christ the Conqueror of Hades, to assist their brethren in the Church, to aid those who find themselves plunged into the black hole of depression, doubt, confusion, despair."[60] Speyr was apparently one of those "certain souls" who had the "privilege" to share in the Lord's descent into hell to some extent along with many saints and mystics in history, who bore such a sharing in the spiritual night on behalf of others. However, as pointed out by Shelly Rambo, another interpreter who engages with this question, this point makes it extremely difficult to translate the Holy Saturday pattern of Christian witness more broadly into ordinary Christian life.[61]

---

58. Balthasar, *Mysterium Paschale*, 181. Italics added.

59. Saward, *The Mysteries of March*, 126–29. Also see Thomas Aquinas, *The Three Greatest Prayers*, 63–64.

60. Saward, *The Mysteries of March*, 127.

61. Rambo, *Spirit and Trauma*, 69–70.

Perhaps we should rather respect the fact that we can follow the Lord only "at a distance" on Holy Saturday, as Balthasar says. After all, even Mary could not follow him into hell. In her visions, Speyr often talked about how Mary was outside hell.[62] Rather, her suffering on this day is characterized by not knowing what is happening behind the stone of the tomb or in hell and not being able to participate in her son's suffering and death. In this sense, Mary and the rest of the followers stand at the same place: at the tomb of the dead Lord. Though she does not know what is happening, she is not in despair. On the other hand, such a deep sorrow and grief as expressed in the image of the *Pietà* seems to reject a naïve use of the word "hope." In the end, "waiting in faith" seems to be the only expression we can use to describe Mary on Holy Saturday, if faith is understood as something to encompass a mixture of the aftermath of pain, sorrow, loneliness, obedience, vague hope, and loving trust in God, instead of bland optimism. Speyr writes as follows:

> From Good Friday on the Mother suffers in a new anticipation. The Son's suffering is at an end and she has gone with him to this end. She has tasted abandonment and loneliness. And yet, she knows that he is God and, as God, survives all destruction and death. She cannot imagine the Resurrection, nor does she picture the future to herself. She has only faith, which overcomes every death. And she also knows that, when the Child was given to her long ago, that had not been the beginning of her Son. The Child was not created at his conception. The eternal Son, who always was, came down into her womb. From this she understands that even death cannot end his life. He lived before she bore him; and so he still lives after he has disappeared.[63]

If we locate ourselves in the place of Mary waiting at the tomb, Mary's obedient faith in the Lord can be a source of inspiration and motivation for small acts of charity and solidarity. Thus Balthasar concludes his presentation of Speyr's approach to Holy Saturday as follows:

> What follows from all this for us? Let us leave it to the theologians to discuss the dogmatic aspects. *We, however, like Mary and most Christians, cannot follow Christ on this last way. We remain awake at the grave with the other holy women:* What can we do? Many things. In our lives, revive the spirit of solidarity, this power to share the burden of another, to pray with fervor--and such prayer is unfailing--so that our brothers and sisters

---

62. For example, Speyr, *Kreuz und Hölle* I, 135, 139.

63. Speyr, *Handmaid of the Lord*, 133.

would not be lost in the end . . .We simply attempt to put into action the small things that are possible for us.[64]

We are not all given the mystical gift to share in the dark night on behalf of others, and such a horrible experience cannot be sought for its own sake. Nevertheless, there are many things we can do, such as praying for each other and sharing the burden of another (as expressed in the tradition of meditation on hell mentioned above), as Balthasar proposes here.

Balthasar's View of Childlikeness

As we noted earlier, for Balthasar, the Marian attitude means "feminine" receptivity. There is another important characteristic he attributes to this receptivity: "childlikeness." The topic of childlikeness has been largely ignored by Balthasar's critics, even though it runs through his theology. (Childlikeness is an interesting characteristic to examine, considering the adjectives often used by his critics to describe him and his writings: "oppressive," "aristocratic," "authoritarian," "elitist," "overarching," "epical" and so forth.) Nevertheless, a few scholars have actually said that Balthasar himself possessed the heart of a child throughout his life. Saward is one of those few,[65] and writes as follows:

> I do not just mean that "despite" or "in addition to" the adult grandeur of his achievement he retained a childlike simplicity. That is true, but it is not the whole truth. *In Balthasar the child's heart shapes and orders the mind.* In the *Theological Aesthetic* it is young, uncluttered eyes which see the splendid form of revelation. In the *Theo-dramatic*, a child is caught up into the drama of Christ's self-giving love. In the *Theologic* a little one lets himself be led by the Holy Spirit into all the truth of the Father's Word made flesh.[66]

This statement from Saward echoes Peter Henrici's words, "for all his greatness and towering knowledge, he was able to remain 'uncomplicated,' humble, indeed, childlike."[67] This point seems to be symbolically suggested by the fact that his last book, which was lying on his desk on the day of his

---

64. Balthasar, "Theologie des Abstiegs zur Hölle," 146.

65. As for other exceptions, see Cihak, *Balthasar and Anxiety*, 237–40; Henrici, "Hans Urs von Balthasar," 7–43; Howsare, *Balthasar*, 127–28.

66. Saward "Youthful unto Death," 140. Italics added.

67. Henrici, "Hans Urs von Balthasar," 8.

death and was meant to be a Christmas gift to his friends, was exactly on the spirit of childhood[68]: *Unless You Become Like This Child.*[69]

In this short work, Balthasar argues that when Jesus says "whoever does not receive the kingdom of God as a little child will never enter it" (Mark 10:15), he is inviting us to become exactly like *him* (hence the emphasis, "this," in the title).

Balthasar points out the importance of Christ being not only the Son to the Father but also "the Child." As Balthasar says, the Son has "never left the Father's bosom"[70] even after he has grown up as a human being. According to Balthasar, it makes perfect sense for Jesus to encourage childlikeness precisely because he himself shares this nature. Further, the childlikeness Jesus encourages in his followers is not supposed to be mere infantilism but rather a supreme form of *amazement, gratitude, humility,* and *maturity*. It would be relevant to discuss the spirit of childhood in this chapter on the Mother of God, for, first of all, childhood and motherhood are intrinsically interconnected, and secondly we detect in Balthasar's view of the childlike something problematic in a similar way to his view of the feminine.

For example, Balthasar explains how Christ continues to look up to the Father "with eternal childlike amazement."[71] Jesus's word, "the Father is greater than I" (John 14:28), (the word which Arius and his followers once quoted to prove the Son's inferiority to the Father), is interpreted in terms of the child's amazement and pride in his father. In Balthasar's own words, "the comparative is the linguistic form of amazement."[72] This amazement of the Son toward the Father is translated into his human existence, "beginning with the existence of his loving Mother, then passing on to his own existence, finally going from both to all the forms offered by the surrounding world, from the tiniest flower to the boundless skies."[73] Furthermore, this amazement is derived "from the much deeper amazement of the eternal Child who, in the absolute Spirit of Love, marvels at Love itself as it permeates and transcends all that is."[74] Balthasar further describes how human

68. Ibid., 42.

69. Balthasar, *Unless You Become Like This Child.* The following exposition is mostly from this book, but as for other sources where Balthasar explores the theme of the spirit of childhood, see, for example, "The Eternal Child," "Young Until Death" in *Explorations in Theology* V, 205–24; "The Faith of the Simple Ones," in *Explorations in Theology* III, 57–83; *Bernanos*, 322–40.

70. Balthasar, *Unless You Become Like This Child*, 10.

71. Ibid., 44.

72. Ibid., 46.

73. Ibid., 46.

74. Ibid., 46.

erotic love and childlike amazement are connected; "eros can keep alive an awed amazement at one's partner's self-surrender within all the routine of the common life."[75]

For Balthasar, another "childlike" attitude shown by the Son to the Father is that of thanksgiving. Balthasar states that thanksgiving is "the quintessence of Jesus' stance toward the Father."[76] Even when he gives *himself* away (at the Last Supper), he gives thanks to the Father (Mark 14:23; Matt 26:27; Luke 22:17, 19; 1 Cor 11:24). To be a child means to be dependent on another and to receive from others. In the child, to plea and to give thanks can basically coincide. Jesus says, "whatever you ask for in prayer, believe that you have received it, and it will be yours." (Mark 11:24) The Christian as a child of God never outgrows the obligation to give thanks to God, for they receive everything from him including their life and salvation.

Most importantly, Christ's childlike attitude toward the Father can be most poignantly seen in his kenotic obedience during the paschal event. Balthasar writes,

> Jesus, thus, suffers as the Son. In his own prayer, the child's word "Abba!" ("Papa") is first heard on the Mount of Olives (Mk 14:36). Even though the Father can now no longer respond, still *all Jesus' suffering—even to the cry of abandonment on the Cross—is suffered in the spirit of childhood*. And after the Son, *like a lost child in an eerie forest, has been led through all the horrors of Holy Saturday*, he can proclaim triumphantly on Easter Day: "I go up to my Father and your Father" (Jn 20:17).[77]

In short, for Balthasar, the spirit of childhood means "a repetition of the eternal Son's loving readiness to obey the 'command' (*mandatum*) of the Father."[78] Therefore, Christians too "must persevere, together with Christ, in fleeing to the Father, in entrusting ourselves to the Father, in imploring and thanking the Father."[79] Since in Christ the perfect form of maturity and responsibility with regard to his mission is realized, we can say that "Christian childlikeness and Christian maturity are not in tension with one another" and also "the more we identify ourselves with the mission entrusted to us, in the manner of the eternal Son, the more thoroughly do we become sons and

---

75. Ibid., 47.
76. Ibid., 47.
77. Ibid., 61. Italics added.
78. Ibid., 40.
79. Ibid., 40–41.

daughters of the Heavenly Father."[80] Therefore, the notion of the spirit of childhood is the key to the manner in which every Christian is supposed to carry out their mission entrusted to them by God and to persevere in their suffering on the way. In short, Balthasar says that the Christian should carry out their mission and persevere in their suffering in childlike obedience like Christ.

Naturally, Our Lady again is believed to be the one that embodies this childlike obedience of the Christian in the most perfect form (as a creature). Her first consent at the annunciation "presupposes a pure childlike attitude that entrusts everything to the Father,"[81] and she maintained this childlike attitude throughout her life, including at the foot of the cross, where, as we have seen, she consented to participate in the Son's separation from the Father. Balthasar stresses that "all forms of the following of Christ within the Marian Church by carrying Christ's Cross with him. . .are in the end ordered to this highest grace of *childhood*."[82] Balthasar sees such Christian childlikeness not only in Mary but also in basically all other saints.[83] In particular, here we can add another reason for Balthasar's appreciation of St. Thérèse of Lisieux, who is also known as St. Thérèse of the Child Jesus. From her childhood St. Thérèse cultivated a personal relationship with the Child Jesus "in the crib." She also had the spirituality to keep on seeing the unchanging spirit of childhood in Jesus, even on the cross. Balthasar writes, "The darkness over the Head that is wounded and bloody never grows too thick for Thérèse to see a glorious ray of eternal childhood streaming through the lowered eyelids [of Christ] . . .For in her every feeling and action, she aims at being a tiny mirror for the Child."[84] Therefore, in Balthasar's appreciation of the spirit of childhood, we can see another influence of St. Thérèse's "Little Way," (in addition to her "night of nothingness," which we discussed in chapter 2).

In this section, we have discussed how Balthasar views childlikeness. This quality may seem to be a minor point, but still it is worth noting for a balanced view of his writings as a whole. In particular, we would like to point out the excessively romanticized way he speaks about children (the connection between childlikeness and eros, for example). How many people

---

80. Ibid., 41.

81. Ibid., 69.

82. Ibid., 73.

83. Not only the saints. The spirit of childhood is one of the qualities he sees in those whom he admires, including Adrienne von Speyr, Georges Bernanos, and Charles Péguy.

84. Balthasar, *Two Sisters in the Spirit*, 230.

actually agree with his view of children as the ones that readily give thanks for everything they receive and obediently carry out their duties? Something similar can also be said concerning his view of the feminine. As we have mentioned, for Balthasar, Mary represents everything feminine. He writes that Mary "is woman, pure and simple, in whom everything feminine in salvation history is summed up."[85] It is not that we have any objection to calling Our Lady "feminine" or "pure" or "simple." The problem is the way Balthasar seems to lump together all women under the same adjectives. In our age, how many women actually want to be called "pure and simple"? Some may, but not all. Lucy Gardner, for example, critiques the essentialist and over-simplistic way in which Balthasar presents Mary as "Woman" per se:

> What are "enlightened" intellects, of howsoever many schools of thought and shades of opinion, to make of this strange, even distasteful, deployment of a certain essentialization of "woman" and "femininity" in a hermeneutic which seems capable of eliding all women (in the Bible and beyond) with this one woman (Mary) merely on account of an apparently over-simplistic linkage between biological, social, psychological, and grammatical "gender?" Similarly, we may ask: what are readers of a critical or post-critical generation to make of Balthasar's apparently naïvely literal, uncritical readings of the Gospel stories, combined as they are with an insistence on unrecorded psychological "facts?"[86]

Therefore, we detect something similarly naïve and over-simplistic in the way Balthasar speaks about both children and women. It would be natural to anticipate that this tendency would also affect his engagement with the reality of human suffering, which we will discuss below.

Conclusion: Balthasar's Problematic View of Sexual Differentiation

In this chapter, we have been mainly discussing the Marian principle presented by Balthasar as the role model of Christian faith. It is basically characterized by obedient faith and loving consent in a feminine and childlike manner, and Our Lady embodied it to the fullest even at the culmination of her anguish of losing her son. However, unsurprisingly Balthasar's portrayal

85. Balthasar, "Our Lady in Monasticism," 52. Quoted by Gardner in "Balthasar and the Figure of Mary," 66.

86. Gardner, "Balthasar and the Figure of Mary," 66–67.

of the suffering obedience of Mary causes uneasiness among his critics. As we stated at the beginning, for Balthasar, Mariology is clearly located within both Christology and ecclesiology. It is no surprise, then, that the criticism raised against Balthasar's portrayal of Mary is not particularly a critique of his Mariology in itself but rather reflects the criticism raised in other areas of his theology. We will discuss two issues below: the exegetical question and his view of the "feminine." Obviously, neither of them is an issue merely limited to his portrayal of Mary.

Let us start with the less significant point: the exegetical question, particularly regarding John 19:26: "Woman, behold your son," which is an important verse for Balthasar's portrayal of Mary as participating in the abandonment experienced by Christ on the cross. This interpretation is certainly a unique one, and some would quickly take issue with it and object to such a seemingly "cruel" portrayal of Christ.[87] How could the loving Son of God abandon his own Mother? However, we also have to note that this portrayal of the community of love and forsakenness between the Son and the Mother is exactly rooted in his Christology, which is anchored in his Trinitarian theology. This drama of love and abandonment between the Son and the Mother would not make sense at all without the Trinitarian form of love and abandonment between the Father and the Son. Therefore, if we do not accept this Trinitarian form in the first place, we certainly could deny this double abandonment of the Son and the Mother, but if we accept the former, we could admit that Balthasar may be consistent about his logic of love and abandonment after all: if love is truly strong, it can afford to be abandoned. Mary is not forced to share in this night of separation. As Balthasar and Speyr meditate on the unimaginable sorrow of Our Lady, she would certainly do anything to take her son's place if she could, but she must let it happen out of love and obedience. (We come back to this point

---

87. One straightforward line of interpretation from St. Augustine to St. Thomas Aquinas is that here Jesus is worried about his mother's future so he is leaving her to the care of his closest friend. On the other hand, Raymond Edward Brown, for example, does not support this view, because it seems "to reduce Johannine thought to the level of the flesh and to ignore the distancing from the concerns of natural family that took place at Cana 2:4." (Brown, *The Death of the Messiah* vol. II, 1021.) Brown himself sees this verse (and the verse following) as the establishment of a new relationship which goes beyond the natural family. Also, he pointed out that these verses evoke the image of Lady Zion's giving birth to a new people in the messianic age, and of Eve and her offspring. (See Brown, *The Gospel According to John [XIII-XXI]*, 926.) For a survey of some Marian interpretations of this passage, see, for example, Collins, "Mary in the Fourth Gospel." Also, for a somewhat Balthasarian mariological reflection on these verses as the third of the seven last words of Jesus, see Neuhaus, *Death on a Friday Afternoon*, 71–101. (Neuhaus too talks about Mary's *kenosis* mirroring Christ's.)

later in chapter 5, when we discuss Balthasar's emphasis on the Eucharist as sacrifice.)

It would also be helpful here to note that Balthasar is not the only one that emphasizes the forsakenness of Mary at the foot of the cross and sees it as a parallel of the Son's abandonment by the Father. For example, as pointed out by some,[88] Chiara Lubich, the twentieth-century Catholic activist and founder of the Focolare movement, emphasizes the abandonment of Mary by the Son in a strikingly similar way to Balthasar and Speyr. No direct influence between them appears to have been confirmed, which makes the similarity all the more interesting. For Lubich and her Focolare movement, "Jesus Forsaken" and "Mary Desolate" are the main sources of inspiration. She too reads John 19:26 as depriving Mary of her maternity toward Jesus and thus her passion is fused with his.[89] It is relevant for our discussion to note that it has been testified that some of those who are going through their own dark night of faith in the Focolare movement actually find hope and consolation in the figure of Mary forsaken along with her son.[90]

Now, let us turn to the second issue: Balthasar's view of the "feminine" understood as "receptive" and "obedient." This is the most problematic one and most critiques regarding his portrayal of Mary seem to be more or less related to this point. It is actually Balthasar himself who has laid the foundation for such criticism by incorporating his own rather outdated view of sexual differentiation into his Mariology. As we noted at the beginning, while Balthasar appreciates Vatican II's acknowledgement that Mary is the archetype of the church, he has also attempted to "correct" it by bringing in the man-woman aspect to Mariology. Mary, for Balthasar, is "the Woman,"

88. For example, see O'Byrne, *Model of Incarnate Love*, 46; Langan, *The Catholic Tradition*, 448n97.; de Maeseneer, "Review Symposium," 104.

89. Lubich writes, "In that moment Mary, in an abyss of suffering whose depths we cannot measure, experiences the trial of losing the fruit of her womb, Jesus, the one who she could say was her purpose and work. It seems Jesus is almost depriving Mary of her maternity toward him and transferring her motherhood to someone else, to John, in whom Jesus saw all of us. And Mary becomes mother to the whole of humanity, mother of the Church. She pays for this with her own darkest desolation. She is alone, without Jesus. She is the Desolate. Here she lives the so-called 'night of the spirit,' because her heart echoes Jesus' cry on the cross, 'My God, my God, why have you forsaken me?' (Mt 27:46) Mariologists say that this was the moment the Virgin Mary reveals God's plan for her. His plan blossoms in full. Here she associates herself with Christ and fuses her passion with his, for the redemption of the human race." Lubich, *Mary*, 63–64.

90. Lubich writes, "In those moments [of the "night of the spirit"], along with Jesus forsaken, it is the Desolate that can be of light to their soul. It is from her that they learn to 'stand upright' at the foot of the cross, while in deep agony of the soul, completely accepting God's will just as Mary did." (Ibid., 64–65)

and she can represent the whole of humanity at the annunciation precisely because of her gender, for Balthasar analogically characterizes the Creator-creation relationship by using sexual differences. As we have mentioned above, he develops the idea that Mary represents the whole human race in response to God the Creator to the notion that the whole creation is "feminine" in terms of its "obedient," "receptive," and "open" relationship to God. For him, to be a man is to give while to be a woman is to receive. What Balthasar actually aims to do with such a sexual differentiation is to argue how the man-woman relationship is "fruitful" exactly because of their different and complementary roles. Unsurprisingly, however, such an essentialist kind of categorization has invited much criticism.[91] In Balthasar's theology of sexual differentiation, as pointed out by his critics, primacy is preserved for the man, and the woman is always secondary, in other words, an "answer" to the man, even though he stresses that the man and the woman are equal. Also, as can be seen in the ecclesial structure composed of the Marian principle (representing the feminine/lay) and the Petrine principle (the masculine/office), although Balthasar himself tries to stress that the Marian principle embraces the Petrine principle (hence, the feminine principle is more comprehensive than the masculine), in reality, it has the effect of limiting the role of women. It has also been pointed out that Balthasar's view of sexual differentiation will ultimately undermine one of the goals of Vatican II, namely, the integration and maturation of the laity.[92] After all, in this system, while the man can be both masculine and feminine, the woman is forever only feminine. To make matters worse for Balthasar, his tendency not to explain why he says what he says (the tendency most strongly criticized by Kilby) is most apparent in his way of sexual differentiation, as he never explains why the role of the woman is to receive in the first place.[93] Therefore, (rather to our disappointment), there is no way to defend Balthasar from the critique that he limits the role of women, whatever his actual intention is. His theology of sexual differences is probably the most criticized area and it is beyond our scope and interest to consider all the critiques raised against it, but let us mention some which seem to be relevant for our topic: Mary's obedient consent and Christian suffering.

For example, Lucy Gardner and David Moss have pointed out that Mary's consent, which Balthasar's Mariology so emphasizes, is actually

91. Most notably from David Moss and Lucy Gardner, Corinne Crammer, Michelle A. Gonzalez, Tina Beattie, and Karen Kilby.

92. See Imperatori-Lee, "The Use of Marian Imagery in Catholic Ecclesiology since Vatican II," 92.

93. See Kilby, *Balthasar*, 142–46.

not recorded.[94] This silence on her side is particularly conspicuous in her "consent" at the foot of the cross, which is supposed to be so crucial for his Mariology. Her silence certainly could mean many things including her complete obedience as Balthasar interprets, but it could also suggest other possibilities such as her voice being *silenced*. It has also been pointed out that his theology is not helpful for the cause of social justice, which includes improvement of gender equality. Corinne Crammer, for example, writes, "Whatever his intentions may have been, Balthasar's theology does not serve the cause of justice for women well but rather provides theological justification for social inequality."[95] We agree that this kind of attitude, despite his opposite intentions, could be "hijacked to support an unjust *status quo*," as Gerard O'Hanlon strongly argues.[96] This is true of his presentation of the Marian and Petrine principles, for instance; to those who wish to simply make women shut up, Balthasar has given a convenient means, whether he notices or not. As O'Hanlon writes, Balthasar's naiveté "is illustrated in particular by his remarks on the Church and structural change."[97] If we return to the figure of Mary and consider how her "obedient" suffering in "silence" could be simply used to justify women's unjust suffering, we can share these moral concerns raised by his critics.

If we reject Balthasar's view of sexual differentiation, we might also have to anticipate a question to be raised against the validity of the project of this book: would it be possible to reject his view of sexual differentiation and still argue that his theology tells us something significant about human suffering? We anticipate this question because it has been pointed out by many that his entire theology is "gendered" and his view of sexual difference permeates his theology. Because of this strongly "gendered" characteristic, some even imply that his entire theology could be in danger of falling apart because of his flawed view of sexual differences. Gardner, for example, writes:

> The fabric of Balthasar's theological argument is at once remarkably plastic and yet frighteningly fragile: able to encompass and account for literally everything it might encounter, and yet so tightly woven in ever greater intensities that one minor fault or imbalance might seem to threaten the whole edifice. . .it is tempting to wonder whether his theology must, as it were, stand or fall today by the accuracy or acceptability of its account of

94. Gardner and Moss, "Something like Time; Something like the Sexes," 136–37.

95. Crammer, "One Sex or Two?," 107.

96. O'Hanlon, "Theological Dramatics," 110.

97. Ibid., 110.

sexual difference in which woman appears to be always second, receptive, responsive, response, never first-always man's, never her own self, always eliding with difference.[98]

However, at least we do not share this concern. Despite his indefensible view of women and the fact that his theology is strongly coloured by his view of sexual differences, we still argue that his theology of Holy Saturday has important implications for the issue of suffering. This is largely because we do not think that the conclusion we draw from Balthasar's theology concerning the issue of Christian suffering is necessarily affected by whether or not his view of sexual differentiation is problematic. We do not see any reason why our emphasis on the in-betweenness of Holy Saturday, or on the aspect of waiting, should be affected by his outdated view of women.

If we have to characterize the mystery of Holy Saturday with one word, that would be *waiting*. In silence, we could add. This silent waiting is what really distinguishes Holy Saturday from Good Friday and Easter Sunday, both of which are more or less characterized by "cries" (the cry of dereliction on the one hand, and the cry of joy on the other.) That is what Christ was "doing" in *Sheol* and what Mary was doing at the tomb, and this is what the church liturgically does every year on Holy Saturday. The Roman Missal clearly says, "On Holy Saturday the Church *waits at the Lord's tomb* in prayer and fasting, meditating on his Passion and Death and on his Descent into Hell, and awaiting his Resurrection."[99] This emphasis on waiting could have important implications for the issue of suffering in Christian discipleship, which is the topic of the next chapter.

98. Gardner, "Balthasar and the Figure of Mary," 77.

99. *The Roman Missal*, 374.

4

Holy Saturday and the "Tragic" Christian

Introduction

IN THE PREVIOUS CHAPTER, WE DISCUSSED THE PERFECT OBEDIENCE OF Mary, the Mother of God and also the very first disciple, consistently held even in the midst of suffering and godforsakenness. Mary is the perfect role model of Christian discipleship and shows the way to persevere obediently in our suffering. However, all other Christians are quite different from Mary, who is the immaculately conceived one (hence *Ecclesia Immaculata*). Balthasar emphasizes that in reality the church is made up of sinners. He writes of "the irreducible dialectic peculiar to the Church's existence and resting on her twofold reality" as follows:

> The Church is *both eternal and temporal, infallible and fallible, immaculate in herself and yet sinful in her members.* In her first aspect, the Church requires the most childlike obedience and an open love for the truth entrusted to her, a truth she freely dispenses and simply is-in her deepest identity as Bride and Body of Christ, as communion of saints, and as "love." In her second aspect, the Church requires open judgment, criticism, and even humiliation, things the Christian cannot spare the Church provided he lays claim to his part in the burden of guilt. . . . Every apologetical approach that seeks to argue away the Church's aspect of being sinful in her members in fact harms the Church more than it helps her.[1]

The awareness of this twofold reality of the church and its members permeates Balthasar's writings, so he writes extensively on the church as

---

1. Balthasar, *Bernanos*, 109–10. Italics added.

Casta Meretrix ("chaste whore").[2] Christian life and discipleship is characterized by a paradoxical twofoldness in many ways. The Christian is a "justified sinner," forgiven but not exempt from judgment, redeemed by Christ but still exposed to sin as long as they live in this world.

We would like to explore this paradoxical existence of the Christian on the basis of Balthasar's writings specifically by connecting his theology of Holy Saturday with another innovative area of his theology, namely his theological engagement with tragedy. His engagements with Holy Saturday and tragedy are both quite novel and exploratory in their nature, and Balthasar himself does not make the connection explicitly. However, we see a profound link between these two areas of his theology, and we believe this way of reading him would eventually deepen our understanding of Christian suffering and discipleship. First of all, Balthasar sees something fundamentally "tragic" in the in-between state of the Christian existence, which is torn between the truth of Christ and the law of this world. This in-between state has been caused by nothing other than the new creation in Christ (2 Cor 5:17), which has been brought by his death and resurrection. Now, as we saw in chapter 1, for Balthasar, the starting point of the new creation is Christ's descent into hell. In other words, hell is the turning point of the old and new aeon, and Christ himself went through this transition in utter passivity.

Thus, Balthasar presents a significant connection between Christ's waiting for the resurrection in hell on Holy Saturday and the fundamentally "tragic" state of the Christian torn between the old aeon and the new. As a paradoxical being in transition, the Christian believes their victory is both already there and not there yet. In this sense, the Christian still lives in Holy Saturday. We believe this notion deepens our understanding of suffering in the Christian life, because now we can translate the meaning of suffering into "tragic waiting," which avoids explaining away the subjective reality of suffering and at the same time maintains the hope of finding its salvific meaning by relating it to Christ's suffering. Our conclusion will be that this "tragic waiting" in our lives, which is represented by Holy Saturday, now can be seen in a christological light.

We believe such an exploration can make a contribution both to the scholarship on Christian discipleship and suffering and to the scholarship on Balthasar because, first of all, the issue of human suffering has always been an important topic for Christian theology, and also because not all Balthasarian scholars agree that he makes significant contributions to this

---

2. Balthasar, *Explorations in Theology* II, 193–288.

issue. Some scholars read him sympathetically,[3] but his commentators are often critical of his treatment of human suffering. We could largely summarize the critiques into two points: first, Balthasar does not really engage with concrete social and historical contexts despite his seemingly deep concern, and secondly, he presents too positive a view of human suffering and tragedy. More often than not, these two criticisms seem to be made together.

We will carefully consider whether or not these critiques about his treatment of the question of human suffering and evil are legitimate and also examine whether or not the argument of this book can stand them. Concerning the first criticism, there is no point in arguing for the opposite. It is true that Balthasar did not spend much ink on *concretely* applying his theology to the social, political, or economic problems of his time. However, the fact that he explores such interests in art and literature rather than concrete social or historical contexts does not necessarily undermine the relevance of his theology to "the real world." The second point is more complex, but we will eventually present that Balthasar somehow maintains decent respect for the mystery of human suffering.

The section titles of this chapter are as follows: 1) Balthasar and the problem of theodicy, 2) theological engagement with tragedy as a response to evil and human suffering, 3) Balthasar and tragedy—Jesus Christ as "the heir of all the tragedy of the world," 4) "tragedy under grace"—the tragic state of the Christian existence, 5) the tragic nature of Christian life and Holy Saturday, 6) Balthasar and the concrete reality of suffering, and 7) conclusion: And Still We Wait . . .

Balthasar and the Problem of Theodicy

We have repeatedly stated that this book attempts to examine Balthasar's theology of Holy Saturday and present its implications for Christian suffering. Here let us clarify further why such connections are valid.

As we have pointed out several times, Balthasar himself does *not* try to construct a so-called theodicy. He even presents a critical attitude

---

3. The most recent one is Oglesby, *C. G. Jung and Hans Urs von Balthasar.* This book tries to compare Balthasar's and Jung's ideas on the question of God's involvement with evil. Also, see Tallon, *The Poetics of Evil*, which turns to Balthasar's theological aesthetics as a good resource for theodicy. Also, as we made reference in chapter 1, there is Jacob Friesenhahn, *The Trinity and Theodicy.* Further, the following articles are also relevant: Sutton, "Does God Suffer?"; Sara, "*Descensus ad Infernos*, Dawn of Hope." We will make reference to these works below when it is deemed necessary and relevant for our discussion.

toward theodicy in general at various places.[4] On the other hand, he refers to the problem of evil as a problem "that has acquired an urgency today quite different from the urgency it had in primitive Christian and medieval theology"[5] and it is clear that his *Theo-drama* has the problem of evil and suffering within its scope.

First of all, the existence of God is not really a question for Balthasar, so he does not see the need to justify God in the face of evil. In other words, he does not engage with the Humean question: "Is [God] willing to prevent evil, but not able? Then he is impotent. Is he able, but not willing? Then he is malevolent. Is he both able and willing? Whence then is evil?"[6] Concerning the origin of evil, Balthasar's answer could be classified under the so-called free-will argument.[7] Evil originates in human free will, and human beings are solely responsible for evil. On the other hand, Balthasar shows some affinity with the so-called soul-making argument too, for he stresses that human freedom needs to explore all its possibilities including evil and that salvific "soul-making" can become possible through such an exploration.[8]

As we have already seen in chapter 1, Balthasar explains that it is God himself that has given human beings the perfect freedom to say "No" to him, to choose evil rather than good, and eventually, to choose hell rather than heaven. This gift of freedom itself is considered as an expression of God's kenotic love for humankind, so hell, which is the supreme consequence of perverted human freedom, belongs to God himself. Therefore, within Balthasar's unique Trinitarian framework, when the Father sends the Son to

---

4. For example, Balthasar is critical of the Augustinian kind of harmonic theodicy as he thinks that it throws a "cloak over tragedy" and fails to discern the deep reality of suffering (Balthasar, *The Glory of the Lord* II, 129). Also see Tallon, *The Poetics of Evil*, 117, 124–25, 131–34). It has also been pointed out that he takes a critical attitude toward a Hegelian kind of narrative theodicy as he believes it does not do justice to the particularities of human suffering. However, this is a complex subject, as it also concerns the difficult question of how we view the relationship between Balthasar and Hegel. For an examination of Hegel's theodicy and Balthasar's challenge to it, for example, see O'Regan, "Hegel, Theodicy, and the Invisibility of Waste"; *The Anatomy of Misremembering*, 244–50. In particular, O'Regan points out how the anti-Hegelian element in Balthasar's theology of Holy Saturday can be underscored by Balthasar's challenge to Hegel's theodicy.

5. Balthasar, *Theo-Drama* I, 48. Also, see 48–50.

6. Hume, *Dialogues Concerning Natural Religion*, 106.

7. See Oglesby, *C. G. Jung and Hans Urs von Balthasar*, 103–5. Also, for a summary of Balthasar's understanding of evil, see 27–31, 103–8, and 118–26.

8. He more or less agrees with Irenaeus on this point. See, for example, Balthasar, *Theo-Drama* II, 216.

save the humanity, the Son descends into hell, which is the final destination of the redemptive mission he has received from the Father. As we pointed out then, this Trinitarian structure leads us to see the connection between Balthasar's theology of Holy Saturday and theodicy. As concisely summarized by Aidan Nichols, "the Descent 'solves' the problem of theodicy, by showing us the conditions on which God accepted our foreknown abuse of freedom; namely, his own plan to take to himself our self-damnation in Hell."[9] God can assume the risk of giving his creation the freedom to reject him and to become lost, because he is able to gather this lostness into himself. It is exactly through the Son's descent into hell that such gathering up of the lostness of humanity into God is revealed. In Balthasar's words, God gathers the abyss of the lostness of humanity into "the abyss of absolute love."[10] If we dare present a clear-cut theoretical "answer" to the problem of evil on the basis of Balthasar's theology of Holy Saturday, this is it, more or less.

Further, if we try to provide an answer to the problem of suffering, Jacob H. Friesenhahn has already done so by concluding, "All human suffering and death, conformed by God's grace to the Paschal Mystery of Christ, has ultimate meaning as grounded in the Triune God through the Incarnate Son."[11] Similarly, it has been further stated by Matthew Lewis Sutton that "to comfort, to redeem, to heal, the theology of Holy Saturday as the descent of God into Hell is the only compelling belief in God for us in this postmodern age,"[12] for "the God who suffered the worst of Hell can redeem the worst of human suffering."[13]

We do not totally deny this kind of reasoning. As we detect a deep interest in the reality of evil and human suffering throughout Balthasar's theological corpus, it would not be an exaggeration to say that the question his entire theology really engages with is how God is involved with a world which is so obviously fraught with evil and suffering. After all, in his theology, the cross, the descent into hell, and the resurrection can be considered as the ultimate expression of God's loving involvement with the world, and he discusses how the meaning of human suffering and death can be transformed by relating it to the events of the paschal mystery. Further, we could even say that he is not so much interested in the question concerning the

---

9. Nichols, "Introduction," in Balthasar, *Mysterium Paschale*, 7.

10. Balthasar, *Elucidations*, 52.

11. Friesenhahn, *The Trinity and Theodicy*, 174.

12. Sutton, "Does God Suffer?," 179.

13. Ibid., 172.

cause of suffering as in a transformation of the meaning of suffering on the basis of the paschal mystery.[14] For example, he writes,

> In the end it is unimportant that, in this world as it is, we can-not make a clear-cut distinction between pain that comes from God and pain that is caused by the fault of creatures. What en-compasses both and continues to give everything meaning is the unique Cross of the Son—his triune Cross, let us say—in whose purifying fire suffering and healing are one.[15]

However, while it is meaningful to bear in mind that Balthasar's theol-ogy has the potential to give such an "answer" to the problem of evil and suffering as presented by Friesenhahn and Sutton, we should not simply explain away Balthasar's response to the problem as such. This kind of clear-cut conclusion would not do full justice to his theology. As we discussed in chapter 1, such a simple answer that human suffering can find its meaning in Christ's suffering (that is, the kind of answer that some advocates of divine suffering would give) would be in danger of being what Karen Kilby calls "a cheap move."[16] Further, Balthasar himself is critical of systematic theodicy, which ends up neglecting or ignoring the particularities and contingencies of the reality of human suffering and evil. After all, we could even argue that his entire theological trilogy of aesthetics, dramatics, and logic is permeated with such concerns. Also, more importantly, if we would like to consider the significance of Holy Saturday regarding this matter, we have to consider an approach which makes full use of the unique in-betweeness of Holy Satur-day, which is characterized by silent waiting for the victory, which, in fact, has already come. After all, the cross itself is already an enormous suffering. In order to say that God has suffered the worst, we do not necessarily go further than the cross.

In order to see the connection between this in-between state of Holy Saturday captured by Balthasar and its implications for the issue of suffering in Christian discipleship, we have to examine Balthasar's "tragic" view of Christianity. We will discuss Balthasar's theological engagement with trag-edy, but first let us see how the interaction between theology and tragedy has been effectively sought in recent scholarship. We will also present how this interaction is fundamentally connected with the essence of Holy Satur-day, in other words, the in-betweenness of Holy Saturday. Thus, we will try

14. That is why Friesenhahn is actually forced to switch his agenda from the prob-lem of evil to the transformation of the meaning of suffering, despite the title of his book.

15. Balthasar, *New Elucidations*, 279.

16. See the section "The Trinity and the Problem of Suffering" in chapter 1.

to place our discussion of Balthasar's theological engagement with tragedy in a broader context relevant for us.

Theological Engagement with Tragedy as a Response to Human Suffering

Recently, the genre of tragedy has been gaining recognition in theology as an adequate means to grapple with human existence fraught with evil and suffering without falling into the pitfalls of systematic theodicy.[17] Balthasar is usually considered as a pioneer in this area, along with Donald MacKinnon (1913–1994), who himself is known to be a great admirer of Balthasar.[18]

On the other hand, such an interaction between theology and tragedy has been found problematic by quite a few critics. First of all, there is a long-standing view that Christianity is fundamentally anti-tragic. For example, I. A. Richards clearly juxtaposes tragedy and Christianity when he writes, "Tragedy is only possible to the mind which is for the moment agnostic or Manichean."[19] This kind of juxtaposition has been shared by quite a few authors. George Steiner, for example, declares that tragedy is dead after Christianity, because hope is always present. In his words,

> There has been no specifically Christian mode of tragic drama even in the noontime of the faith. *Christianity is an anti-tragic vision of the world* . . .Christianity offers to man an assurance of final certitude and repose in God. It leads the soul toward justice and resurrection . . .Being a threshold to the eternal, the death of a Christian hero can be an occasion for sorrow but not for tragedy . . .Real tragedy can occur only where the tormented soul believes there is no time left for God's forgiveness. . . .The Christian view knows only partial or episodic tragedy.[20]

However, in classifying Christianity as "anti-tragic" or "untragic" lies a risk of reducing it to a naïve or bland optimism, which is exactly what the Christian theologians who engage with tragedy seek to avoid. For example,

17. For example, see Taylor and Waller, *Christian Theology and Tragedy*; Farley, *Tragic Vision and Divine Compassion*; Tallon, *The Poetics of Evil*.

18. See Taylor and Waller, "Introduction," in *Christian Theology and Tragedy*, 7–8. As a critical examination of Balthasar's theological use of tragedy, see Quash, *Theology and the Drama of History*, 85–118; "Real Enactment"; "Christianity as Hyper-Tragic"; Taylor, "Hans Urs von Balthasar and Christ the Tragic Hero"; *Hans Urs von Balthasar and the Question of Tragedy in the Novels of Thomas Hardy*.

19. Richards, *Principles of Literary Criticism*, 230.

20. Steiner, *The Death of Tragedy*, 331–32. Italics added.

MacKinnon is an exemplary figure who turns to tragedy with keen sensitivity to the reality of human suffering and evil.[21] In particular, it is because of
the Holocaust that MacKinnon examines the tragic element in Christianity
with utmost seriousness.[22] It would be helpful to refer to him here, especially since he reads Balthasar as a theologian who shares the same kind
of sensitivity as his own. MacKinnon believes that Balthasar considers the
horrors of Holocaust with utmost seriousness, even though Balthasar does
not overtly express it in his writings. In MacKinnon's own words,

> In the pages of his work with which we are here concerned
> [*Theo-drama*] there is comparatively little that treats directly of
> these horrors [the Holocaust]; but the nervous tension of the
> whole argument bears witness to *the author's passionate concern
> to present the engagement of God with his world in a way that
> refuses to turn aside from the overwhelming, pervasive real-
> ity of evil.* It is not that Balthasar indulges in any facile cult of
> pessimism; for one thing he is too well schooled in the great
> traditions of European literature for such triviality. It is rather
> that he insists on *a vision that can only be won through the most
> strenuous acknowledgement of the cost of human redemption.*[23]

This "vision that can only be won through the most strenuous acknowledgement of the cost of human redemption" may be called "tragic"
vision, which is definitely one of the reasons for MacKinnon's admiration
of Balthasar. MacKinnon himself writes, "It is part of Balthasar's genius as
a theologian that he has recognized, in Christian history, an *ongoing tragic
dialectic.*"[24] (We will discuss this "ongoing tragic dialectic" captured by
Balthasar in the subsequent sections.)

As many commentators on MacKinnon note, his writings are not systematic or declarative but rather fragmentary and suggestive.[25] One com-
mentator says, for example, "His work, which is probing, interrogative and

---

21. For discussions of MacKinnon's theological engagement with tragedy, see
Waller "Freedom, Fate and Sin in Donald MacKinnon's Use of Tragedy"; Devanny,
"Truth, Tragedy and Compassion." Also for an analysis of how Steiner and MacKin-
non (a literary critic and a Christian theologian) have influenced each other regarding
the question of tragedy through their friendship at the University of Cambridge, see
Ward, "Tragedy as Subclause."

22. MacKinnon, *The Problem of Metaphysics*, 130.

23. MacKinnon, "Some Reflections on Hans Urs von Balthasar's Christology," 165.
Italics added.

24. Ibid., 171. Italics added.

25. See Waller, "Freedom, Fate and Sin in Donald MacKinnon's Use of Tragedy,"
104; Devanny, "Truth, Tragedy and Compassion," 33.

somewhat fragmentary, has a tendency to eschew solution or synthesis in favour of ever more sharply articulated problems and paradoxes."[26] This style seems to be related to his strong insistence that evil or suffering cannot be (or rather, should not be) theologically explained away. This principle is actually a "lesson" which we should learn from tragedy. In MacKinnon's view, tragic literature, which is most characteristically represented by such classic authors as Sophocles and Shakespeare, captures "a presence to the reality of moral evil, to the ways in which its power is experienced as a destructive force which makes the writings of most philosophers and theologians seems somehow trivial."[27] The following passage summarizes his position regarding this matter well:

> It is a lesson to be learnt from tragedy that *there is no solution of the problem of evil*; it is a lesson which Christian faith abundantly confirms, even while it transforms the teaching by the indication of its central mystery. In the Cross the conflicting claims of truth and mercy are reconciled by deed and not by word. The manner of their reconciliation is something which lies beyond the frontier of our comprehension; we can only *describe and redescribe.*[28]

Thus, MacKinnon argues that the only approach allowed for us to deal with the problem of evil and suffering is to "describe and redescribe" concrete particulars (as done in tragic literature) without trying to analyse or explain them presumptuously. In another place, MacKinnon also declares that "it is sheer nonsense to speak of the Christian religion as offering a solution of the problem of evil."[29]

Lying at the core of this insistence is MacKinnon's strong conviction that the story of Jesus himself should be interpreted as a tragedy. He stresses the historical contingency of the event of the cross. It was a particular event after all, which defies philosophical or theological rationalization. Even the glorious victory of the resurrection should not be considered as negation of the horrible suffering of the cross. We should never forget that "the one who is raised is the one who died, who passed through physical agony, and through mental and spiritual dereliction, into the nothingness of death."[30]

---

26. Waller, "Freedom, Fate and Sin in Donald MacKinnon's Use of Tragedy," 104.

27. MacKinnon, *Borderlands of Theology and Other Essays*, 101.

28. Ibid., 104. Italics added.

29. MacKinnon, *Borderlands of Theology and Other Essays*, 92.

30. MacKinnon, "A Master in Israel," 8.

The fact that the resurrected Jesus maintains the marks of the nails on his body vividly illustrates this point.

Moreover, even though the resurrection is a victory, we always have to remember that it was a victory won at great costs. MacKinnon likes to quote a remark made by the great Duke of Wellington that "a victory is the most tragic thing in the world, only excepting a defeat," which he applies to the victory of Christ as well.[31] In particular, MacKinnon remains troubled by the fate of Judas Iscariot, and for him Judas is the proof that Jesus' ministry was "a failure." In his words, "It is in the figure of Judas Iscariot that the failure of Jesus is focused, and the tragic quality of his mission becomes plain."[32] As Jesus himself declares, "It would have been better for that one [Judas] not to have been born" (Matt 26:24). Even in God's great plan of salvation, even after the victory of the resurrection, the question concerning the lostness of Judas remains unsolved. Therefore, for MacKinnon the problem of evil is exactly the problem of Judas Iscariot (largely influenced by Karl Barth on this point).[33] Thus, MacKinnon tries to remind us of the high cost of redemption in terms of the evil deeds done and the suffering of the innocent.

MacKinnon's moral concerns are obvious, but his "tragic" theology has not been free from critique. The most vehement critique comes from David Bentley Hart, who denounces "tragic theology" as a whole (in which not only MacKinnon but also Balthasar is included). In Hart's words, "Simply said, tragic theology lacks theological depth."[34] As to MacKinnon, Hart suspects that he "has not so much read the story of the crucifixion in the light of Attic tragedy as read tragedy in Christian terms."[35] Lying at the core of Hart's critique of tragic theology in general is the concern that Christianity should never be reduced to mere tragedy.

The problem is basically caused by the different interpretations of the word "tragedy" or "tragic."[36] So far, we have rather intentionally avoided defining the word, as it is exactly what we would like to explore in the following sections by examining Balthasar's use of the word in a Christian sense. Eventually, we will see below that the word "tragedy" or "tragic" used in a Christian context is best interpreted as "tragedy under grace" (the expression Balthasar borrows from the German novelist Reinhold Schneider),

31. MacKinnon, *The Problem of Metaphysics*, 126, 131.

32. MacKinnon, "Theology and Tragedy," 168.

33. MacKinnon, *Borderlands of Theology*, 67.

34. Hart, *The Beauty of the Infinite*, 374.

35. Ibid., 383.

36. For example, see Quash, "Four Biblical Characters," 22.

which means something between the mere "tragic" and the "untragic." Such "in-betweenness" detected in the use of the word "tragedy" or "tragic" in a Christian sense is well captured by Ben Quash's statement that "Godly life, in Christian terms, is *hyper*-tragic, not *un*tragic."[37] What he means by the word "hyper-tragic" is explained as follows:

> Rather than stopping short of tragedy, circumventing tragedy, or resting with tragedy, Christianity's doctrine *embraces and heightens* tragedy, in order simultaneously to *acknowledge its full, unmitigated power to disrupt, disturb and destroy, and also to let it mean more than itself.*[38]

Importantly, this statement of Quash's is made on the basis of his critical appreciation of Balthasar's and MacKinnon's use of tragic drama. In short, the tragic sensibility in Christian theology usually seeks to find a middle ground *between* nihilistic pessimism and bland optimism, or between hopeless despair and naive hope.

Furthermore, as we have seen in MacKinnon's tragic sensibility, lying at the center of theological interaction with tragedy is the question of how we view the relationship between the cross and the resurrection. This point brings us to the very topic of this book, namely, the significance of Holy Saturday. We can see how the tragic sensibility in Christian theology is fundamentally connected with Holy Saturday.

First of all, if we take MacKinnon's tragic theology as a warning against simple triumphalism, in other words, a warning against those who rush towards Easter joy too eagerly or hastily, we can see that a similar concern is lying at the core of an emphasis on Holy Saturday as the day of silent waiting and mourning. As a matter of fact, according to MacKinnon, it is from Balthasar that we can learn that we should not forget the lesson about the costs of victory, which MacKinnon likes to see as well-represented in the remark made by the Duke of Wellington.[39] Balthasar definitely has this concern in mind when he argues for the significance of the "passive" waiting on Holy Saturday in contrast to the way the victory of Easter is prematurely celebrated as an "active" event on Holy Saturday by the traditional teachings. In his words,

> We must, in the first place, *guard against that theological busyness and religious impatience* which insist on anticipating the

37. Ibid., 31.

38. Quash, "Christianity as Hyper-Tragic," 77. Italics added.

39. MacKinnon, "Some Reflections on Hans Urs von Balthasar's Christology," 166.

moment of fruiting of the eternal redemption through the temporal passion—on *dragging forward that moment from Easter to Holy Saturday.*[40]

Secondly, in the last analysis, human existence itself has something fundamentally close to the image of Holy Saturday as a day suspended between the suffering of Good Friday and the victory of Easter Sunday. This point has been suggested by Steiner in the following memorable passage:

> *Ours is the long day's journey of the Saturday. Between suffering, aloneness, unutterable waste on the one hand and the dream of liberation, of rebirth on the other.* In the face of the torture of a child, of the death of love which is Friday, even the greatest art and poetry are almost helpless. In the Utopia of the Sunday, the aesthetic will, presumably, no longer have logic or necessity. The apprehensions and figurations in the play of metaphysical imagining, in the poem and the music, which tell of pain and of hope, of the flesh which is said to taste of ash and of the spirit which is said to have the savour of fire, *are always Sabbatarian.* They have risen out of *an immensity of waiting which is that of man.* Without them, how could we be patient?[41]

What Steiner tells us here is that the attempts of Christian theology or tragic literature to grapple with the human reality of suffering, pain, despair, victory, joy and hope "are always Sabbatarian." If we turn our attention to a perspective from the point of view of tragic literature, there is an idea that tragedy actually operates in the borderlands, somewhere in-between.[42] Adrian Poole observes, for example, that tragedy is particularly concerned with imagining the point between here and "elsewhere," or more specifically, between life and death.[43] "There is a world elsewhere"; this is what Shakespeare's Coriolanus proclaims with contempt as he turns his back on ungrateful Rome.[44] Using this expression, Poole says that tragedy can be seen as the place where two "elsewheres" meet and yet are separated.[45] In this sense, tragedy can be seen both as a protest against the present conditions of

---

40. Balthasar, *Mysterium Paschale*, 179. Italics added.

41. Steiner, *Real Presences*, 232. Italics added. As a further theological reflection on this passage, see Lash, "Friday, Saturday, Sunday."

42. See Taylor and Waller, "Introduction," *Christian Theology and Tragedy*, 8–9.

43. Poole, *Tragedy*, 167.

44. Shakespeare, *Coriolanus* III. iii. 137. Quoted by Poole in *Tragedy: Shakespeare and the Greek Example*, 166.

45. Ibid., 167.

human suffering and a yearning for a better future, in other words, located between suffering and victory or between sorrow and joy.[46]

It would also be helpful here to note the view that one important characteristic of tragedy is that it embraces contraries in tension. For example, Helen Gardner, a renowned literary critic, writes, "tragedy includes, or reconciles, or preserves in tension, contraries."[47] These "contraries" could refer to various things: two ideals incompatible with each other, contradictory aspects of human nature (like reason and passion), the contingencies of life and their meaningful coherence, protest and acceptance, despair and hope. We definitely could add to this list the tension between the cross and the resurrection, which we believe to be existent in the very center of the Christian existence, as we will discuss later.

In this section, we have tried to show that there is inherently a deep connection linking the in-betweenness of Holy Saturday and Christian engagement with tragedy. With this broad framework in mind, let us proceed to examine Balthasar's theological engagement with tragedy.

Balthasar and Tragedy: Jesus Christ as "the Heir of All the Tragedy of the World"

Balthasar's approach to tragedy has been critically examined by a few scholars such as Quash and Kevin Taylor.[48] However, in comparison to the amount of scholarly work produced on the topic of his aesthetics or dramatics as a whole, the significance of tragedy or the tragic in Balthasar's theology seems to remain under-appreciated[49] (despite the fact that Balthasar is generally admitted to be a pioneer in the area of intellectual interaction between theology and tragedy, as we have mentioned above.) Below we will try to present how his interest in tragedy is closely related to his theology of Holy Saturday. In the last analysis, we would like to argue that the "tragic" state of Christian existence, which is "torn between" the truth of Christ and the world, is deeply connected with the in-betweenness of Holy Saturday captured by Balthasar. First, we will see Balthasar's use of tragedy or tragic

46. See Taylor and Waller, "Introduction," in *Christian Theology and Tragedy*, 8–9.

47. Gardner, *Religion and Literature*, 24.

48. See Quash, *Theology and the Drama of History*, 85–118; "Real Enactment"; "Christianity as Hyper-Tragic"; Taylor, *Hans Urs von Balthasar and the Question of Tragedy in the Novels of Thomas Hardy*; "Hans Urs von Balthasar and Christ the Tragic Hero." Also see, Block, Jr., "Balthasar's Literary Criticism."

49. See Taylor, *Hans Urs von Balthasar and the Question of Tragedy in the Novels of Thomas Hardy*, 9–12.

drama in general, and then go on to discuss his reading of one specific modern tragic author, namely, Reinhold Schneider (as he has been largely neglected despite his relevance to this topic.)

The significance of tragedy in Balthasar's theology has been concisely summarized by Taylor; Balthasar uses the concept of tragedy in multiple ways without explicitly distinguishing them in his writings—as ontic and historical experience, as a genre of literature, and as a philosophical concept; In particular, Balthasar believes that tragedy reveals the following three aspects of the nature of the world, namely, the dramatic nature of human existence, the existential truths, and the participative distance of humanity from God.[50]

Balthasar covers a wide range of tragic literature, that is, from classic authors such as the great Greek playwrights (Homer, Aeschylus, Sophocles, and Euripides),[51] through Shakespeare,[52] Racine and Corneille, to modern authors such as Dostoyevsky, Paul Claudel, Georges Bernanos, and Reinhold Schneider. It is far beyond the scope or interest of this chapter to engage thoroughly with Balthasar's reading of all these tragic authors. Therefore, for our purpose, let us focus on two relevant aspects: the influence of Hegel on Balthasar's approach to tragedy and Balthasar's Christocentric reading of tragedy.

The significance of the influence of Hegel on Balthasar and its complex nature has been pointed out by many, but especially in his approach to tragedy, the importance of the Hegelian influence cannot be ignored. First of all, Hegel is admittedly the only author who matches Balthasar in the depth and richness of his theological engagement with tragedy. Balthasar himself praises Hegel on this point.[53] Like Balthasar, Hegel had a life-long interest in tragedy, which can be traced from *Early Theological Writings* to *Philosophy of Religion*. Balthasar's high regard for drama itself is apparently influenced by Hegel's aesthetics which values poetic drama as the queen of the arts.[54]

---

50. Ibid., 9–38.

51. For example, for Balthasar's theological engagement with Greek tragedies, see Denny, "Greek Tragedies."

52. Especially, as Taylor points out, while Balthasar's love for the Attic tragedians is obvious, Shakespeare appears in his writings more consistently than any other literary author in the theological trilogy, because Balthasar sees in Shakespeare that the essence of tragedy innovated by the Greek authors is combined with a rich biblical awareness and Christian ethos.

53. He writes, "no thinker before him [Hegel] more profoundly experienced and pondered Christian revelation in dramatic categories." (Balthasar, *Theo-Drama* I, 66.)

54. Hegel writes, "because drama has been developed into the most perfect totality of content and form, it must be regarded as the highest stage of poetry and art

Therefore, it is natural that, as it has been pointed out by Quash, "Hegel accompanies von Balthasar's thought everywhere in his trilogy."[55] However, as is usual with Balthasar's use of Hegel, he borrows basic concepts from Hegel, but modifies them for his own usage, and eventually departs from him.[56]

The categories of "epic," "lyric," and "dramatic" which Balthasar borrows from Hegel[57] are especially relevant for our interest, because it is on the basis of his use of this Hegelian distinction that scholars like Quash eventually critique Balthasar for his "epic tendency," which, in Quash's view, contradictorily exposes itself in his theology of Holy Saturday despite the fact that it is supposed to be the climax of the dramatic perspective.[58] (We will discuss this criticism later in this chapter.) The category of "epic" means a bird's-eye view of history, in which all actions and events are seen as completed. It is the perspective to "smooth out the folds and say that Jesus' suffering is past history."[59] One example of using this perspective is to see Eucharist as a mere memorial. Balthasar also uses this "epic" category to criticize systematic theologies and creeds that speak of God in the third person. This point is clarified further if we consider the category of "lyric," which is placed in opposition to the "epic" and is used to mean "the internal motion of the devout subject, his emotion and submission, the creative outpouring of himself in the face of the vivid re-presentation. . .of what is a past event."[60] In other words, the "lyrical" perspective means to receive Eucharist as a personal participation in the death of Jesus and to build an I-Thou relationship with God (as best realized in Ignatian spirituality). To put it simply, the "epic" and the "lyric" are "objective" and "subjective" perspectives respectively, or to put it even more simply, theology and spirituality. Further, for Balthasar it is the "dramatic" (in other words, his project of *Theo-drama*) that successfully unites both of the "epic" and the "lyric" in a somewhat Hegelian dialectical way. He writes, "We shall not get beyond the

---

generally." (Hegel, *Aesthetics* II, 1158.)

55. Quash, *Theology and the Drama of History*, 12n21.

56. See Quash, *Theology and the Drama of History*. Further, for a very concise summary of the Hegelian influence on Balthasar's approach to tragedy, see Taylor, *Hans Urs von Balthasar and the Question of Tragedy in the Novels of Thomas Hardy*, 34–38.

57. Balthasar, *Theo-Drama* II, 55–57. For Hegel's own distinction between these categories, see Hegel, *Aesthetics* II, 1040–1237. For a summary of exactly how Balthasar adapts Hegel's distinctions to his theological use, see Quash, *Theology and the Drama of History*, 41–51.

58. Quash, *Theology and the Drama of History*, 195. He makes this particular criticism in various other places.

59. Balthasar, *Theo-Drama* II, 54.

60. Ibid., 55.

alternatives of "lyrical" and "epic," spirituality (prayer and personal involvement) and theology (the objective discussion of facts), so long as we fail to include the dramatic dimension of revelation, in which alone they can discover their unity."[61]

In short, in the dramatic perspective both the epic and lyrical perspectives are supposed to be maintained in perfectly balance without collapsing into each other. As Balthasar applies this dramatic perspective theologically, to be an apostolic witness for Christ means to have a dramatic existence, in which the epical and lyrical perspectives are not only unified but also heightened. To put it in a way relevant for our interest, the encounter between divine and human freedom should be explored by such a dramatic perspective, in which the sensitivity to particular individuals and events as well as the view of broad contexts in history can be maintained. As we have already discussed in chapters 1 and 2, for Balthasar, the climax of the encounter of divine and human freedom is Christ's descent into hell on Holy Saturday. It is the most dramatic event of all, where "the epic" and "the lyric," objectivity and subjectivity, and eventually theology and spirituality, are somehow united. Such a unity is best represented by the word "contemplative," which is often used to characterize the Holy Saturday presented by Balthasar, in contrast to Hegel's "speculative" Good Friday.[62] (However, some critics like Quash argue that Balthasar's dramatics, including his interpretation of Holy Saturday as its climax, may not be so faithful to this dramatic perspective after all. We will discuss this point later.)

On the other hand, while for Hegel tragedy (and more broadly, art) becomes surpassed by Christianity and ultimately by philosophy, Balthasar departs from him by taking the position that Christianity sustains tragedy. This point is closely related to his Christocentric reading of tragedy which we will discuss next.

Balthasar's Christocentric reading of tragedy is most clearly seen in the following statement: "Jesus Christ is the heir of *all the tragedy of the world*, that of the Greeks as well as that of the Jews, that of the so-called unbelievers as well as that of the so-called believers."[63] In the last analysis, for Balthasar, all tragedies, both in literature and in history, are ultimately christological. To put it more specifically, all tragedies or all human suffering both before and after Christ culminate in and are surpassed by the cross and the descent

---

61. Ibid., 57.

62. See Balthasar, *Mysterium Paschale*, 62–66, 172. Also see, de Lubac, "A Witness of Christ in the Church," 284–85.

63. Balthasar, *Explorations in Theology* III, 400. Italics added. For a critical examination of this statement, see Taylor, "Hans Urs von Balthasar and Christ the Tragic Hero."

into hell. As we can see from this statement, like MacKinnon, Balthasar reads the Christian gospel as a tragedy. However, in comparison to MacKinnon, Balthasar's Christocentric emphasis is obvious, which allows him to escape the criticism presented by Hart against MacKinnon[64] (mentioned in the section above). (Certainly, whether such a Christocentric reading does full justice to originally non-Christian tragedies would be another matter.)

The key concept that connects the classic tragic drama with the paschal mystery is what Balthasar calls "opaque guilt," the best illustration of which is found in Sophocles's *Oedipus*.[65] King Oedipus committed the most atrocious crimes imaginable: murdering his own father and marrying his own mother. The tragedy lies in the fact that he did all this without knowing it. Where does his guilt actually lie? Is he completely guilty? It was he himself that committed these crimes and yet it was done under the influence of an inherited curse. By the expression, "opaque guilt," Balthasar means opaque causality in which the distinction between human freedom and determined fate is blurred. Human acts are strangely both free and determined, therefore an individual is both guilty and innocent. Balthasar observes that this ambiguous causation in tragedy is quite close to the Christian concept of original sin. In traditional Christian theology, each individual is considered as being under the influence of collective guilt and yet still morally responsible for their own deeds. Further, this closeness between opaque guilt and original sin allows Balthasar to see tragic figures in the Old Testament (most notably Job, Samson, Jeremiah, Hagar, and so forth) in parallel with characters in Greek tragedies (Hecuba, Hercules, Cassandra, Andromache, and so forth),[66] and eventually to reach Jesus Christ as "the heir of *all the tragedy of the world*, that of the Greeks as well as that of the Jews."[67]

Jesus Christ not only inherits all the tragedy of the world but also *surpasses* it. He does so by "simultaneously fulfilling them" by his own "tragedy," namely, the cross and the descent into hell. Only Christ, the one who is completely sinless and thus completely innocent, can free this world from the tragically tangled knots of guilt and innocence. Only he is the true *deus ex machina theatri* (not in the sense of a cheap plot criticized by Aristotle.) Thus, even the most horrible tragedy of the *Trojan Women* is encompassed by the tragedy of Christ.

---

64. See Taylor, *Hans Urs von Balthasar and the Question of Tragedy in the Novels of Thomas Hardy*, 32.

65. Balthasar, *Explorations in Theology* III, 394–95.

66. Ibid., 398–400.

67. Ibid., 400.

Now, it is not difficult to see that this idea has the potential to be a con-soling answer to the problem of suffering,[68] because now we could believe that however deep in hell we may feel we are, Christ has descended even deeper. There is no tragedy in this world that is not encompassed within the tragedy of Christ. In relation to this point, Balthasar likes to quote from Claudel, who writes, "the poor man. . .has no friend to rely on except one poorer than himself."[69] Similarly, as we saw in chapter 2, Balthasar likes to evoke the image of the lonely sinner in hell with the even lonelier Savior be-side them. Christ is always the "poorer" and "even lonelier" man beside us. Hence, as we have discussed at the beginning of this chapter, some scholars try to explain away Balthasar's "theodicy" by simply concluding that now we can believe that even the worst suffering of hell has been redeemed by Christ's suffering. However, this simplification actually ends up being what we might call an "epic" theodicy, which could not escape the criticism that Balthasar pays little respect to concrete and particular suffering in reality. It is true that Balthasar argues in this direction to some extent and he certainly presents the idea that we can find meaning in our suffering by relating it to the paschal mystery, but we should also note that he is attentive to the concrete reality of human suffering in his own way. In order to argue for this point further, we need to explore the nature of Balthasar's conception of post-Easter "tragedy." While tragedy or human suffering could be mitigated and minimized by reference to the paschal mystery, the status of tragedy itself is actually heightened after Christ. Similarly, human suffering is intensified in a way, and moreover, is given a positive meaning. In stark contrast to those who have declared that Christianity and tragedy are incompatible with each other (from Hegel to Steiner), for Balthasar, it is actually Christianity that will sustain tragedy.[70] This position is exactly shared by MacKinnon, who writes, "Christianity, properly understood, might provide men with a faith through which they are enabled to hold steadfastly to the significance of the tragic."[71] In the last analysis, Balthasar believes that Christian existence is fundamentally tragic. We will discuss this point by examining his reading of the German Catholic novelist, Reinhold Schneider.

---

68. See Taylor, "Hans Urs von Balthasar and Christ the Tragic Hero," 144–46; *Balthasar and the Question of Tragedy in the Novels of Thomas Hardy*, 186–90.

69. Claudel, "Mother of Perpetual Help." Conclusion of Part I of the Corona Po-ems, quoted by Balthasar in *Theo-Drama V*, 312.

70. For example, see Balthasar, *Theo-Drama II*, 49–51.

71. MacKinnon, *The Problem of Metaphysics*, 135.

"Tragedy under Grace": The Tragic State of the Christian Existence

Balthasar calls the fundamental situation of the church "tragic," because it is formed out of Jews and Gentiles in the first place, in other words, *"unification in the state of being torn."*[72] He explores the "tragic" dimension of Christian existence in various places. For example, he writes as follows:

> The Cross has removed the wall of division, as the Letter to the Ephesians says, in the tortured flesh of Christ. And yet this wall seems to be set up higher and more unsurmountably than ever. The Cross is judgement and therefore division: one thief is on the left, and another is on the right. But it is wholly dialectical: Jesus openly makes a promise to the thief on his right and says nothing to the thief on his left. But in order that the thief on the right may win the promise, Jesus unites himself in secret with the thief on the left in the solidarity of being rejected. *The Christian is exposed to this situation of being torn; and what other name than tragic could one find for this*, if one looks back to the Greek stage?[73]

This tragic state of "being torn" needs examining further. It would be helpful to turn to the German novelist, poet, and playwright, Reinhold Schneider (1903–1958), whose portrayal of the "tragic" Christian existence in many of his works is much appreciated by Balthasar.[74] How he reads Schneider to explore the tragic dimension of Christian existence has hardly ever been investigated,[75] but it is relevant for our discussion. (For example, the image of the two thieves on the right and the left is pursued in his analysis of Schneider.[76]) Eventually, examination of his reading of Schneider helps us to see how Balthasar views the relationship between tragedy and the Christian, or tragedy and grace. Schneider basically sees a paradoxical relationship between tragedy and grace, and so does Balthasar. This point

---

72. Balthasar, *Explorations in Theology* III, 405. He discusses this point further in "Church of Jews and Gentiles-Today" in *New Elucidations*, 60–74.

73. Balthasar, *Explorations in Theology* III, 406. Italics added.

74. See Balthasar, *Tragedy Under Grace*; *Explorations in Theology* III, 471–93. Also see *Theo-Drama* I, 119–23.

75. Kevin Taylor briefly mentions Balthasar's reading of Schneider, but only to criticize the aristocratic tendency in his reading. Also John R. Cihak gives a short summary of Balthasar's use of Schneider as far as it is related to the topic of "anxiety" in Cihak, *Balthasar and Anxiety*, 43–50.

76. Balthasar, *Tragedy under Grace*, 132–57.

further helps us to see the implications his theology provides for the issue of Christian suffering.

First of all, it is intriguing to see how Schneider's view of the tragic developed during the course of his life.[77] Schneider's life can be divided into three stages depending on his view on the tragic: 1) the period of a tragic, nihilistic view of life (from his childhood to his conversion to Catholicism in 1933), 2) the period of an *anti-tragic* view of Christianity (from 1933 to around 1948), and 3) the period of a *tragic* view of Christianity (from around 1948 to his death). In Schneider's own words, these three stages are described as follows: "At first, I overestimated the earthly power, because I had not yet seen the living reality of God. Then, I came to underestimate the earthly power, because the power of God devoured it. Finally, I understood that a human being must control it in front of God."[78] In his youth, Schneider was hugely influenced by both Miguel de Unamuno and Schopenhauer, both of whom led him to believe that "the tragic was the deepest essence of existence."[79] After his conversion to Catholicism, however, this interest in tragedy lost its melancholic nature and somehow flowed into "an Augustinian idea of struggle, into a striving toward salvation on the part of the whole of history."[80] Now, for Schneider, Christ on the cross "has taken tragedy on himself and thus withdrawn it from the world."[81] He even declared, "as soon as Christ appears, the whole tragic world perishes: the terrible confusion is no longer possible. As soon as the tragedian meets Christ, he loses his ability to write tragedy."[82] Then both his earlier interest in tragedy and his Christian faith become somehow merged, and he declares, "*Christianity has given a metaphysical answer to the tragic, but it has not abolished it. The tragic remains a basic phenomenon of our existence and history as a*

---

77. See Kihachi Shimomura, *Ikirareta Kotoba*, 195. For further reference on Schneider's life and works, there seems to be no English secondary source available apart from the translation of Balthasar's work on him. As to German sources, see, for example, Scherer, *Tragik vor dem Kreuz*.

78. Schneider, *(Lebensbericht) Schulfunk (22.9.1953)*, 3. Quoted by Scherer in *Tragik vor dem Kreuz*, 130, and by Shimomura in *Ikirareta Kotoba*, 195: "Erst überschätzte ich die irdische Macht, weil ich die lebendige Wirklichkeit Gottes noch nicht sah; dann unterschätzte ich sie, weil die Macht Gottes sie aufzehrte. Endlich verstand ich, daß der Mensch sie verwalten soll vor Gott."

79. Balthasar, *Tragedy under Grace*, 283.

80. Ibid., 118.

81. Schneider, *Tagebücher 1930–1935*, 610. Quoted by Balthasar in *Tragedy under Grace*, 283.

82. Schneider, *Tagebücher 1930–1935*, 670. Quoted by Balthasar in *Tragedy under Grace*, 283.

contradiction of life."[83] Schneider also wrote to a friend in 1950, "For a long time I used to think that Christianity and tragedy were incompatible, but now I see that Christianity is something fundamentally tragic. The fate of the truth is death."[84]

It is worth noting that Schneider himself had an anti-tragic view of Christianity (more or less in accord with Steiner's point of view) before he came to regard it as tragic, even though this period of the anti-tragic view of Christianity happened to coincide with the most difficult time of his life under the Nazi regime.[85] Schneider is surely well aware that the joy and hope based on the Christian good news should not be undermined. Rather, his use of the word "tragic" is actually intended for something between tragic and untragic, as we have already noted in the section above. This point is related to why Balthasar approves of Schneider's tragic vision. Now let us examine how Schneider exactly uses the word "tragic" in a Christian sense and how Balthasar appreciates it.

Balthasar approvingly quotes the following sentence of Schneider's: "the Christian stands in a thoroughly dramatic, indeed, tragic relationship to the world: he must represent in the world something that is not of the world."[86] In other words, the Christian is called "tragic" because they find themselves constantly torn between the truth, which is Christ, and the world, which has fallen away from God and now stands against Christ. Schneider further explains,

> For the Christian, there is both *a tragedy under grace* and *a graceless tragedy*. Tragedy under grace is what is experienced by the man who wants to do the truth and is brought down because truth cannot be done in this world; graceless tragedy is the lot of the man who does not want the truth.[87]

---

83. Schneider, *Der Christliche Protest*, 75. Italics added: "Das Christentum hat eine metaphysische Antwort auf das Tragische gegeben, aber es hat das Tragische nicht aufgehoben. Es bleibt als Lebenswiderspruch ein Grundphänomen unseres Daseins und der Geschichte."

84. Schneider, *Briefe an einen Freund (Otto Heuschele)*, 147. Quoted by Scherer in *Tragik vor dem Kreuz*, 80: "ich hielt lange Christentum und Tragik für unvereinbar; nun sehe ich, daß das Christliche das eigentlich Tragische ist. Das Schicksal der Wahrheit ist der Tod."

85. See Shimomura, *Ikirareta Kotoba*, 196.

86. Schneider, *Rechenschaft*, 22. Quoted by Balthasar in *Tragedy under Grace*, 119.

87. Schneider, *Rechenschaft*, 23. Quoted by Balthasar in *Theo-drama* I, 120. Italics added.

In short, the tragic state of "being torn" between Christ and the world within Christian life is called a "tragedy under grace" and it is definitely distinguished from a "graceless tragedy" of the non-Christian, let alone what Steiner calls "absolute or pure tragedy."[88] In particular, for Schneider, this tragic state of the Christian is expressed symbolically by Jesus standing before Pontius Pilate.[89] The "fettered King," who "will prove the world wrong about sin and righteousness and judgement" (John 16:8), stands powerless and defenceless before the administration of secular power.

This reference to power is significant for Schneider, as most of his works focus on the tragedy inherent in the exercise of power by Christians, who have the duty and/or desire to bring the truth of the gospel into the world and yet fail to do so because of the tragic dilemma on earth where they find themselves. Schneider does not believe that power is evil per se, but still, as Balthasar points out, "The burning concrete question posed by Schneider is this: Concrete history applies force, but the gospel forbids the use of force—does not every Christian who intervenes actively in concrete history, therefore, become guilty in relation to the gospel?"[90] Schneider explores such a Christian dilemma on a grand scale, for example, in the dramas surrounding three popes in the past (Celestine V and Boniface VIII in *Der große Verzicht* [the great renunciation], and Innocent III in *Innozenz and Franziskus* [Innocent and Francis]).[91] Using the real life story centered around Celestine V's abdication of the papacy in 1294 and the subsequent downfall of Boniface VIII after his manipulative acquisition of the office from Celestine V, Schneider attempts to "uncover the enormous tragedy of the existence of the one who bears office and to make visible the deep ecclesial guilt that consists in the mutual exclusion of action and contemplation."[92] On the other hand, with Innocent III, "the pope with Celestine's heart and Boniface's deeds,"[93] Schneider further portrays this tragic tension existent within the Church.

Schneider's dramatic portrayal of the tragic struggles of the popes in the past helps us to understand further what Balthasar means when he says

88. Steiner, "Tragedy Reconsidered," 29–44.

89. Schneider, *Rechenschaft*, 23. See Balthasar in *Theo-Drama* I, 120–22.

90. Balthasar, *Tragedy Under Grace*, 128.

91. Balthasar says these two dramas form "a kind of *summa* of Reinhold Schneider's view of the world." (Balthasar, *Tragedy Under Grace*, 221.) Balthasar's summaries of the synopses of *Der große Verzicht* and *Innozenz III* are respectively in *Explorations in Theology* III, 476–82, 482–93; *Tragedy under Grace*, 220–28, 229–44.

92. Balthasar, *Tragedy Under Grace*, 228.

93. Ibid., 229.

the church is, and eventually all individual Christians are, fundamentally tragic. He mentions the dramas of these three popes as good examples of the innate tragedy within the church itself, which seeks to exercise power in this world, though it has its origin in the powerlessness of the cross.[94] Specifically, the "innate tragedy" refers to a disquieting possibility that "the Church becomes the true Oedipus" for the church could end up exposing its own guilt in its eager attempts to re-establish order in society.[95] He writes, "Wherever the Church rejects the powerlessness of the Cross, which is offered her and imposed upon her, she reaches out to take hold of power, and the face of Satan glimmers in her."[96] Another such tragic example is found in the trial and execution of St. Joan of Arc, who "was more innocent than Antigone . . .but her judges [those who held hierarchical office in the Church] were more guilty than Creon."[97] The tragedy of St. Joan of Arc is portrayed not only in Schneider's work but also in the work of Georges Bernanos (another twentieth-century Catholic novelist admired by Balthasar). In his studies on Bernanos, Balthasar takes up the similar, disquieting thought that we may see "the face of Satan glimmer[ing]" in the church;

> But what if sin lives in the Church herself, if sin anchors itself most securely precisely where the Church is most vulnerable-in her hierarchical structure? What if the horror occurs that the face of Satan should begin to glimmer in the very heart of that Trinitarian image, which is the relationship of ecclesial obedience?[98]

These innate tragedies within the church can happen because the church is tragic "in its innermost being," to the extent that it believes itself "*to be redeemed once and for all,*" when, in truth, the church is different from its archetype, Virgin Mary (*Ecclesia Immaculata*).[99] All of this points to the idea that the church (and the individual Christian) remains exposed to sin as long as it is in this world. At the same time, the church (and the individual Christian) is already redeemed and forgiven because of faith in Christ. Eventually, it is this paradoxical double existence of the Christian that both Schneider and Balthasar mean when they say Christianity (or the church or the Christian) is fundamentally "tragic."

94. Balthasar, *Explorations in Theology* III, 406–7.

95. Ibid., 411.

96. Balthasar, *Tragedy Under Grace*, 212.

97. Balthasar, *Explorations in Theology* III, 407.

98. Balthasar, *Bernanos*, 279.

99. Balthasar, *Explorations in Theology* III, 409.

This point brings us to what we would like to discuss further, namely, Balthasar's deep concern for Christian life. We will argue that he takes the possibility of the Christian committing sin with utmost seriousness and that this point is an important aspect of his theology of Holy Saturday.

The Tragic Nature of Christian Life and Holy Saturday

In various places in chapters 1 and 2, we repeatedly referred to the concept of "distance" in Balthasar's theology, but now we can see that it contains the most serious meaning. For example, now it makes perfect sense to read the following statement of Adrienne von Speyr (approvingly quoted by Balthasar) in the context of the tragic situation of the Christian: "*the greater a man's intimacy with the Lord, the greater the danger that he will become estranged.*"[100] Though this sentence reveals the kind of idea which is found problematic by Balthasar's critics including Pitstick,[101] it would make perfect sense if we consider the tragic possibility that "the face of Satan glimmers" at the center of the church, or even in the life of the most pious Christian, as suggested by Balthasar. As a matter of fact, the Christian can be even more vulnerably exposed to sin than non-believers, exactly because only they can be tempted to believe that they are redeemed once and for all and to forget their paradoxical status as "*Simul iustus et peccator*" or a "justified sinner."

Further, it is in this context of the tragic Christian existence that we should remember the emphasis made by Balthasar that there was no heaven or purgatory or hell (as *Gehenna*) before Christ's descent into *Sheol*. As we have seen in chapter 2, these three afterlife states are considered as its results, and therefore, "Christological concepts." In other words, our free decision-making starts to have real consequences only after the event on Holy Saturday. Now our Yes and No have eternal effects, which could actually weigh the most heavily on Christians themselves. Also, in relation to this point, we have seen in chapter 2 how the reverse side of Balthasar's famous "hope" for universal salvation is the possibility of the Christian's complete rejection of God. This possibility too, which Pitstick argues cannot exist,[102] will make sense if we think of such a tragic situation for the Christian.

On the other hand, we should never forget that the Christian can be called tragic only in the sense of "tragedy under grace." Despite the fact that the Christian existence fundamentally has a tragic element of being torn

---

100. Speyr, *I Korinther*, 348. Quoted by Balthasar in *Theo-drama* V, 288. Italics added.

101. See Pitstick, *Light in Darkness*, 273–74.

102. See the section "'Hope' for Universal Salvation" in chapter 2.

between the truth of Christ and the power of the world, the Christian always has the privilege of relating their own tragedy to the tragedy of Jesus Christ. As we have mentioned above, the paschal mystery has shown the way for the Christian to have their own suffering mitigated by reference to Christ. Such a way of consolation has been made possible by nothing other than grace.

In order to pursue further this double status of the Christian expressed as "tragedy under grace," let us turn to St. Paul. After all, the kind of a tragic struggle of a Christian portrayed by Schneider and appreciated by Balthasar can be traced back to St. Paul. In particular, 2 Corinthians is relevant for our discussion here, as St. Paul deals with the tragic tension existent in Christian life while referring to the cross and the resurrection.

The significant connection between tragedy and 2 Corinthians has been pointed out by David Ford, for example. He says this epistle shows "the tragic being taking into a transformation which sharpens rather than negates it, while yet rendering the category of the tragic inadequate by itself."[103] As Ford points out, St. Paul is acutely aware that (in a similar way to MacKinnon in this context) a simple triumphalist understanding of the resurrection should be denied. In St. Paul's words, he is "always carrying in the body the death of Jesus, so that the life of Jesus may also be made visible in our bodies" (2 Cor 4:10). As Ford says, "the Resurrection message has sent him even more deeply into contingency, weakness and suffering."[104] As Ford points out, the new contingency is the Gospel itself, which opens up the new possibility of tragedy. As St. Paul writes, those who preach Christ can be "a fragrance from death to death" or "a fragrance from life to life" depending on those who listen (2 Cor 2:16). In this context again, we can remind ourselves of Balthasar's emphasis that heaven, hell (as *Gehenna*), and purgatory are the results of Christ's descent into *Sheol*.

Further, we have to note the tension St. Paul describes within the Christian themself. He writes, "Even though our outer nature is wasting away, our inner nature is being renewed day by day" (2 Cor 4:16). This tension is caused exactly by the new creation in Christ (2 Cor 5:17), which has been brought by his death and resurrection. After all, as St. Paul writes in various places, to live as a Christian means to participate in the death and resurrection day by day. To be a Christian means to be "buried with him [Christ] by baptism into death, so that, just as Christ was raised from the dead by the glory of the Father, so we too might walk in newness in life" (Rom 6:4). St. Paul also declares, "I die every day!" (1 Cor 15:31). What

103. Ford, "Tragedy and Atonement," 123.

104. Ibid., 123.

St. Paul tries to describe through all these words is nothing other than the paradoxical double existence of the Christian.[105] Referring to these verses, Balthasar himself writes that "Christian existence is one of transition and separation. . .of longing and sighing because the old man is in the process of disappearing, but the new man is still hidden from view."[106] This language of "transition" brings us back to the image of Holy Saturday. Surely St. Paul himself does not use the image of Holy Saturday but what he suggests in his epistles is unquestionably related to it. In the Christian existence, the glory of Easter is still "hidden."[107] As it is written, "You have died, and your life is hidden with Christ in God. When Christ who is your life is revealed, then you also will be revealed with him in glory" (Col 3:3).

Furthermore, in the last analysis, such a paradoxical nature of Christian existence can be traced back to Jesus himself and therefore there is hope that it can be redeemed and consecrated. We remember Jesus mysteriously declaring, "I *have conquered* the world!" (John 16:33)[108] even before he was handed over to be crucified. Further, in chapter 2, in our analysis of the concept of "sin-in-itself" and Balthasar's reading of St. John of the Cross, we discussed the "in-between" state of Jesus in hell on Holy Saturday, which Balthasar fully appreciates by using the concepts of "objectivity" and "subjectivity." On Holy Saturday, Christ himself sinks into the silent abyss of hell suffering in solidarity with sinful humanity while subjectively waiting for the victory, which, in objective reality, has already arrived. Does this passive waiting in silence for the subjectively hidden victory not represent the tragic tension within Christian existence very well? After all, the real strength of Balthasar's theology of Holy Saturday is that it shows us that this "tragic" waiting itself can be given christological meaning. It is significant that he concludes his *Mysterium Paschale* with the image of the Christian stretched out on the cross, which is "formed by the crisscrossing beams of the old aeon and the new."[109] He further writes that

> the Church, and Christians, can occupy no determinate place within the *Mysterium Paschale*. Their place is neither in front of the Cross nor behind it, but on both its sides: without ever settling for the one vantage point or the other they look from now one, now the other, as ceaselessly directed. And yet *this see-saw* by no means lacks a support, because the Unique One is the

---

105. See Ford and Young, *Meaning and Truth in 2 Corinthians*, 132.

106. Balthasar, *The Christian State of Life*, 218–19.

107. See Balthasar, *The Glory of the Lord* VII, 354–68.

108. Italics added.

109. Balthasar, *Mysterium Paschale*, 264.

identity of Cross and Resurrection, and Christian and ecclesial existence is disappropriated into him[110]

This state described as a "see-saw" is exactly what we have been calling the "tragic" state of the Christian existence. The Christian's life is like a "see-saw" swaying between the cross and the resurrection, death and life, or the old aeon and the new, but this see-saw is always supported by Christ himself who went through both. We can see that this is another way of expressing "tragedy under grace."

What is further important is that, through all this exploration, the reality of the Christian existence itself, which is tragically torn between forgiveness and judgment, suffering and victory, and despair and joy, becomes clarified in the life of Christian faith. Our existence is represented by Holy Saturday. As best represented by Steiner's famous passage we mentioned above, nothing can be said on Friday, the day of great suffering itself. We cannot even afford to try thinking about the meaning of such suffering. On Sunday, nothing needs to be said. Great joy overwhelms the memory of the suffering in the past. Therefore, any decent "theodicy" project, or the earnest questioning of God and search for meaning in suffering, belongs fundamentally to Saturday. This is why we have been hesitant to accept in its totality the kind of "theodicy" which simply claims that even the worst suffering of hell can be redeemed by Christ's descent into hell (as suggested by a few scholars regarding this subject). If we do not appreciate the waiting in silence, which is the real unique point of Holy Saturday, which is "tragic" waiting in silence characterized by hidden but undoubtedly present victory, there may be no point in discussing the significance of Holy Saturday at all. We could simply stop at the foot of the cross, the horror of which is itself great enough to encompass the worst human suffering.

The Christian is a paradoxical being. Christians believe that their victory is both already there and not there yet. Christians are forgiven their sin, but yet still exposed to sin, therefore not exempt from judgment. Christians can believe that their suffering is already redeemed by Christ in an objective sense, but still the pain of their suffering remains subjectively. This tension between the objective meaning of redemption and the subjective reality of sin and suffering is well captured by Balthasar's theology of Holy Saturday without compromising it. It is for this reason that we believe that it can provide one ideal approach to the issue of suffering in Christian discipleship.

---

110. Ibid., 266. Italics added.

Balthasar and the Concrete Reality of Suffering

Thus, in this chapter, we have attempted to present the connection between Balthasar's interest in tragedy, with his emphasis on the tragic element in the Christian existence, and his deep concern for Christian life, the "tragic" state of which is considered as best represented by Holy Saturday. Now, in order to strengthen our argument further, let us turn to the response of his critics concerning his engagement with tragedy, or more broadly, his treatment of the reality of human suffering.

For example, commentators on Balthasar have been critical of the way he heightens the status of tragedy and seems to give too positive a meaning to tragedy and human suffering. This is especially so since Balthasar ultimately locates human suffering within the infinite distance between the Father and the Son within the Trinity. He is accused of divinizing and eternalizing suffering even though its ugliness and horror should never be affirmed. In chapter 1, we discussed this kind of criticism as far as it is concerned with his Trinitarian theology and Christology, and argued that he could escape it with his subtle and nuanced approach.

Here let us discuss what his critics say about his attention to the concrete and the particular. MacKinnon praises Balthasar for his "remorseless emphasis on the concrete."[111] However, as evidenced by Quash's comment on MacKinnon's appraisal, some critics have questioned exactly "how remorseless this emphasis on the concrete really is."[112] This point is related to the Hegelian categories Balthasar makes use of in his dramatics, namely, the distinction of the three categories: the "epic," the "lyric," and the "dramatic," which we have mentioned above. Quash, while critically appraising Balthasar's use of drama and tragedy in comparison with Hegel, points out that Balthasar himself still falls prey to the same "epic" tendency as Hegel, even though he apparently tries to resist it. In particular, Quash's critique that is most relevant for our discussion is that it is exactly in his theology of Holy Saturday that Balthasar's "epic" tendency is most explicitly revealed. Quash writes,

> Even in this most innovative area of his theology von Balthasar tries to control the dazzling darkness with strategies that mitigate the drama. The hell of von Balthasar's theology is *outside* and *beyond* our time. It is narrated in "epic" time . . . The irony of von Balthasar's theology is that at the moment when it aims

111. MacKinnon, "Some Reflections on Hans Urs von Balthasar's Christology," 167.

112. Quash, "Hans Urs von Balthasar," 120.

most concretely to concern itself with struggle, suffering and death, it also becomes most mythological.[113]

Quash further explains what he means by "mythological." He says, "Attention is diverted from the struggles and suffering that characterize the social and material aspects of human history, and the structural and political aspects of sin are not considered."[114] This critique of Quash's echoes Gerard O'Hanlon's comment that "from one who is so conscious of the reality of evil there is a curious lack of engagement with the great modern structural evils."[115]

In the same direction as Quash and O'Hanlon, Taylor, who focuses his work on Balthasar's use of tragedy, points out the limitations of Balthasar's conception of tragedy and argues that despite his deep interest in tragedy and his desire to engage with the reality of the world, aristocratism and anti-modernism can be detected in his writings, marring his theological work.[116] Even when he engages with modern authors such as Claudel, Bernanos, and Schneider ("anti-modern" authors), his aristocratic and anti-modern preference is obvious. Taylor argues that Balthasar's "dislike for the common" (most notably exposed in his underestimation of modern novels) leads to a failure to fully engage with the reality of creaturely freedom despite his seemingly opposite intentions. He also accuses Balthasar of ignoring the diversity of suffering in reality and failing to respect its mystery.

Why do such opposing views exist in interpreting Balthasar? Did someone like MacKinnon simply overlook this contradiction or read his own agenda into Balthasar? There is no point in denying that Balthasar fails to explicitly engage with "the social and material aspects of human history, and the structural and political aspects of sin." That is simply something he does not do in his writings.[117] Considering the nature of the activity of the secular institute (the Community of St. John) that Balthasar established

---

113. Quash, *Theology and the Drama of History*, 194–95. He makes this point at various other points.

114. Ibid., 216.

115. O'Hanlon, "Theological Dramatics," 109.

116. Taylor, *Hans Urs von Balthasar and the Question of Tragedy in the Novels of Thomas Hardy*, 183–216.

117. In relation to this, he actually makes critical comments on so-called political theology. "in no way can the whole theology of the New Testament—its theology of the Cross and Resurrection—be reduced to political theology. . .Political struggle is given as a charge to the Christian. But he must know that the kingdom of God is not established (in Marxist fashion) within the structures of the world." (Balthasar, *A Short Primer for Unsettled Laymen*, 124–25.)

with Speyr,[118] he did not attempt to engage with the actual problems of his age in a practical way either. Even when he shows the concern that sin might reside in the church itself (as we have seen above), he does not go on to criticize the hierarchical structure of the church. Further, when we discussed his outdated view of sexual differentiation in chapter 3, we pointed out the criticism that his theology is not really helpful for the cause of social justice, which includes gender equality, and it even has the potential danger of being "hijacked to support an unjust *status quo*."[119]

It is a serious issue for this book, for if such a criticism is valid, then what kind of implications would his theology have for Christian suffering and discipleship? We still believe that Balthasar's theology of Holy Saturday could offer a message of hope for those who are in the midst of suffering. Nevertheless, we also have to admit that he does not engage with the actual problems of his age in an explicit way. To put it more specifically, his primary interest apparently does not lie in offering "practical solutions" to social, political, or economic problems. Considering his critical attitude toward political theology or feminism, we could even conclude that he believes that it should not be his job. Rather, his main interest seems to be how we can find meaning in the suffering that is already here and inescapable. This attitude can be found in many of his writings. Take a look, for example, at his essay, "Loneliness in the Church," which is related to the topic of this book. The essay starts by describing the problem of the church in his day: "Many Christians today feel lonely in the Church. In fact, it would not be too much to say: they feel isolated *from* the Church."[120] He then goes on to explain why it should be the case. His answer is that the church originates in loneliness and abandonment (of the Son, the Mother, and also John). Though it may be frustrating for some readers who seek a more practical means to deal with their loneliness and to be liberated from it in a concrete way, Balthasar says as follows:

> Those who belong to the Church should be deep enough Christians to know that loneliness in the Church belongs to her essence. This means that the ecclesial loneliness the Christian feels is a part of his growth in Christ, and so he should have no reason to see his loneliness as an excuse for indulging in a false pathos

118. The purpose of this secular institute was to let its members live a life of holiness in the midst of the secular world while continuing with their ordinary vocations and occupations in society. For a report of the activities of this secular institute, see Balthasar, *Our Task*, 118–79; Greiner, "The Community of St. John," 87–101.

119. O'Hanlon, "Theological Dramatics," 110.

120. Balthasar, *Explorations in Theology* IV, 261.

against the Church as she currently exists or establishing a sec-
tarian pseudo-or anti-church against the *Catholica*.[121]

If Balthasar does not offer concrete solutions to the problems of his
age (or our age), is there nothing at all that his theology could teach us
about suffering? This would not necessarily be the case, for there is another
point to consider: are some sufferings in this world not inescapable after all?
There certainly is suffering (physical, mental, or spiritual) to which there
is no solution, probably, except prayer. The loss of our beloved one is one
such case, and that is exactly what, for example, the grief and solitude of
Our Lady on Holy Saturday represents. There is also another fundamental
question: why should we suffer in the first place? In the case of the inescapable and inexplicable kind of suffering, the only approach we could take is
to persevere in prayer. Is it to this kind of suffering, then, that Balthasar's
theology of Holy Saturday could offer something hopeful? We believe so.
For some, such kinds of suffering which keep on haunting us after the actual
event might be classified as "trauma." Inspired by Balthasar's and Speyr's
theology of Holy Saturday as the day between death and life, Shelly Rambo,
for example, has proposed a theology of "remaining" as an approach to the
experience of living in the aftermath of trauma.[122] Therefore, after we have
done everything not to fall into futile resignation and thus to avoid surrendering to unjust suffering, and after we make sure that perseverance is really
the only approach possible, that is where the significance of his approach to
human suffering can be relevant.

Lastly, regarding the scope and diversity of actual human suffering
Balthasar deals with, we would like to stress again how relevant the hell
Balthasar explores is for our contemporary mind, as we discussed in chapter
2. The variety of negative feelings Speyr experienced in her mystical visions
seems to include many of the so-called "modern" phenomena: emptiness,
loneliness, futility, despair, and so forth. Further, by referring to such mystics as St. John of the Cross and St. Thérèse of Lisieux, we have explored the
reality of hell in terms of the dark night of the soul, which has an existential
dimension in terms of the sinner's personal and spiritual relationship with
God. In other words, contrary to Quash's claim that Balthasar's hell is "*outside* and *beyond* our time*," we have presented that the reality of the hell
explored in his theology of Holy Saturday is actually *inside* and *within* our
time. No wonder quite a few scholars turn to Christ's descent into hell as the
theme most relevant for the postmodern age.[123]

121. Ibid. 283–84.

122. Rambo, *Spirit and Trauma*.

123. For example, see Sutton, "Does God Suffer?," 177. Also, we reflected on the

Conclusion: And Still We Wait . . .

In this chapter, we have discussed how Holy Saturday represents the tragic and paradoxical state of Christian existence torn between the old and new aeons, between Christ and the world, and between suffering and victory. This point has huge implications for Christian discipleship and suffering. In chapter 3, we explored Mary's Holy Saturday on the basis of Balthasar's Mariology. While discussing Mary's perfect obedience, maintained even in the midst of horrible suffering and godforsakenness, as the role model of Christian discipleship, we pointed out Balthasar's problematic view of the woman and sexual differentiation. We saw that his theology has the potential danger of being used to bolster the unjust status quo in society, including gender inequality, if placed in the wrong hands. Despite this weakness, however, we stated that his theology of Holy Saturday, which captures well the transition from the cross to the resurrection, could still tell us something important about Christian discipleship and suffering. We have explored this point further in this chapter, where we have connected Balthasar's theology of Holy Saturday with another major innovative area of his theology, namely, his theological engagement with tragedy. We have explored the Christian's Holy Saturday existence on the basis of his "tragic" view of Christianity. We have argued that Balthasar sees a paradoxical relationship between tragedy and grace, while discussing another concern raised against Balthasar by his critics, namely the fact that he does not engage with the concrete reality of human suffering despite his apparent interest in it. We have agreed that his treatment of human suffering could be insufficient for those who seek practical solutions to their problems and his theology should definitely not be used to justify any unjust status quo or to encourage unnecessary resignation in the face of suffering. Nevertheless, we have argued that his theology could convey a hopeful message to those who are forced to face inexplicable and inevitable suffering. In the last analysis, his theology of Holy Saturday helps our understanding of Christian discipleship and suffering because it clearly presents the fundamental framework of the paradoxical existence of the Christian, which helps us to locate our suffering and to find its positive meaning. Let us clarify this point further below.

First of all, the connection between Holy Saturday and Christian life drives home to us the fundamental twofoldness inherent in Christian existence. We often hear the paradoxical expression "already but not yet" as the characteristic of the victory hidden in the Christian existence, but this point becomes clearer if we relate it to Holy Saturday, the day between the cross

relevance of hell in our age in chapter 2.

and the resurrection, in other words, the day on which the transition from the old aeon to the new took place. The new creation has caused the "tragic" twofold state of the Christian being torn between Christ and the world. In Balthasar's own words, "we exist in a process of transition that Christ has carried out and (solely thereby) has made available to us: "Put off the old nature with its practices and put on the new nature (Col 3:9)."[124] As we repeatedly pointed out, it is in hell on Holy Saturday that Christ carried out this transition: "The turning point [where the old has been changed into the new] lies in Christ, or, more exactly, in the drama of the Paschal transition from Good Friday to Easter Sunday."[125]

This awareness of the double existence in transition permeates Balthasar's writings, and he discusses Christian discipleship and suffering on the basis of such awareness.[126] The Christian has been assigned a mission from God to accomplish in the world. Solidarity with the world is also what Balthasar encourages on the basis of this in-between state of the Christian. In his words,

> It is precisely this Christian existence at the turning point of the Eons that is emphatically an existence for the world, a living in solidarity with the world beyond all active, apostolic activity.[127]

To put it differently, the Christian, as a being in transition who belongs to Christ but is also part of the created world, holds a unique responsibility to deal with the problems in the world. Balthasar writes, "it is because they are rooted in eternal life that the Church and Christians acquire strength to carry out their mission in *this* world; they are otherworldly, but they are also this-worldly, addressing the world and its issues."[128]

This status of transition further suggests that the Christian has no privileged place to boast about in God's salvific plan for humankind. As we have already seen in this chapter,

---

124. Balthasar, *You Crown the Year with Your Goodness*, 107.

125. Balthasar, *Explorations in Theology* IV, 463.

126. For example, we can clearly see this awareness in the following places in his writings: "Eschatology in Outline" in *Explorations in Theology* IV, 457–67; "Church and World" and "Joy and Cross" in *Truth is Symphonic*, 90–107, 152–69; *The Christian State of Life*, 210–24; *Mysterium Paschale*, 262–66; "Living in the Interstices," "The Logic and Ethics of the Forty Days," "The Future has Already come," "Waiting for God," and "Jesus Christ and the Foundation of the Church" in *You Crown the Year with Your Goodness*, 16–26, 104–14, 243–51, 251–57, 319–23.

127. Balthasar, *Explorations in Theology* IV, 465.

128. Balthasar, *You Crown the Year with Your Goodness*, 323.

the Church, and Christians, can occupy no determinate place within the *Mysterium Paschale*. Their place is neither in front of the Cross nor behind it, but on both its sides: without ever settling for the one vantage point or the other they look from now one, now the other, as ceaselessly directed.[129]

Rather, as St. Paul writes, the only thing that the Christian can boast about is the cross (Gal 6:14). In relation to this point, as we have already discussed, the possibility of hell, or separation from God, paradoxically weighs most heavily on Christians themselves. This point justifies the view that Christian existence is tragic.

If Christian discipleship is placed in this context of the transition from the old aeon to the new, so is Christian suffering. The awareness of life in transition enables us to translate the meaning of suffering into "tragic waiting," while facing the full reality of suffering and at the same time highlighting the victory hidden but already present. Today, we still have to wait for the victory, which has already come in an objective sense but remains hidden within our lives in this world. We can be patient because Christ has already done the waiting in the hell of absolute loneliness.

This idea explains why the paradoxical coexistence of suffering and joy is possible in Christian life (the kind we have seen in the case of the dark night of the soul experienced by St. Mother Teresa in chapter 2). Balthasar writes,

> Now, in the "Church between the times," the paradox between Cross and joy reaches its full dimensions, because the Church can never see the Cross as something that lies behind it as an accomplished fact in past historical time, any more than it can regard its sinfulness as a closed issue in the past. It can never establish itself so completely in the Easter event—and hence in Easter joy—that it no longer needs to be continually accompanying Jesus on the way to the Cross . . .It is due to this strange paradox that Christian joy has a uniquely burning and consuming quality.[130]

The paradoxical coexistence of suffering and joy in Christian life also explains why Christians have to suffer for the sake of this world. Balthasar reminds us that "the joy that Christians have is both a gift and *a responsibility* . . .Amid all the fear that characterizes our time, we Christians are summoned to live in joy and to communicate joy—joy in spite of fear, joy

129. Balthasar, *Mysterium Paschale*, 266.

130. Balthasar, *Truth is Symphonic*, 168.

in the midst of fear."[131] After all, as Jesus himself has declared, the Christian is essentially "the light of the world" (Matt 5:14). As Balthasar reminds us, all that Christians possess is intended for those who do not have it, and Christians are those who bring "Easter joy in the midst of the passion of humanity."[132] Therefore, the Christian who has the privilege of finding positive meaning in their suffering by relating it to the paschal mystery can (and should) assume the responsibility to deal with the suffering in the world by communicating love and joy, which is inexhaustible as it is rooted in God himself. This way of finding positive meaning in suffering has nothing to do with masochism or distortion of the good news of Christianity. It is not blurring the distinction between suffering and joy. Rather, this paradoxical coexistence of suffering and joy can only be possible if the suffering really *is* suffering.

In sum, despite his lack of engagement with the "concrete" problems in reality, Balthasar's theology of Holy Saturday presents us with the framework to clarify the in-between state of the Christian existence, which helps our understanding of Christian discipleship and the role of suffering in it. The Christian's Holy Saturday, which is characterized by "tragic" waiting, can be endured because Christ himself has already endured the waiting on Holy Saturday in hell. This gives the Christian both a privilege and a responsibility as the one who has to follow Christ while living and acting in solidarity with this world.

In the next chapter, we will explore how we liturgically live out what we have just discussed about Christian discipleship and suffering in the light of Holy Saturday. We will see that the "in-between" existence of the Christian is supported and sustained by the Eucharist, which is "the source and summit of the Christian life."

---

131. Balthasar, *You Crown the Year with Your Goodness*, 31. Italics added.
132. Ibid., 31.

5

Holy Saturday and the Eucharist

Introduction

FINALLY, BEFORE WE CONCLUDE OUR BOOK, LET US EXPLORE THE CONNEC-
tion between Holy Saturday and the Eucharist, "the source and summit
of the Christian life."[1] It seems only appropriate to end this book with a
chapter on the Eucharist, not only because it is the center of Christian discipleship, but also because we have been stressing the importance of the
liturgical framework within which Balthasar is developing his theology of
Holy Saturday. As we mentioned in the introduction, liturgically speaking
(particularly since the liturgical reforms of the 1950s[2]), Holy Saturday is the
day on which we celebrate no Mass (until the evening when we celebrate the
Easter Vigil Mass), or we could even say it is the day which is characterized
by its very absence. Probably, this point has been one of the reasons why
the connection between Holy Saturday and the Eucharist has rarely been
explored in depth, while the obvious connection between the significance
of the Eucharist (the "bodily" fruit of our salvation accomplished by the
paschal mystery of the Lord, who sacrificed himself out of self-giving love)
and Balthasar's interpretation of Christ's descent into hell on Holy Saturday
(as the culmination of his self-giving love) has been pointed out by some.[3]

An examination of Balthasar's theology of the Eucharist would be an
immense task in itself. As is usual with his treatment of important themes,
the theme of the Eucharist is scattered through his theological corpus,[4] and

1. *Catechism of the Catholic Church*, §1324, quoting from *Lumen Gentium*, n.11.

2. See footnote 34 in the Introduction.

3. For example, see Healy, *The Eschatology of Hans Urs von Balthasar*, 205–9;
Pitstick, *Light in Darkness*, 249–50.

4. For example, he discusses the Eucharist in depth in the following works:

it is almost always present in his thoughts. As it is far beyond the scope of this chapter to discuss all the elements of Balthasar's theology of the Eucharist, we will just focus on the aspects most relevant to the mystery of Holy Saturday, such as its sacrificial significance, its connection to Mariology, its emphasis on "bodiliness," its aspect as an *anamnesis*, its eschatological dimension, and its importance as the source of the Christian mission. While examining these aspects, we will explore how the mystery of Holy Saturday has a central place in Balthasar's theology of the Eucharist as well as how it could help deepen our understanding of the mystery of the Eucharist. In the last analysis, we will see that the central aspects of Balthasar's theology of Holy Saturday—namely self-giving love, solidarity, and waiting—are all unified in the Eucharist. Based on these explorations, we will reaffirm that the mystery of Holy Saturday has deep implications for Christian discipleship.

The section titles of this chapter are as follows: 1) the Eucharist as sacrifice, 2) the Eucharist as an *anamnesis* and a foretaste of heaven, 3) the Eucharist and the mystery of Holy Saturday, 4) the Eucharist and the Christian's Holy Saturday experience, and 5) conclusion: the "in-between" existence sustained by the living Christ.

The Eucharist as Sacrifice

Let us start by discussing the Eucharist as a sacrifice. We cannot emphasize too much the sacrificial significance of the Eucharist.[5] At the beginning of the article on the sacrament of the Eucharist, the Catechism of the Catholic Church states that Christians "participate with the whole community in the Lord's own sacrifice by means of the Eucharist."[6] The church is born out of the Christ's saving sacrifice on the cross and the whole community of the church is built on the participation in this once-and-for-all sacrifice. This

---

"Eucharistic Congress 1960," in *Explorations in Theology* II, 503–13; "The Mass, a Sacrifice of the Church?," *Explorations in Theology* III, 185–243; "Spirit and Institution," in *Explorations in Theology* IV, 209–60; "The Mystery of the Eucharist," in *New Elucidations*, 111–26; "Flesh Becomes Word," and "By Water, Blood, and Spirit," in *You Crown the Year with Your Goodness*, 146–55; "The Holy Church and the Eucharistic Sacrifice." As to the secondary sources on Balthasar's theology of the Eucharist, see, for example, Healy and Schindler, "For the Life of the World," and Healy, "Christ's Eucharist and the Nature of Love."

5. For Balthasar's thoughts on this aspect of the Eucharist, see his longest writing on the Eucharist, "The Mass, a Sacrifice of the Church?," in *Explorations in Theology* III. For a concise summary of Balthasar's thoughts on the Eucharist as a sacrifice, see O'Donnell, *Hans Urs von Balthasar*, 121–25.

6. *The Catechism of the Catholic Church*, §1322.

fundamental idea lies at the center of Balthasar's theology of the Eucharist as well, so he himself declares that,

> no other thought is so persistent and so penetrating in the Roman Canon as the idea that the Church offers a sacrifice to God the Father, presents it and recommends it to him, asks him to accept it, urges it upon him and gives many reasons for this, urgently and almost anxiously, as if the all-decisive question for her salvation and for that of her children were that God should accept this sacrifice of hers. Other motifs are not lacking—the glorification of God, the *memoriale* of Christ, the gathering of all the living and departed believers in Christ, the uniting with the fellowship of the saints in heaven—but these motifs, which cannot be separated from the first motif mentioned, take their place within this as integrating parts and aspects.[7]

The emphasis on the sacrificial significance is a distinctive characteristic of his theology of the Eucharist and it is closely connected with many of the important (and sometimes problematic) themes in his theology which we have already discussed in the previous chapters, such as the close link between love and abandonment, the emphasis on "passivity" in obedience, and his notion of "passive" femininity. For Balthasar, all these themes take a "bodily" form in the sacrament of Eucharist, which is the embodiment of Christ's self-giving love for the world.

It is also worth noting that Balthasar's account of the Eucharist as a sacrifice can be considered as an exception in the trend of the twentieth-century Catholic eucharistic theology, which increasingly distanced itself from the concept of communion in and through sacrifice, and turned toward a bifurcation of sacrifice and communion (with God and neighbors).[8] Further, this point is relevant for our purpose of presenting a connection between the mystery of the Eucharist and that of Holy Saturday based on Balthasar's theology. Balthasar's notion of sacrifice is developed on an existential (rather than cultic) interpretation of the term, and it is considered as an important aspect of every loving relationship. For Balthasar, the central aspect of Christ's sacrifice is that he suffered the sinner's absolute loneliness for our sake (on the cross and in hell). In the Eucharist, we are invited to share sacrificially in Christ's loneliness somehow. As Balthasar says, "Seeing from the stance of the self-giving Lord, sharing in his suffering is part of

---

7. Balthasar, *Explorations in Theology* III, 185.

8. This point has been made by Matthew Levering in *Sacrifice and Community*, 25, note 75.

eucharistic fellowship with him."[9] That is also why Balthasar calls the church a "community out of loneliness,"[10] and even says "loneliness in the Church belongs to her essence."[11] In his words,

> The essence of the Church's community, which is more deeply socially bonded and rooted than any other earthly and fleshly community, flows out of the most extreme and exquisite loneliness imaginable, in which but one man, "for the sake of the many," becomes the ultimate individual of all, utterly abandoned by God and man alike. *How could the birthmark of this origin not continually brand such a community!*[12]

Thus, on the basis of his distinctive theology of the cross, Balthasar holds together the aspects of the Eucharist as a sacrifice (absolute loneliness) and communion (built on such loneliness). Let us discuss it further below.

Going back to the subject of the Eucharist as a sacrifice *offered by* the church, for Catholics, Christ's saving sacrifice on the cross is not merely commemorated in the Eucharist but also actually "re-presented" on the altar (we will discuss later the Eucharist as an *anamnesis*). According to the traditional teaching of the Catholic Church (reaffirmed by the Council of Trent), Christ's bloody sacrifice on the cross is really made present and offered in an "unbloody" manner through the ministry of priests, so "the sacrifice of Christ and the sacrifice of the Eucharist are *one single sacrifice.*"[13]

While working in this traditional framework, the first point Balthasar makes about the church's Eucharistic offering of Christ's sacrifice is that we must always assign the priority in the Eucharist to the action of Christ himself, for no one else but him is in the position to offer sacrifice in a real sense of the word. The church is a community of sinners, so the sacrifice of the church herself can never measure up to the sacrifice of Christ. Our salvation depends solely on the action of God in Christ, and Christ has already accomplished the redemption without our initiative or consent. Thus it is a *fait accompli*, which we can only fully accept or reject. While emphasizing this point, Balthasar deals with the classical question concerning the Eucharist offered by the church as a sacrifice: if Christ alone offered the

9. Balthasar, *New Elucidations*, 121.

10. He explores this aspect of the church in "Loneliness in the Church" in *Explorations in Theology* IV, 261–98.

11. Ibid., 283.

12. Ibid., 271–72.

13. See *Catechism of the Catholic Church*, n.1367, quoting from Council of Trent (1562) *Doctrina de ss. Missae sacrificio*, c. 2: DS 1743.

sacrifice on the cross, in what sense can this one and same sacrifice be offered by the church? In the last analysis, Balthasar's answer to this question
lies in the "passive" "feminine" receptivity of faith, the best model of which
has been presented by the Virgin Mary.[14] (Certainly we should never forget
that Balthasar describes Christ himself being utterly obedient in a "passive," "receptive," and "feminine" way to God the Father in the first place.)
For Balthasar (and even more so for Speyr), Eucharistic theology is closely
linked with Mariology. For Balthasar, the original form of the sacrifice of
the Mass was most clearly presented by Our Lady, who consented to participating in her son's abandonment at the foot of the cross, by herself being
"abandoned" by him (as discussed in chapter 3).[15] In Balthasar's words,

> I believe that the expression "sacrifice of the Mass" will remain
> obscure so long as we have not encountered that veiled woman
> at the foot of the Cross, who is the Mother of the Crucified and
> at the same time the icon of the Church. She is present at the
> self-gift of the Son, not able to intervene; but she is far from
> passive; a superhuman action is asked of her: consent to the sac-
> rifice of this man who is the Son of God but also her own son.
> She would prefer a thousand times over to be tortured in his
> place. But this is not what is demanded of her; she has only to
> consent to it. Actively, she must let herself be stripped. She must
> repeat her initial Yes up to the end, but this end was virtually
> included in the first impulse. This acquiescence of the Mother
> is the original form, reserved for the pure creature, of participa-
> tion in the sacrifice of Christ.[16]

In this mariological insight, we can see Balthasar's distinctive characterization of faith as loving obedience to God's will. Mary's *fiat* at the Annunciation, "Here am I, the servant of the Lord; let it be with me according
to your word" (Luke 1:38), is the attitude to be shared by every Christian,
at every stage of their life including when offering the sacrifice of the Mass,
that is, the sacrifice of Christ. In fact, the only thing we can bring to the
Eucharist is our loving obedience to God's will. Balthasar states that "the
true contribution of the Church" is always "the obedience that assents to the
one thing that counts in God's eyes: the sacrifice of the Son."[17] The example
of Mary at the foot of the cross is important and relevant for the Church

14. We have discussed Balthasar's distinctive Mariology in chapter 3.

15. Concerning this topic, see Balthasar and Speyr, *To the Heart of the Mystery of
Redemption*, 45–49.

16. Ibid., 46–47.

17. Balthasar, *Explorations in Theology* III, 237.

(the Bride of Christ), because her suffering is based on her love for her son. Mary's suffering comes from the fact that she herself would do anything to suffer and die in the place of her son, but all she can do is to silently "let it be," that is, let him die for the salvation of the humanity.[18] Likewise, the church, and each member of the church, must consent to the sacrifice of the Son (the Beloved Bridegroom) with the pain in the heart that we can do nothing but to consent to this sacrifice, each time we celebrate the Mass. For Balthasar, this is one of the central aspects of the *anamnesis*: we must relive the pain of having to let our beloved Christ die. It is true that we are living in the age after the resurrection and ascension, and Balthasar is certainly aware of this fact and he does not neglect any sense of thanksgiving or joy, but he still insists that

> We must—not as sinners, but in the Spirit of the Bride-Church— share in experiencing the absolute pain that we must allow the Beloved Christ to keep his own will to die a vicarious death. The sword must penetrate us at this thought. The necessity of experiencing this together with the contemporaries . . . remains the decisive and ultimate proof of the *distinction* between the sacrifice of Christ and the sacrifice of the Church in the same historical and "mystical" act of sacrifice.[19]

With such a loving, obedient, faithful attitude, every time we partici- pate in the sacrifice of the Eucharist, we become "contemporary" with the loving sacrifice of Christ so that his self-giving becomes our own. Through the Eucharist, we die to our own self and let Christ live within us, so that we can obediently follow his footsteps as his disciples and live for the mission assigned to us. Since, for Balthasar, the central aspect of Christ's sacrifice is that he renounced his intimacy with the Father in order to go through the sinner's absolute loneliness to the fullest (that is, to the descent into hell), the Christian faith and mission is also supposed to entail a certain sense of loneliness based on love and communion. That is why Balthasar says the loneliness is the essence of the church and the dark night of the soul is an important concept for Balthasar's idea of Christian suffering and mission

18. In addition to the example of Our Lady, borrowing from Speyr's insight, Balthasar also refers to the examples of the two other Marys in the Gospels (Mary of Bethany and Mary Magdalene) as they are the ones who let Christ accomplish his mission despite their wishes to prevent him from suffering or to stay with him. No doubt these female examples reinforce Balthasar's description of the ideal attitude of the church as being "feminine." See Balthasar, *Explorations in Theology* III, 224–28, 236–37; Balthasar and Speyr, *To the Heart of the Mystery of Redemption*, 47–49; Speyr, *Three Women and the Lord*.

19. Balthasar, *Explorations in Theology* III, 233.

(as we have seen in chapter 2), and consequently that is why he says that the Eucharist "presupposes the descent into hell (mine and yours)."[20] (We will come back to this point later.)

Further, any discussion of the Eucharist as a sacrifice would not be complete without mentioning the Eucharist as a meal. The Eucharist is a sacrificial meal of the new covenant, and Christ has offered himself as our food and nourishment: "my flesh is true food and my blood is true drink" (John 6:55). Both the elements of a sacrifice and a meal form the mystery of the Eucharist, for the completion of the saving sacrifice is the meal or the banquet where we are invited to consume the body and blood of Christ. As St. John Paul II has said, "The saving efficacy of the sacrifice is fully realized when the Lord's body and blood are received in communion. The Eucharistic Sacrifice is intrinsically directed to the inward union of the faithful with Christ through communion."[21]

It is further important to note that through our communion in his body and blood, Christ grants us his Spirit.[22] According to the *Roman Missal*, the celebrant prays "grant that we, who are nourished by the Body and Blood of your Son and filled with his Holy Spirit, may become one body, one spirit in Christ."[23] We have been discussing how Christ and the church co-offer the one and same sacrifice at the altar in the Mass, but, as Balthasar himself reminds us, "it is ultimately only through the working of the Holy Spirit that one can understand the unity in antithesis between Christ and the Church."[24] In sum, by eating and drinking the body and blood of Christ, the church is incorporated into the mystical body of Christ. Literally speaking, we become what we eat.

Here we have to pause to note that the importance of the physical acts of eating and drinking in the celebration of the Eucharistic banquet is related to the significance of bodiliness. Despite the common critique that his theology is "other-worldly" or lacking in concreteness as we have discussed in the previous chapter, Balthasar himself constantly insists on the importance of bodiliness. He is also consistently critical of any spirituality which tends to flee from the physical world. When we say "the body of Christ," "the church as the body of Christ," the word "body" should never be merely symbolically taken. As a Catholic theologian, Balthasar takes the mystery of the incarnation with utmost seriousness. The emphasis on "bodiliness"

20. Balthasar, "Receiving the Tradition," 167.

21. John Paul II, *Ecclesia de Eucharistia*, n.1382.

22. Ibid., n.17.

23. This is from the Eucharistic Prayer III. See *The Roman Missal*, 687.

24. Balthasar, *Explorations in Theology* III, 241.

is also related to Balthasar's anthropology and his view of spirituality. His is an anthropology of "unity-in-duality" according to which corporeal and spiritual perception are inextricably intertwined with one another.[25] In his words, "What is at stake is always man as a spiritual-corporeal reality in the concrete process of living. This is evident in Jesus himself, the archetypal 'whole man,' who does not 'exist as the union of two parts or two "substances," he is the one whole man, embodied soul and besouled body.'"[26] (We will discuss this point further below when we discuss the question of the body on Holy Saturday.) For Balthasar, wherever there is the spirit, there is always a dynamism by which the spirit seeks to manifest itself in a bodily form: "if the spirit is to express what is most essential to it, it must descend into its own flesh."[27] To translate it into our everyday language, love is only proved by "bodily" deeds. That is why God's Word became flesh in the first place, and we continue to encounter in the Eucharist the incarnate Son of God, who remains willing to give up and distribute his body among his followers, even after the resurrection and ascension.[28] Balthasar writes,

> Jesus's Eucharistic gesture of self-distribution to his Apostles, and through them to the world, is a definitive, eschatological and thus irreversible gesture. The Father's Word made flesh is

25. See Fields, "Balthasar and Rahner on the Spiritual Senses," 240. Further, Mark McInroy discusses in depth Balthasar's anthropology of "unity-in-duality" and argues for its significance for his use of the doctrine of spiritual senses. In particular, McInroy argues that (inspired by Karl Barth and Gustav Siewerth) Balthasar integrates the spiritual senses into a "personalist" anthropology according to which they are bestowed upon the human being in the encounter with the neighbor. See McInroy, *Balthasar on the Spiritual Senses*, 94–121.

26. Balthasar, *The Glory of the Lord* I, 384.

27. Balthasar, *You Crown the Year with Your Goodness*, 147.

28. In relation to the connection between this particular importance of the Eucharist and the anthropology of "unity-in-duality" mentioned above, it is worth noting that Balthasar turns to the French poet Paul Claudel's insight on this point. Balthasar notes that, for Claudel, "The Eucharist, in particular, is the adaptation of our being to God by the descent of the Word into our senses, indeed, into our substance, which is something even below the senses. Not only does Spirit speak to spirit, but Flesh speaks to flesh. 'Our flesh has ceased being an obstacle; it has become a means and a mediation. It has ceased being a veil to become a perception.' It must, like it or not, learn to taste, to taste how God tastes—God himself, our means of sustenance, who has now become 'accessible to our bodily organs.'" (Balthasar, *The Glory of the Lord* I, 401–2.) Balthasar integrates Claudel's view of the Eucharist into his own theology. For them, the supreme union of the spiritual and corporeal perception is realized in the Eucharist. For Balthasar's engagement with Paul Claudel on the matter of the Eucharist, See *The Glory of the Lord* I, 399–405. Also, see McInroy, *Balthasar on the Spiritual Senses*, 116–20.

definitively given and distributed by him and is never to be taken back. Neither the Resurrection from the dead nor the "Ascension" as "going to the Father" (Jn 16:18) are a countermovement to Incarnation, Passion, and Eucharist.[29]

The resurrection and ascension do not mean a withdrawal of the Father's gift, his Son, from us. On the contrary, as the Farewell Discourse in the Gospel of John (John 14: 16, 19, 28; 16:16) clarifies, through the sending of the Holy Spirit, they enable us to enjoy a new kind of intimacy with the incarnate Son of God through the Eucharist. Therefore, the emphasis on the "bodiliness" of the Eucharist helps us to see all the mysteries (incarnation, passion, Eucharist, resurrection, and ascension) somehow unified. The one and same body has gone through all these events. As the mark of the wounds on the body of the risen Lord signifies, "The Crucified, and he alone, is the Risen One."[30] This risen body is also the body distributed to us each time we celebrate the Eucharist. Thus, we continue to recall and relive all these mysteries again and again when we celebrate the Eucharist, but we do so with the eyes looking ahead into the glorious future. Let us discuss the temporal dimensions of the Eucharist further in the next section.

The Eucharist as an Anamnesis and a Foretaste of Heaven

First, let us pause to consider the Eucharist as an *anamnesis*. The word *anamnesis* entails more than a mere remembrance of the past. It is a concept which entails memory, experience, and hope, so it essentially covers all three temporal dimensions: the past, present, and future.[31] St. Paul has perfectly expressed the aspect of the *anamnesis* of the Eucharist in the following single sentence, which we cite in the liturgy of the Eucharist in the Mass: "For as often as you eat this bread and drink the cup, you proclaim [in the present] the Lord's death [in the past] until he comes [in the future]." (1 Cor 11:26). In the Eucharist, the once-and-for-all past event of salvation (the loving sacrifice of the Lord) is re-represented at the altar here and now with the anticipation of his Second Coming and the final kingdom. In Balthasar's words,

> In the ever-present Anamnesis ("Do this in memory of me," I Cor 11:25) of the self-sacrifice of God's love (*unde et memores*),

29. Balthasar, *New Elucidations*, 117.

30. Ibid., 120.

31. O'Collins, *Catholicism*, 74.

the living and resurrected Christ becomes present (Mt 18:20)—but present "until he comes again" (I Cor 11:26), and therefore not looking backward, but with eyes set forward, into the future and full of hope.[32]

Thus, we can see that the past, the present, and the future (that is, the past, present, and future of Christ and his church) are all woven together in the celebration of the Eucharist. We cannot fully appreciate the profound mystery of the Eucharist without considering this dynamism, but also it is particularly important to us because it is closely related to the "in-between-ness" of the Christian existence. In the previous chapter, we have discussed how Balthasar presents the Christian's "life in transition" between the old and new aeon has already been assumed by Christ himself in the transition from Good Friday to Easter Sunday in the paschal mystery. We have further argued that, for Balthasar, this awareness of the in-betweenness is inseparable from the Christian sense of solidarity with the world. Bringing this insight into the aspect of the *anamnesis* in the Eucharist will eventually help us to appreciate further both the mystery of the Eucharist and that of Holy Saturday. After all, we celebrate the Eucharist as an existence "in-between." Alternatively, we could even say that our "in-between" existence is supported and sustained by the Eucharist.

The Eucharist is an *anamnesis* of the incarnation and the paschal mystery. As the traditional Eucharistic hymn *Ave Verum Corpus* goes, the body we receive in the Eucharist is the "true body born of the Virgin Mary" (*Ave verum corpus natum ex Maria Virgine*), the body that "truly suffered, was sacrificed on the cross for humankind" (*vere passum, immolatum in cruce pro homine*), the body "from whose pierced side water and blood flowed" (*cuius latus perforatum fluxit aqua et sanguine*). It is also the glorious body that was resurrected and ascended into heaven.

However, in a manner somewhat similar to his objection to rushing towards the Easter joy while neglecting the silent pause on Holy Saturday, Balthasar reminds us that even though we celebrate the Eucharist on the day of the resurrection and the body of Christ we receive in the Eucharist is the body of the risen Christ, it is still the Lord's death that we proclaim (as we have pointed out in the previous section). He says, "Even from the outlook of Easter, the Eucharist is still the 'anamnesis of the Passion.'"[33]

The passion was anticipated by the Last Supper.[34] Before he is passively "handed over" to his death, Jesus actively hands himself as food to his

32. Balthasar, *Love Alone is Credible*, 89.

33. Balthasar, *Explorations in Theology* IV, 272.

34. Balthasar, *New Elucidations*, 113. Cf. *Ecclesia de Eucharistia*, n.3: "The

disciples, saying "This is my body which is given for you" (Luke 22:19) and "This is my blood of the covenant, which is poured out for many" (Mark 14:24). In Balthasar's words, Jesus "is at once *a disposer* (as institutor of the Eucharist, the new covenant in his blood) and *the disposed of* (in obedience to the hour, when, at the Father's disposition, he will be handed over.)"[35] The Last Supper displayed the self-giving spirit in which Jesus was ready to suffer. His Eucharistic gesture of self-distribution preceded the passion and "thus shows that his free self-surrender is also the essential reason and prerequisite for the fact that the subsequent horrible event can acquire its meaning of universal salvation."[36]

Further, the memorial of the Last Supper itself already contains a hope for the eschatological future, as the Jesus himself there directed his disciples' attention to the heavenly banquet in the eschatological future[37]: "I tell you, I will never again drink of this fruit of the vine until that day when I drink it new with you in my Father's kingdom" (Matt 26:29).[38] Therefore, as the *Catechism of the Catholic Church* states, "the Eucharist is also an anticipation of the heavenly glory,"[39] and "Whenever the Church celebrates the Eucharist she remembers this promise and turns her gaze 'to him who is to come.'"[40] Thus the Eucharist has a deeply eschatological dimension. Although this dimension has long been recognized since the days of the church fathers, there has recently been a "rediscovery" and deepening of this dimension.[41]

Before the current trend, Balthasar was well aware of the importance of this dimension in the Eucharist.[42] For example, he writes, "It is the Eucharist . . .that must reveal the most profound truth about heaven's presence to earth."[43] Further, inspired by Speyr, he says, "Christ's return to the world has

---

institution of the Eucharist sacramentally anticipated the events which were about to take place."

35. Balthasar, *Mysterium Paschale*, 97. Italics added.

36. Balthasar, *New Elucidations*, 114.

37. See *Catechism of the Catholic Church*, §1403.

38. cf. Luke 22:18, Mark 14:25.

39. *Catechism of the Catholic Church*, §1402.

40. Ibid., § 1403.

41. Apparently, this trend has been shared by various denominations.

42. For example, see Balthasar, *Theo-Drama* V, 118–141, 411–417, and 470–487. For the secondary sources on the connection between the Eucharist and eschatology in Balthasar, see Ciraulo, "Sacramentally Regulated Eschatology in Hans Urs von Balthasar and Pope Benedict XVI"; Healy, "Christ's Eucharist and the Nature of Love," 13–17; Healy, *The Eschatology of Hans Urs von Balthasar*, 192–200.

43. Balthasar, *Theo-Drama* V, 416.

already begun in the Eucharist."[44] Through the Eucharist, we experience a foretaste of heaven. For Balthasar, heaven means the loving communion of the Trinity. For him, eschatology and the Trinity are inseparable. As we have mentioned in chapter 2, Balthasar has reconstructed the traditional four last things (death, judgment, heaven, and hell) by focusing on the Triune God himself, who is revealed in Jesus Christ:

> God is the "last thing" of the creature. Gained, he is heaven; lost, he is hell; examining, he is judgment; purifying, he is purgatory. To him finite being dies, and through and to and in him it rises. But this is God as he presents himself to the world, that is, in his Son, *Jesus Christ*, who is the revelation of God and therefore the whole essence of the last things.[45]

We have to pause here to note that the Eucharist has its origin in the Trinity. First of all, the Son is "the Father's substantial Eucharist."[46] As we have seen in chapter 1, in the initial *kenosis* within the inner life of the Godhead, in other words, the eternal generation of the Son by the Father, the Son's response to the Father is eternal *thanksgiving*. On the other hand, for the world, the Son is Eucharist in the sense of a self-giving love. These two aspects of the Eucharist are realized at the same time by the Son giving up his own body and pouring out his blood for the world, because the Son thankfully fulfils the Father's will to gather the humankind into the eternal life of the Trinity by doing so. We discussed in chapter 1 the Son's two-fold love for the Father and for the world, which is revealed in the paschal mystery, but now we can see it again here in the form of Eucharist. In the last analysis, through the Eucharist we are invited to participate into the loving communion with the eternal life of the Trinity. Thus, the Eucharist becomes the meeting point between heaven and earth.

This idea has been further affirmed by St. John Paul II and further liturgically explored in depth by Pope Emeritus Benedict XVI. In his encyclical letter *Ecclesia de Eucharistia*, St. John Paul II discusses "the eschatological thrust which marks the celebration of the Eucharist,"[47] and says that "the

---

44. Ibid., 130. Cf. *Catechism of the Catholic Church*, §1404. It is also important to note that the part of the *Theo-Drama* V where he discusses the deep connections among the Trinity, eschatology, and sacraments happens to be one of the places where he most frequently quotes from Speyr. She emphasizes that the Eucharist (along with the other sacraments) has its origin in the Trinity and the Christian participates into the loving communion with the Trinity through the Eucharist.

45. Balthasar, *Explorations in Theology* I, 260–61.

46. Balthasar, *New Elucidations*, 120.

47. *Ecclesia de Eucharistia*, n. 18.

eschatological tension kindled by the Eucharist expresses and reinforces our communion with the Church in heaven."[48] Further, Benedict XVI has been known for his emphasis on the liturgical continuity between the last things and the sacraments. It would be helpful and relevant to refer to his theology of the liturgy briefly here, as the affinity between Benedict XVI's and Balthasar's eschatology has been pointed out by some.[49] Benedict XVI's theology of the liturgy is imbued with eschatology. He describes liturgy as "a kind of anticipation, a rehearsal, a prelude for the life to come, for eternal life."[50] He also emphasizes that the liturgy is not something invented by human minds but something "given" to the church. He says, "The life of the liturgy does not come from what draws upon the minds of individuals and planning groups. On the contrary, it is God's descent upon our world, the source of real liberation."[51] Further, "the uniqueness of the Eucharistic liturgy lies precisely in the fact that God himself is acting and that we are drawn into that action of God."[52] Because it is God who is working in the liturgy of the Eucharist, we can truly be transformed and incorporated into the body of Christ, so the liturgy itself becomes inseparable from the eschatological hope. As Benedict XVI reminds us, "the Blessed Sacrament contains a dynamism, which has the goal of transforming mankind and the world into the New Heaven and New Earth, into the unity of the risen Body."[53] Further, such transformation and incorporation leads us into the communion of saints, for it is "a drive toward union, the overcoming of the barriers between God and man, between 'I' and 'thou' in the new 'we' of the communion of saints."[54] Further, we have to note that the eschatological hope grounds not only the communion of saints but also the Christian sense of responsibility for the world today, which lies at the core of the Christian mission. St. John Paul II said,

48. Ibid., n. 19.

49. For example, see Ciraulo, "Sacramentally Regulated Eschatology in Hans Urs von Balthasar and Pope Benedict XVI," 226: "the Trinitarian liturgy of Balthasar becomes the actual, postconciliar liturgy for Benedict . . . Balthasar and Benedict should be considered as two sides to the same coin . . . Balthasar's side begins by looking up toward God, Benedict's begins by looking down toward the church on earth." On the other hand, we have to note that some scholars point out the differences between the two. For example, see Hofer, "Balthasar's Eschatology on the Intermediate State."

50. Ratzinger, The Spirit of the Liturgy, 14.

51. Ibid., 168.

52. Ibid., 174.

53. Ibid., 87.

54. Ibid., 87.

A significant consequence of the eschatological tension inherent in the Eucharist is also the fact that it spurs us on our journey through history and plants a seed of living hope in our daily commitment to the work before us. Certainly the Christian vision leads to the expectation of "new heavens" and "a new earth" (Rev 21:1), but this increases, rather than lessens, *our sense of responsibility for the world today.*[55]

This point brings us back to the conclusion of the previous chapter. We have argued that the Christian, as a being in transition who belongs to Christ but is also part of the created world, holds a unique responsibility to deal with the problems in the world. In Balthasar's words, "it is because they are rooted in eternal life that the Church and Christians acquire strength to carry out their mission in *this* world; they are otherworldly, but they are also this-worldly, addressing the world and its issues."[56] Also, we have argued that the Christian has a privilege of seeking support and consolation in the paschal mystery.

What we have discussed in this section affirms and reinforces these arguments from the previous chapter from the perspective of the liturgy of the Eucharist. Through the lens of the Eucharist as an *anamnesis* of the incarnation and the paschal mystery and a foretaste of heaven, we can clearly see that the Christians are rooted in the living memory of the incarnation and the paschal mystery, while looking ahead into the eschatological future, when Christ will come again and we will be invited for the final heavenly banquet. Most importantly, now we can add that this in-between status of the Christian is supported and strengthened by a daily encounter with the living Christ, who is really present in the Eucharist. In the previous chapters, we emphasized the element of waiting in Christian life (hence the importance of the Holy Saturday perspective for the Christian existence), but now we can see that through the Eucharist this waiting becomes "confident waiting 'in joyful hope for the coming of our Saviour, Jesus Christ.'"[57] This confidence and hope becomes the powerful source for the Christian to go out into the world on a mission and to build a community. It is further relevant for our discussion that Balthasar declares that "Christian community is established in the Eucharist, which presupposes the descent into hell (mine and yours)."[58] Let us explore below the profound connection between the mystery of the Eucharist and the descent into hell.

---

55. *Ecclesia de Eucharistia*, n. 20.

56. Balthasar, *You Crown the Year with Your Goodness*, 323.

57. *Ecclesia de Eucharistia*, n. 18.

58. Balthasar, "Receiving the Tradition," 167. Italics added.

The Eucharist and the Mystery of Holy Saturday

How does the mystery of the Eucharist and the descent into hell relate to each other? This question has not yet been explored in full depth either in the scholarship or in the life of the church. Every year, through the absence of liturgy, with the altar left bare, we relive the "empty, wordless pause of Saturday,"[59] the day on which the Son of God was dead with the dead. To contemplate on the mystery of the Eucharist from this "empty, wordless pause of Saturday" helps us to appreciate the depth of the kenotic love of the Triune God, which literally went the way of love to the end (John 13:1). As we have seen in chapter 1, for Balthasar, the descent into hell marks the final point of the economic mission of the Son hence the climax of his kenotic obedience. It then naturally follows that, for Balthasar, the descent into hell is also central to the mystery of the Eucharist, which is the embodiment of the Son's willingness to be disposed of for the sake of salvation of humanity. Further, as we have discussed above, the central aspect of Christ's sacrifice was a renunciation of his intimacy with the Father, his experience of absolute loneliness of the sinner, which reached its climax in hell. Therefore, we could conclude that, for Balthasar, the Eucharist is effectively the sacrament of the descent into hell.[60]

However, there is also the difficult question of the body on Holy Saturday. As we have mentioned in the first section of this chapter, Balthasar takes "bodiliness" seriously, but how could the mystery of Holy Saturday be called "bodily," if we understand that Christ's dead body lay in the tomb, while his soul was in *Sheol* going through the *visio mortis*? According to Pitstick's critical analysis concerning this point,

> It may be that the Eucharist's reception of its efficacy from Christ's descent [into hell] contributes to Balthasar's reluctance to discuss Christ's descent in relation to the separation of His body and soul in death. . . .if the Eucharist is the sacrament of Christ's body and blood, soul and divinity, how can this sacrament represent Christ's descent if His body and soul were separated during it?[61]

Here Pitstick seems to suggest that the close connection Balthasar evidently sees between the Eucharist (the sacrament of Christ's body and blood) and Christ's descent into hell cannot be justified, because Christ's body did not participate in the descent into hell.

---

59. Balthasar, *Explorations in Theology* IV, 401.

60. Pitstick agrees on this point as well. Pitstick, *Light in Darkness*, 249.

61. Ibid., 250.

However, what we should take into full account here is that, as we have mentioned in the first section of this chapter, Balthasar's is an anthropology of "unity-in-duality" according to which corporeal and spiritual perception are inextricably intertwined with one another. In other words, his is a non-dualistic anthropology according to which the human being is understood as being fundamentally united in body and soul. This idea lies at the core of Balthasar's thanatology as well as his interpretation of the descent into hell. For him, it is not just the body that suffers death but the body-soul complex in its totality.[62] Death is characterized by the loss of spiritual-corporeal integrity and consequently the loss of all relationality,[63] rather than a simple "separation" of body and soul.[64] That is why Balthasar criticizes the traditional, rather dualistic image of Christ's descent into hell as his soul seems "too active" or rather "too alive" as if it were an entity completely separated

---

62. For example, see Balthasar, *Theo-Drama* IV, 130. Also, see *Explorations in Theology* IV, 411. Further, Jennifer Newsome Martin discusses this point in the context of comparison between Balthasar's and Bulgakov's theologies of death in *Hans Urs von Balthasar and the Critical Appropriation of Russian Religious Thought*, 131–37.

63. For Balthasar, corporeality and relationality are closely interlinked. For example, we can clearly see this link in his discussion of the spiritual senses in *The Glory of the Lord* I, 365–425. Also see McInroy, *Balthasar on the Spiritual Senses*, 94–121.

64. It is also worth noting here that only in this non-dualistic anthropology Speyr's mystical insights about hell make sense as well. She reflects on the question of Christ's "bodily state" in hell as well as "hell and the body (*Leib*)," which would be an irrelevant question for a clear-cut dualistic anthropology (See Speyr, *The Passion from Within*, 153–58; Speyr, *Kreuz und Hölle* II, 124–25). For example, Speyr says, "Somehow I receive a body for hell, so I can say and hear something at all. But this body is not my own, because the senses are cut off. This body is alien to me, as I am alien to myself, this body does not possess my experiences. The irritation in hell is the expression of this discrepancy between my body and my spirit." (Speyr, *Kreuz und Hölle* II, 125.) Further, Speyr attempted to describe how in hell Christ's "bodily state becomes very different from what it was in life." In particular, asked by Balthasar how Christ can experience in hell evil as a quality-in-itself, that is, as something completely nonrelational, Speyr responded, "*Because he has been robbed of his Eucharist.*" (Speyr, *The Passion from Within*, 157.) She further explained what she meant by this remark as follows: "The Cross lies behind him and is no longer relevant. And his physical being with its striving seems at this moment left behind with men in the Eucharist, in the same way as his martyred body has been left behind on the Cross. Whatever united him with God the Father and with mankind, everything horizontal and vertical, has been left behind." (Speyr, *The Passion from Within*, 158.) Speyr further expresses the Lord's experience of absolute loneliness in hell with a "bodily" expression: "In hell, however, when I accompany the Lord on Holy Saturday, I no longer know: Will I be hungry? Will I be thirsty? Must I dress up? Eat? Or must I withdraw completely into myself? Be body to such a degree that I no longer know the needs and questions concerning them." (Speyr, *The Passion from Within*, 158.)

from the dead body in the tomb.[65] (As we have seen in the previous chapters, even though the first emphasis of the traditional teachings of the descent into hell was that Christ was really dead, the traditional image of Christ's soul in hell is filled with "action": he preaches to the dead, he delivers the just of the Old Testament out of *Sheol*, and he even fights with the Devil.)

According to Balthasar, it is crucial for our salvation that Christ experienced and encountered the reality of human death "as a whole," that is, body and soul, for that is how he has overcome human death: "by allowing the horror of death to penetrate his innermost, loving heart and showing that, dying, buried and descending to the underworld, he had a longer breath than death and hell."[66] In other words, "he stood *under* death and not *above* it."[67] To neglect this point would eventually lead to downplaying both the mystery of the Trinity and the supreme sovereignty of the Triune God, for "the perfect self-alienation of the experience of hell is the function of the incarnate Christ's obedience, and this obedience is once more a function of his free love for the Father"[68] and also "by going all the way to the outermost alienation, God himself has proven to be the Almighty who also is able to safeguard his identity in non-identity, his being-with-himself in being lost, his life in being dead."[69]

What we have to consider further here is how it is relevant for the mystery of the Eucharist that Christ really went through the finality of death. This point is directly related to the importance of contemplating on the mystery of the Eucharist from the empty and silent liturgical pause of Holy Saturday. Such an attempt has hardly ever been done, both in the scholarship and in the life of the church, but Balthasar and Speyr have given enough insights for us to explore profound connections between the mystery of the Eucharist and the mystery of Holy Saturday. We do not claim in any way that these connections are dogmatically necessary or central. Rather, we would like to

---

65. In relation to this point, Balthasar would probably side with the medieval, Franciscan depictions of the dead body of Christ, which often portray Jesus as pale, rigid, and even, already corrupting. It would also be relevant to note here that, in contrast to the Franciscan tradition, many Byzantine depictions intimate that his dead body is in some sense still alive. (Concerning this contrast, see Grumett, *Material Eucharist*, 67–8.) This point is evidently connected with the contrast between the Eastern and Western tradition concerning Holy Saturday as well, as we pointed out in the introduction to this book (the former with the emphasis on the victory of Easter, the latter on silence).

66. Balthasar, *You Crown the Year with Your Goodness*, 117.

67. Ibid., 116.

68. Balthasar, *Explorations in Theology IV*, 411.

69. Ibid., 413.

propose that such connections provide profound ways to contemplate on the mystery of the Eucharist while being faithful to the church's liturgical tradition. We also believe that these connections reinforce our thesis that Balthasar does *not* try to present a radical reinterpretation of the doctrine of the descent into hell in contrast to the tradition of the church but rather tries to appreciate the "in-between" state of Christ in *Sheol* on Holy Saturday while being faithful to the tradition of the church.

Going back to the question we raised in the introduction to this book, if only the explicitly triumphant image of Christ in hell were true to the tradition of the church (as Pitstick emphatically has argued), how could we explain the liturgical silence on Holy Saturday? Why would not the church simply celebrate Christ's triumphant descent into hell instead of keeping this "mourning period" before Easter and waiting at the tomb with sorrowful Mary (whose title becomes "Our Lady of Solitude" on Holy Saturday)? This empty and silent space in the liturgical calendar contains the mystery of the decisive turning point from death to life, from the old aeon to the new. According to Balthasar, on Holy Saturday, the incarnate Son of God went through the whole reality of death, that is, the sheer "passivity" of death, both in body and soul. In other words, he encountered death "without any hope of the resulting hiatus ever being bridged: there was no hope of ever closing the rift opened up by this death."[70] The unbridgeable gap between death and life was bridged solely by a completely free and gracious act of God the Father. We do not know exactly how or at which moment the unbridgeable was bridged.[71] Only the incarnate Son of God is "the continuity" between death and life, the old aeon and the new, "the connecting thread linking ruin and rising, which does not break even in death and hell."[72] This "continuity" do we still witness every time we celebrate the Eucharist, in which the living Lord is truly present. Without the acute awareness of the unbridgeableness between death and life, or without the empty and silent pause of Holy Saturday, we cannot truly appreciate the joy of Easter or eventually the mystery of the Eucharist. And it is this logically inexplicable but unbreakably firm "continuity" of Christ's that supports the Christian's life in transition between the old aeon and new. As we have mentioned above, Balthasar insists that "Christians too should celebrate the Mass with death in mind, *with a view to* death and not simply *in the wake of* it."[73] By saying

70. Balthasar, *You Crown the Year with Your Goodness*, 90.

71. No human being witnessed the actual moment of the resurrection. The disciples only encountered the "resurrected" Christ.

72. Ibid., 91.

73. Ibid., 116.

this Balthasar is not belittling the joy of Easter. Rather, what he means is that the meaning of death has been transformed completely by Christ's descent into hell and his resurrection from there. Thanks to the paschal mystery, our journey into hell can now be our ascension as well. Through the Eucharist, we become incorporated into Christ's ascent.[74]

The Eucharist and the Christian's Holy Saturday Experience

Next, let us explore below what implications the connection between the mystery of the Eucharist and the mystery of Holy Saturday provide for Christian discipleship, based on what we have been discussing in this and the previous chapters. Every time we receive the Eucharist, the body of Christ, we are incorporated into the church, the mystical body of Christ. Nourished by the body and blood of Christ and filled with his Holy Spirit, we become one body and one spirit in Christ. As Christ, the head of the church himself, lived a life of perfect self-giving love, which culminated in his sacrifice on the cross and the descent into hell, the members of his body, Christians, are also invited through the Eucharist to live a life of self-giving love, which is what Christian discipleship is all about. As we have already briefly mentioned, Balthasar says that *our own* descent into hell is a presupposition of the Eucharist. In his words,

> The Christian, however, must open his heart and allow himself to be most intimately affected, challenged, hurt. God in Christ went to the place of the loneliest sinner in order to communicate with him in dereliction by God. *Christian community is established in the Eucharist, which presupposes the descent into hell (mine and yours).* No flight into an abstract unity is permitted there.[75]

This passage suggests that there are deep connections among the Eucharist, the descent into hell, the Christian mission and community. According to Balthasar, Christians are invited to descend into their own hell for the sake of their brethren somehow. This is the attitude of selflessly caring about those who are the most alienated from God even to the point

74. In relation to this point, it is worth noting that early Christians literally took the Eucharist as a matter of life and death. This point has been made clear by David Grumett's study about how the Eucharistic practice has been developed through practices surrounding death (such as the viaticum, feeding the dead, and burial) since the early Christian times. See Grumett, *Material Eucharist*, 191–232.

75. Balthasar, "Receiving the Tradition," 167. Italics added.

of forgetting our own salvation. As we have already seen in the previous chapters, many saints (and other Christians) have followed his footsteps and willingly descended into their own hell for the sake of their brethren. The experience of the dark night of the soul is a typical example of the descent into hell, but the idea can be applied more widely to our daily life on a smaller scale. As Balthasar reminds us, the church is also "lonely in an internal and qualitative sense" because to be sent out into the world "as lambs among wolves" is an essential part of the Christian mission, as shown in Jesus' own words.[76] If the Christian mission is essentially about trying to reach the loneliest sinner, that is, the sinner who shuts out themselves from God's saving grace, it is not at all an easy, pleasant task. It means that we should willingly give up our own comfortable territory and go even to where God seems to be absent, or where he is actively rejected or hated (in other words, hell on earth) for the sake of the Christian mission. This idea sounds somewhat similar to one of Pope Francis's messages. He has said that we should "break the habit of conveniently placing ourselves at the center" and "open ourselves to the peripheries, also acknowledging that, at the margins too, even one who is cast aside and scorned by society is the object of God's generosity. We are all called not to reduce the Kingdom of God to the confines of the "little church"—our "tiny little church"— but to enlarge the Church to the dimensions of the Kingdom of God."[77] Pope Francis has also said in the same speech, "the banquet of the Lord's gifts is universal, for everyone. Everyone is given the opportunity to respond to the invitation, to his call."[78] As we have seen in the previous chapters, a practical result of Christ's descent into hell on Holy Saturday is our duty to hope for universal salvation. That means to hope that everyone will eventually respond to such an invitation to the final banquet of the Lord.

Further, let us explore below how the "Holy Saturday perspective" we presented in the previous chapters can be relevant for contemplation of the mystery of the Eucharist. In order to do so, let us reflect on the story of the two disciples on the road to Emmaus narrated in the Gospel of Luke (Luke 24:13–35). This story has often been studied, discussed, and meditated upon because of its significance for the Eucharistic theology as well as for Christian discipleship.[79] For example, St. John Paul II declared in his apostolic letter *Mane Nobiscum Domine* for the year of the Eucharist that

76. Balthasar, *Explorations in Theology* IV, 276.

77. Pope Francis, *Angelus*, n.p.

78. Ibid.

79. For example, see John Paul II, *Mane Nobiscum Domine*; Nouwen, *With Burning Hearts*; Kasper, *Sacrament of Unity*, 38–45.

"the image of the disciples on the way to Emmaus can serve as a fitting guide for a Year when the Church will be particularly engaged in living out the mystery of the Holy Eucharist."[80] At another occasion, he had also said "whenever the Church celebrates the Eucharist, the faithful can in some way relive the experience of the two disciples on the road to Emmaus: 'their eyes were opened and they recognized him' (Lk 24:31)."[81]

It is a story with many deep implications for the mystery of the Eucharist and Christian discipleship; It is a story about an encounter with Jesus in our journey of faith (v. 15); It is a story about the presence of the risen Christ accompanying us, though hidden from our eyes (v. 16); It is a story about how the Scriptures testify about Jesus Christ (v. 25–27); it is a story of our prayer and invitation to the Lord ("Stay with us") and his acceptance (v. 29); It is a story about recognizing the Lord in the breaking of the bread (v. 30–31); It is a story of transformation of sadness into Easter joy (v. 32–34); and finally, it is also a story about mission, going into the world with burning hearts to proclaim the good news (v. 35). These are merely a few obvious aspects of this great story.

What is further important for our exploration of connections between Holy Saturday and the Eucharist is that this story of the road to Emmaus captures well the Holy Saturday experience of a Christian. Referring to the Emmaus story as a biblical passage related to the descent into hell, Pope Emeritus Benedict XVI explained that, to these two disciples, "something like the death of God has happened: the point at which God finally seemed to have spoken has disappeared. The One sent by God is dead, and so there is a complete void."[82] Though this episode itself took place in the evening of the Sunday of the resurrection and the two disciples had already heard about the women's visit to the empty tomb and their encounter with the angels, they themselves still lived in Holy Saturday. They remained skeptical about the good news they had heard. They were not aware that the risen Lord himself was walking beside them, accompanying them in their journey, so, for them, the joy of the Easter was not there yet. Using Balthasarian terms, we could say that the risen Christ was objectively present in their midst but subjectively still hidden.

The story portrays the "in-between" emotional state of those who suffered a devastating loss, that is, a process of gradual change from despair to joy; at first, when Jesus joined them and asked them what they were discussing, their hearts were so filled with disappointments, sorrow, bitterness,

---

80. John Paul II, *Mane Nobiscum Domine*, n. 2.

81. John Paul II, *Ecclesia de Eucharistia*, n. 6.

82. Ratzinger, *Introduction to Christianity*, 295.

and grief that they were incapable of recognizing him: "their eyes were kept from recognizing him" (v. 16); Then while Jesus was "opening the scriptures" (v. 32) to them, explaining that it was actually the will of God that "the Messiah should suffer these things and then enter into his glory" (v. 26), their hearts were "burning within" them, but their eyes remained blind. Then the story captures the dramatic moment of recognition of the risen Lord in the breaking of the bread. It is significant that Luke writes "he took bread, blessed, and broke it, and gave it to them" (v. 30), exactly to echo the actions of Jesus at the Last Supper: "Then he took a loaf of bread, and when he had given thanks, he broke it and gave it to them, saying, 'This is my body, which is given to you. Do this in remembrance of me'" (22:19).[83] The two disciples recognized the Lord because of their memory of these actions: "Then their eyes were opened, and they recognized him" (v. 31). Then, at this moment the Lord vanished from their sight, but their hearts were now so filled with joy and happiness that they ran back to Jerusalem and told the eleven Apostles of their meeting with the risen Lord. Thus, in a sense, the story of the two disciples on the road to Emmaus can be considered as a story of recognition of the resurrected Christ in the Eucharist based on the memory of the passion (as the Last Supper understood as the anticipation of the passion) and as a story of sadness changed into joy based on such a recognition after the Holy Saturday experience.

An important point worth noting is that the Lord vanishes exactly at the moment the disciples recognize him in the breaking of the bread: "they recognized him; and he vanished from their sight" (Luke 24:31). Henri J. M. Nouwen, for example, says that this very sentence "leads us right into the mystery of communion."[84] In Nouwen's words, "Precisely when he becomes most present to them, he also becomes the absent one."[85] This point touches one of the most sacred aspects of the mystery of the Eucharist: the most intimate communion with Christ is the one that happens in his absence. Going back to the two disciples on the road to Emmaus, they had no full communion with Christ when they had him in front of their eyes. They even mourned his absence. Then, after the moment of the recognition of him in the breaking of the bread, he vanishes from their sight, but they do not even feel sad or lonely. Instead, they look at each other and say, "Were not our hearts burning within us while he was talking to us on the road, while he was opening the scriptures to us?" (v. 32) Now they have a deep

83. Also see the multiplication of the loaves (Luke 9:16).

84. Nouwen, *With Burning Hearts*, 90.

85. Ibid., 90.

spiritual awareness that he dwells in their innermost being. They have been incorporated into him. Now he lives in them. Nouwen further writes,

> When we eat of his body and drink of his blood, we accept the loneliness of not having him any longer at our table as a consoling partner in our conversation, helping us to deal with the losses of our daily life. It is the loneliness of the spiritual life, the loneliness of knowing that he is closer to us than we ever can be to ourselves. It's *the loneliness of faith*.[86]

The usage of the word "loneliness" here is somewhat reminiscent of Balthasar's when he says that loneliness is "deeply stamped for her [the church] as the source of her community."[87] As we have seen above, this is the kind of loneliness that can be a basis for the Christian mission. Balthasar says, "the saints found the Church. They receive her from the Lord in the loneliness of their hearts and spread her out into the world as *communio*."[88] In the Emmaus story, the two disciples' recognition of the resurrected Lord in the breaking of the bread prompts them to return to Jerusalem and to seek out the other disciples, who had been dispersed on Holy Saturday. Likewise, our daily encounter with the Lord in the Eucharist prepares us for going out into the world on a mission and for building communities where we go. We have been discussing the significance of the Eucharist as sacrifice in this chapter, but we also have to stress here that it is communion that is born out of participation in the Eucharistic sacrifice.

Finally, this whole story can be read as a liturgy. The story has the fundamental structure of the liturgy: the gathering, the liturgy of the word, with readings, homily and general intercessions, and the liturgy of the Eucharist, with the presentation of the bread and wine, the consecratory thanksgiving, and communion, followed by the dismissal.[89] Therefore, it can be read as a story about the liturgy and how it transforms the believer and sends them on a mission into the world. We go to the Mass in the midst of our daily cares including all kinds of disappointments, expectations, sadness, happiness, worries, and hopes. So often we become too preoccupied with ourselves to recognize Jesus Christ, who accompanies us in our journey of life. Then in the Mass we encounter and recognize him, the summit of which is the celebration of the Eucharist, and get transformed. As Benedict XVI reminds us, "the goal of the Eucharist is our own transformation, so that we become 'one

---

86. Ibid., 93–94. Italics added.

87. Balthasar, *Explorations in Theology* IV, 275.

88. Ibid., 294.

89. See *Catechism of the Catholic Church*, §1346.

body and spirit' with Christ (cf. I Cor 6:17)."[90] Through this transformation, our personal cares, burdens, and sufferings too receive meaning and consolation in relation to Christ. Further, thanks to such transformation through the Eucharist, we learn to share the burdens and sufferings of our brethren (in other words, to go through our dark night of the soul or to descend into our own hell for our brethren) as well. Most importantly, the liturgical aspect affirms the church's and Christian's in-between status further. After all, we relive this Emmaus story again and again through the liturgy on a smaller scale. That is why, though we are certainly living in the age after the resurrection and have the privilege to look at everything in the light of Easter, it still makes sense to discuss our Holy Saturday experience.

Conclusion: The "In-between" Existence Sustained by the Living Christ

In this chapter, using Balthasar's theology of the Eucharist as a guide, we have discussed some aspects of the mystery of the Eucharist through the lens of Holy Saturday. As we stated at the beginning, the theme of the Eucharist is scattered through his theological corpus and it is almost always present in his thoughts. It is only natural then that we see here again some common ideas which we have already discussed in relation to the other areas of his theology: the close link between love and abandonment, the emphasis on "passivity" in obedience, and his concept of "passive" femininity. In particular, here again we can critique Balthasar's characterization of the ecclesial attitude as being "passive" and "feminine," which is imported directly from his distinctive Mariology, which we discussed in chapter 3.

On the other hand, while exploring the profound connections between the mystery of Holy Saturday and the Eucharist, which is "the source and summit of the Christian life," we have affirmed that Christians liturgically live out the "in-between" existence, which we discussed in chapter 4. Also, by focusing on the sacrificial significance of the Eucharist, which, according to Balthasar, presupposes *our* descent into hell, we have further clarified that suffering (when persevered for the sake of our brethren) is an essential part of Christian discipleship. Also, going back to the question concerning the liturgical pause or "mourning period" that the church respects every Holy Week, we have affirmed that the appreciation of this empty, silent pause of Holy Saturday is necessary for us to fully appreciate the mystery of the Eucharist, for it is the day to remember that the essentially unbridgeable gap between death and life, the cross and the resurrection, the old aeon and

---

90. Ratzinger, *The Spirit of the Liturgy*, 86.

new, was bridged by God the Father in Christ. Only the incarnate Son of God presents to the believers the logically inexplicable "continuity" between death and life. The Christian's life is literally nourished and sustained by a daily encounter with the living Christ in the Eucharist. Thus, from a liturgical perspective, we have reinforced our thesis that Holy Saturday has deep implications for Christian discipleship.

Lastly, before we conclude this chapter, let us go back to the aspect of waiting, which we have been highlighting in this book, and which unifies the mystery of the Eucharist and Balthasar's interpretation of the mystery of Holy Saturday. In the last analysis, these two mysteries reveal God as *the God who waits*.[91] After all, to love and to wait is interlinked. ("Love is patient." [1 Cor 13:4])[92] St. John Paul II once said, "Jesus waits for us in this sacrament of love [the Eucharist]."[93] Balthasar concludes one small essay on the Eucharist with the image of the Lord knocking on the door, waiting to be let in: "Listen! I am standing at the door, knocking; if you hear my voice and open the door, I will come in to you and eat with you, and you with me" (Rev 3:20).[94] As the disciples on the road to Emmaus, we too are required to respond to this voice of the Lord, "Stay with us" (Luke 24:29).

91. For a profound exploration of this theme, see Vanstone, *The Stature of Waiting*.

92. For example, see Vanstone, *The Stature of Waiting*, 96: "Where love is, action is destined to pass into passion: working into waiting."

93. John Paul II, *Dominicae Cenae*.

94. Balthasar, *L'Eucharistie*, 26.

Conclusion

As the conclusion of this book, let us summarize how we have maintained the approach and scope stated in Introduction as well as how we have answered the questions.

We stated that our focus is on Holy Saturday rather than the descent into hell, in contrast to the previous studies on Balthasar's theology of Holy Saturday. As we clarified then, we have explored the significance of Holy Saturday by dividing it into three kinds: Christ's descent into hell, Mary's waiting at the tomb, and the Christian's "tragic" existence. We have also stated that we would pay full respect to the genre within which Balthasar is working. Since his style is a contemplative combination of theology and spirituality, we have selected the sources we deal with accordingly. As a result, we have valued the writings of Adrienne von Speyr, St. John of the Cross, and St. Thérèse of Lisieux in this book.

We also set the following specific questions: what kind of implications can Balthasar's theology of Holy Saturday provide for Christian discipleship? how does Balthasar's theology of Holy Saturday help Christians to find meaning and hope in their suffering? As a response to these questions, we have pointed out how the dark night of the soul is one distinctive example of Christian suffering and discipleship. There has been shown a way to persevere in the seeming absence of God or loss of faith for the sake of brethren.

We further attempted to answer these questions by connecting Balthasar's interpretation of Christ's descent into hell with his "tragic" view of Christianity. We argued that Balthasar's theology of Holy Saturday presents us with a framework to clarify the in-between state of Christian existence. The Christian's Holy Saturday, which is characterized by "tragic" waiting in transition from the old aeon to the new, can be endured because of Christ's waiting in hell on Holy Saturday. This gives the Christian both a privilege and a responsibility as the one who has to follow Christ while living and acting in solidarity with this world. Further, by exploring the profound connections between Holy Saturday and the Eucharist, which is "the source and summit of the Christian life," we reaffirmed, this time from a liturgical perspective, that Holy Saturday has deep implications for Christian discipleship. We argued that the empty and silent pause of Holy Saturday is necessary for a full appreciation of the mystery of the Eucharist, and that Balthasar's theology of Holy Saturday is faithful to the church's liturgical tradition in this sense.

On the other hand, we also discussed some serious issues and concerns raised against Balthasar. In chapters 1 and 2, we dealt with the three main concerns about his treatment of the Trinity, Christology, and soteriology: first, whether he has the tendency to bring a rupture into the eternally blissful unity within the Trinity and eventually ends up elevating and divinizing suffering; secondly, whether he confuses the divinity and humanity of Christ; and thirdly, whether his theology inevitably leads to admitting universal salvation in a systematic sense. Regarding these three concerns, we stated our position that in general he takes a subtle and nuanced approach and he is apparently aware of these issues himself. (Basically, even his critics can only criticize his *tendency*.) We further argued that he is rather consistent with his logic of kenotic love and also that he is sensitive to the paradoxical mystery of love and faith. On the other hand, in chapters 3 and 4, we dealt with other concerns raised against his theology. We criticized his view of sexual differentiation which is interlinked with his Mariology. In relation to this point we even admitted that Balthasar's theology potentially has the danger of being used to justify the unjust status quo if placed in the wrong hands. We also admitted that he does not engage with the concrete reality of human suffering in an explicit way so it could seem to be insufficient to those who want practical solutions to their problems.

Despite all this, we still affirm that Balthasar's theology of Holy Saturday, with its distinctive emphasis on the "in-betweenness," does provide profound implications for Christian discipleship; the Christian, whose existence is characterized by the ongoing transition from the old aeon to the new, thus still living in the "between" time, can be patient in their long waiting because of Christ's waiting in hell on the first Holy Saturday.

Bibliography

Adams, Marilyn McCord. *Horrendous Evils and the Goodness of God*. Ithaca, NY: Cornell University Press, 1999.

Alfeyev, Hilarion. *Christ the Conqueror of Hell: The Descent into Hades from an Orthodox Perspective*. Crestwood, NY: St. Vladimir's Seminary Press, 2009.

Aquinas, Thomas. *Summa Theologiae*, Blackfriars edition. Edited by Thomas Gilby and T. C. O'Brien. Translated by John Fearon, et al. London: Eyre & Spottiswoode, 1964–1981.

———. *The Three Greatest Prayers: Commentaries on the Our Father, the Hail Mary and the Apostles' Creed*. Translated by Laurence Shapcote. London: Burns, Oates & Washbourne Ltd., 1937.

Arendt, Hannah. *Between Past and Future: Six Exercises in Political Thought*. London: Faber and Faber, 1961.

Augustine. *Expositions of the Psalms 33–50 III/16*. Edited by John E. Rotelle. Translated by Maria Boulding. Hyde Park, NY: New City, 2000.

Balthasar, Hans Urs von. "Adrienne von Speyr über das Geheimnis des Karsamstags." *Internationale Katholische Zeitschrift Communio* 10 (1981) 32–39.

———. *Bernanos: An Ecclesial Existence*. Translated by Erasmo Leiva-Merikakis. San Francisco: Ignatius, 1996.

———. *The Christian State of Life*. Translated by Mary Frances McCarthy. San Francisco: Ignatius, 1983.

———. *Cosmic Liturgy: The Universe According to Maximus the Confessor*. Translated by Brian E. Daley. San Francisco: Ignatius, 2003.

———. *Credo: Meditations on the Apostles' Creed*. Translated by David Kipp. Edinburgh: T. & T. Clark, 1990.

———. *Dare We Hope "That all Men be Saved"? With a Short Discourse on Hell*. Translated by David Kipp and Lothar Krauth. San Francisco: Ignatius, 1988.

———. *Does Jesus Know Us—Do We Know Him?* Translated by Graham Harrison. San Francisco: Ignatius, 1983.

———. "Einleitung." In *Kreuz und Hölle I: Die Passionen*, by Adrienne von Speyr, 5–14. Einsiedeln, Switzerland: Johannes Verlag, 1966.

———. *Elucidations*. Translated by John Riches. London: SPCK, 1975.

———. *Engagement with God*. Translated by John Halliburton. London: SPCK, 1975.

———. *Explorations in Theology I: The Word Made Flesh*. Translated by A. V. Littledale and Alexander Dru. San Francisco: Ignatius, 1989.

———. *Explorations in Theology II: Spouse of the Word*. Translated by A. V. Littledale, et al. San Francisco: Ignatius, 1991.

———. *Explorations in Theology* III: *Creator Spirit*. Translated by Brian McNeil. San Francisco: Ignatius, 1993.

———. *Explorations in Theology* IV: *Spirit and Institution*. Translated by Edward T. Oakes. San Francisco: Ignatius, 1995.

———. *Explorations in Theology* V: *Man Is Created*. Translated by Adrian Walker. San Francisco: Ignatius, 2014.

———. *First Glance at Adrienne von Speyr*. Translated by Antje Lawry and Sergia Englund. San Francisco: Ignatius, 1981.

———. *The Glory of the Lord: A Theological Aesthetics* I: *Seeing the Form*. Edited by Joseph Fessio and John Riches. Translated by Erasmo Leiva-Merikakis. Edinburgh: T. & T. Clark, 1982.

———. *The Glory of the Lord: A Theological Aesthetics* II: *Studies in Theological Style: Clerical Styles*. Edited by John Riches. Translated by Andrew Louth, et al. Edinburgh: T. & T. Clark, 1984.

———. *The Glory of the Lord: A Theological Aesthetics* III: *Studies in Theological Style: Lay Styles*. Edited by John Riches. Translated by Andrew Louth, et al. Edinburgh: T. & T. Clark, 1986.

———. *The Glory of the Lord: A Theological Aesthetics* IV: *The Realm of Metaphysics in Antiquity*. Edited by John Riches. Translated by Brian McNeil, et al. Edinburgh: T. & T. Clark, 1989.

———. *The Glory of the Lord: A Theological Aesthetics* V: *The Realm of Metaphysics in the Modern Age*. Edited by Rian McNeil and John Riches. Translated by Oliver Davies, et al. Edinburgh: T. & T. Clark, 1991.

———. *The Glory of the Lord: A Theological Aesthetics* VI: *Theology. The Old Covenant*. Edited by John Riches. Translated by Brian McNeil and Erasmo Leiva-Merikakis. Edinburgh: T. & T. Clark, 1991.

———. *The Glory of the Lord: A Theological Aesthetics* VII: *Theology: The New Covenant*. Edited by John Riches. Translated by Brian McNeil. Edinburgh: T. & T. Clark, 1989.

———. *The Grain of Wheat: Aphorisms*. Translated by Erasmo Leiva-Merikakis. San Francisco: Ignatius, 1995.

———. *Heart of the World*. Translated by Erasmo S. Leiva. San Francisco: Ignatius, 1979.

———. "The Holy Church and the Eucharistic Sacrifice." *Communio: International Catholic Review* 12 (1985) 139–45.

———. "Ist der Gekreuzgte 'selig'?" *Internationale katholische Zeitschrift Communio*, 16 (1987) 107–9.

———. *L'Eucharistie: Don de l'Amour*. Translated by Jean-Pierre Fels. Chiry-Ourscamp, France: Editions du Serviteur, 1994.

———. *Love Alone is Credible*. Translated by David C. Schindler. San Francisco: Ignatius, 2004.

———. *The Moment of Christian Witness*. Translated by Richard Beckley. San Francisco: Ignatius, 1994.

———. *My Work: In Retrospect*. Translated by Cornelia Capol. San Francisco: Communio, 1993.

———. *Mysterium Paschale: The Mystery of Easter*. Translated by Aidan Nichols. Edinburgh: T. & T. Clark, 1990.

————. *New Elucidations*. Translated by Mary Theresilde Skerry. San Francisco: Ignatius, 1986.

————. "Our Lady in Monasticism." *Word & Spirit 10* (1988) 52–56.

————. *Our Task: A Report and a Plan*. Translated by John Saward. San Francisco: Ignatius, 1994.

————. *Razing the Bastions: On the Church in This Age*. Translated by Brian McNeil. San Francisco: Ignatius, 1993.

————. "Receiving the Tradition: Communio: A Program." *Communio 33* (2006) 153–69.

————. *A Short Primer for Unsettled Laymen*. Translated by Mary Theresilde Skerry. San Francisco: Ignatius, 1985.

————. *Theo-Drama: Theological Dramatic Theory I: Prolegomena*. Translated by Graham Harrison. San Francisco: Ignatius, 1988.

————. *Theo-Drama: Theological Dramatic Theory II: The Dramatis Personae: Man in God*. Translated by Graham Harrison. San Francisco: Ignatius, 1990.

————. *Theo-Drama: Theological Dramatic Theory III: The Dramatis Personae: The Person in Christ*. Translated by Graham Harrison. San Francisco: Ignatius, 1992.

————. *Theo-Drama: Theological Dramatic Theory IV: The Action*. Translated by Graham Harrison. San Francisco: Ignatius, 1994.

————. *Theo-Drama: Theological Dramatic Theory V: The Last Act*. Translated by Graham Harrison. San Francisco: Ignatius, 1998.

————. *Theo-Logic: Theological Logical Theory I: Truth of the World*. Translated by Adrian J. Walker. San Francisco: Ignatius, 2000.

————. *Theo-Logic: Theological Logical Theory II: Truth of God*. Translated by Adrian J. Walker. San Francisco: Ignatius, 2004.

————. *Theo-Logic: Theological Logical Theory III: The Spirit of Truth*. Translated by Graham Harrison. San Francisco: Ignatius, 2005.

————. "Theologie des Abstiegs zur Hölle." In *Adrienne Von Speyr und Ihre Kirchliche Sendung: Akten D. Röm. Symposiums, 27–29. September 1985*, edited by Hans Urs von Balthasar, et al., 138–46. Einsiedeln, Switzerland: Johannes Verlag, 1986.

————. *The Threefold Garland: The World's Salvation in Mary's Prayer*. Translated by Erasmo Leiva-Merikakis. San Francisco: Ignatius, 1982.

————. *Tragedy Under Grace: Reinhold Schneider on the Experience of the West*. Translated by Brian McNeil. San Francisco: Ignatius, 1997.

————. *Truth is Symphonic: Aspects of Christian Pluralism*. Translated by Graham Harrison. San Francisco: Ignatius, 1987.

————. *Two Sisters in the Spirit: Thérèse of Lisieux and Elizabeth of the Trinity*. Translated by Donald Nichols, et al. San Francisco: Ignatius, 1992.

————. *Unless You Become Like this Child*. Translated by Erasmo Leiva-Merikakis. San Francisco: Ignatius, 1991.

————. *The Von Balthasar Reader*. Edited by Medard Kehl and Werner Löser. Translated by Robert J. Daly and Fred Lawrence. Edinburgh: T. & T. Clark, 1982.

————. *The Way of the Cross*. Translated by Rodelinde Albrecht and Maureen Sullivan. London: Burns & Oates, 1969.

————. *You Crown the Year with Your Goodness: Radio Sermons*. Translated by Graham Harrison. San Francisco: Ignatius, 1982.

Balthasar, Hans Urs von, and Adrienne von Speyr. *To the Heart of the Mystery of Redemption*. Translated by Anne Englund Nash. San Francisco: Ignatius, 2010.

Balthasar, Hans Urs von, and Joseph Ratzinger. *Mary the Church at the Source.* Translated by Adrian Walker. San Francisco: Ignatius, 2005.

Block, Ed, Jr. "Balthasar's Literary Criticism." In *The Cambridge Companion to Hans Urs von Balthasar,* edited by Edward T. Oakes and David Moss, 207–23. Cambridge: Cambridge University Press, 2004.

Brenan, Gerald. *St. John of the Cross: His Life and Poetry.* Cambridge: Cambridge University Press, 1973.

Bro, Barnard. *The Little Way: The Spirituality of Thérèse of Lisieux.* Translated by Alan Neame. London: Darton, Longman & Todd, 1979.

Brown, Raymond Edward. *The Death of the Messiah: From Gethsemane to the Grave: A Commentary on the Passion Narratives in the Four Gospels.* Vol. 2 of the Anchor Bible Reference Library. London: Doubleday, 1994.

———. *The Gospel According to John (XIII–XXI).* Vol. 29A of the Anchor Bible. New York: Doubleday, 1970.

Buchan, Thomas. *Blessed is He who has Brought Adam from Sheol: Christ's Descent to the Dead in the Theology of Saint Ephrem the Syrian.* Piscataway, NJ: Gorgias, 2004.

Catechism of the Catholic Church. Vatican: Libreria Editrice Vaticana, 1993. http://www.vatican.va/archive/ENG0015/_INDEX.HTM.

Catechism of the Council of Trent. Translated by John A. McHugh and Charles J. Callan. New York: Joseph F. Wagner, 1923.

The Catholic Encyclopedia. New Advent, 2012. http://www.newadvent.org/cathen/.

Cihak, John R. *Balthasar and Anxiety.* London: T. & T. Clark, 2009.

Ciraulo, Jonathan Martin. "Sacramentally Regulated Eschatology in Hans Urs von Balthasar and Pope Benedict XVI." *Pro Ecclesia: A Journal of Catholic and Evangelical Theology* 24.2 (2015) 216–34.

Claudel, Paul. *Coronal.* Translated by Sister Mary David. New York: Pantheon, 1943.

Collins, R. F. "Mary in the Fourth Gospel—A Decade of Johannine Studies." *Louvain Studies* 3 (1970) 99–142.

Crammer, Corinne. "One Sex or Two? Balthasar's Theology of the Sexes." In *The Cambridge Companion to Hans Urs von Balthasar,* edited by Edward T. Oakes and David Moss, 93–112. Cambridge: Cambridge University Press, 2004.

D'Costa, Gavin. *Christianity and World Religions: Disputed Questions in the Theology of Religions.* Oxford: Wiley-Blackwell, 2009.

———. "The Descent into Hell as a Solution for the Problem of the Fate of the Unevangelized Non-Christians: Balthasar's Hell, the Limbo of the Fathers and Purgatory." *International Journal of Systematic Theology* 11, no. 2 (2009) 146–71.

Denny, Christopher D. "Greek Tragedies: From Myths to Sacraments?" *Logos: A Journal of Catholic Thought and Culture* 9, no. 3 (2006) 45–71.

Devanny, Christopher. "Truth, Tragedy and Compassion: Some Reflection on the Theology of Donald MacKinnon." *New Blackfriars* 78, no. 911 (1997) 33–42.

Eliot, T. S. *The Cocktail Party.* London: Faber and Faber, 1950.

Ephrem the Syrian. *Hymns on the Nativity.* Translated by Kathleen E. McVey. New York: Paulist, 1989.

Faber, Frederick William. *At the Foot of the Cross; or, the Sorrows of Mary.* London: Thomas Richardson and Son, 1858.

Falconer, Rachel. *Hell in Contemporary Literature: Western Descent Narratives Since 1945.* Edinburgh: Edinburgh University Press, 2007.

Farley, Wendy. *Tragic Vision and Divine Compassion: A Contemporary Theodicy.* Louisville, KY: Westminster John Knox, 1990.

Fields, Stephen. "Balthasar and Rahner on the Spiritual Senses." *Theological Studies* 57 (1996) 224–41.

Ford, David F. "Tragedy and Atonement." In *Christ, Ethics and Tragedy: Essays in Honour of Donald MacKinnon,* edited by Kenneth Surin, 117–30. Cambridge: Cambridge University Press, 1989.

Ford, David F., and Frances Young. *Meaning and Truth in 2 Corinthians.* London: SPCK, 1987.

Francis, Pope. *Angelus.* October 12, 2014. http://www.news.va/en/news/angelus-12-october-2014.

————. *Urbi et Orbi Message of Pope Francis.* March 31, 2013. https://w2.vatican.va/content/francesco/en/messages/urbi/documents/papa-francesco_20130331_urbi-et-orbi-pasqua.html.

Friesenhahn, Jacob H. *The Trinity and Theodicy: The Trinitarian Theology of von Balthasar and the Problem of Evil.* Farnham, UK: Ashgate, 2011.

Gardiner, Anne Barbeau. "Anne Barbeau Gardiner Answers Jacques Servais." *New Oxford Review* 69, no.8 (2002) 42–45.

————. "The Dubious Adrienne von Speyr." *New Oxford Review* 69, no.8 (2002) 31–36.

Gardner, Helen. *Religion and Literature.* London: Farber and Farber, 1971.

Gardner, Lucy. "Balthasar and the Figure of Mary." In *The Cambridge Companion to Balthasar,* edited by Edward T. Oakes and David Moss, 64–78. Cambridge: Cambridge University Press, 2004.

Gardner, Lucy, and David Moss. "Something like Time; Something like the Sexes—an Essay in Reception." In *Balthasar at the End of Modernity,* edited by Lucy Gardner, et al., 69–137. Edinburgh: T. & T. Clark, 1999.

Gardner, Lucy, et al., eds. *Balthasar at the End of Modernity.* Edinburgh: T. & T. Clark, 1999.

Görres, Ida Friederike. *The Hidden Face: A Study of St Thérèse of Lisieux.* Translated by Richard Winston and Clara Winston. New York: Pantheon, 1959.

Granados, José. "Mary and the Truth about Life." In *Mary, God-bearer to a World in Need,* edited by Maura Hearden and Virginia M. Kimball, 23–41. Eugene, OR: Wipf & Stock, 2013.

Greiner, Maximilian. "The Community of St. John: A Conversation with Cornelia Capol and Martha Gisi." In *Hans Urs von Balthasar: His Life and Work,* edited by David L. Schindler, 87–101. San Francisco: Ignatius, 1991.

Griffiths, Paul J. "Is there a Doctrine of the Descent into Hell?" *Pro Ecclesia* 17, no. 3 (2008) 257–68.

Grumett, David. *Material Eucharist.* Oxford: Oxford University Press, 2016.

Hart, Addison Hodges. *Knowing Darkness: On Skepticism, Melancholy, Friendship, and God.* Grand Rapids: Eerdmans, 2009.

Hart, David Bentley. *The Beauty of the Infinite: The Aesthetics of Christian Truth.* Grand Rapids: Eerdmans, 2003.

Healy, Nicholas J. "Christ's Eucharist and the Nature of Love: The Contribution of Hans Urs von Balthasar." *The Saint Anselm Journal* 10.2 (2015) 1–17.

————. *The Eschatology of Hans Urs von Balthasar: Being as Communion.* Oxford: Oxford University Press, 2005.

Healy, Nicholas J., and David L. Schindler. "For the Life of the World: Hans Urs von Balthasar on the Church as Eucharist." In *The Cambridge Companion to Balthasar*, edited by Edward T. Oakes and David Moss, 51–63. Cambridge: Cambridge University Press, 2004.

Hegel, G. W. F. *Aesthetics: Lectures on Fine Art*. Vol. 2. Translated by T. M. Knox. Oxford: Clarendon, 1975.

Henrici, Peter. "Hans Urs von Balthasar: A Sketch of His Life." In *Hans Urs von Balthasar: His Life and Work*, edited by David. L. Schindler, 7–43. San Francisco: Ignatius, 1991.

Hofer, Andrew. "Balthasar's Eschatology on the Intermediate State: The Question of Knowability." *Logos* 12:3 (2009) 148–72.

Howsare, Rodney. *Balthasar: A Guide for the Perplexed*. London: T. & T. Clark, 2009.

Hume, David. *Dialogues Concerning Natural Religion*. London: 1779.

Hunt, Anne. *The Trinity and the Paschal Mystery: A Development in Recent Catholic Theology*. Collegeville, MN: Liturgical, 1997.

———. *The Trinity: Insights from the Mystics*. Collegeville, MN: Liturgical, 2010.

Imperatori-Lee, Natalia M. "The Use of Marian Imagery in Catholic Ecclesiology since Vatican II." PhD diss., University of Notre Dame, 2007.

John of the Cross, *The Complete Works of St. John of the Cross*. Edited by E. Allison Peers. Translated by P. Silverio de Santa Teresa. London: Burns Oates, 1943.

John Paul II. *Dominicae Cenae*. February 24, 1980. https://w2.vatican.va/content/john-paul-ii/en/letters/1980/documents/hf_jp-ii_let_19800224_dominicae-cenae.html.

———. *Ecclesia de Eucharistia*. April 17, 2003. http://www.vatican.va/holy_father/special_features/encyclicals/documents/hf_jp-ii_enc_20030417_ecclesia_eucharistia_en.html.

———. "Hell is the State of Those who Reject God." In *L'Osservatore Romano Weekly Edition in English*, July 28, 1999. https://www.ewtn.com/library/PAPALDOC/JP2HEAVN.HTM#Heaven.

———. *Mane Nobiscum Domine*. October 8, 2004. https://w2.vatican.va/content/john-paul-ii/en/apost_letters/2004/documents/hf_jp-ii_apl_20041008_mane-nobiscum-domine.html.

———. "My God, My God, Why Have You Forsaken Me?" General Audience on November 30, 1988. http://w2.vatican.va/content/john-paul-ii/it/audiences/1988/documents/hf_jp-ii_aud_19881130.html.

———. "Purgatory is Necessary Purification." In *L'Osservatore Romano Weekly Edition in English*, August 4, 1999. https://www.ewtn.com/library/PAPALDOC/JP2HEAVN.HTM#Purgatory.

———. *Redemptoris Mater: on the Blessed Virgin Mary in the Life of the Pilgrim Church*. March 25, 1987. http://w2.vatican.va/content/john-paul-ii/en/encyclicals/documents/hf_jp-ii_enc_25031987_redemptoris-mater.html.

———. *Salvifici Doloris*. February 11, 1984. https://w2.vatican.va/content/john-paul-ii/en/apost_letters/1984/documents/hf_jp-ii_apl_11021984_salvifici-doloris.html.

Johnston, Philip S. *Shades of Sheol: Death and Afterlife in the Old Testament*. Leicester, UK: Apollos, 2002.

Kasper, Walter. *Sacrament of Unity: The Eucharist and the Church*. Translated by Brian McNeil. New York: Crossroad, 2004.

Kelly, Anthony. *Eschatology and Hope*. New York: Orbis, 2006.

Kerr, Fergus. "Adrienne von Speyr and Hans Urs von Balthasar." *New Blackfriars* 79, no. 923 (1998) 26–32.

Kilby, Karen. *Balthasar: A (Very) Critical Introduction*. Grand Rapids: Eerdmans, 2012.

———. "Evil and the Limits of Theology." *New Blackfriars* 84, no. 983 (2003) 13–29.

———. "Hans Urs von Balthasar on the Trinity." In *The Cambridge Companion to the Trinity*, edited by Peter C. Phan, 208–22. Cambridge: Cambridge University Press, 2011.

Kvanvig, Jonathan L. *The Problem of Hell*. Oxford: Oxford University Press, 1993.

Langan, Thomas. *The Catholic Tradition*. Columbia, MO: University of Missouri Press, 1998.

Lash, Nicholas. "Friday, Saturday, Sunday." *New Blackfriars* 71, no. 836 (1990) 109–19.

Lauber, David. *Barth on the Descent into Hell: God, Atonement and the Christian Life*. Burlington, VT: Ashgate, 2004.

Leahy, Brendan. *The Marian Profile: In the Ecclesiology of Hans Urs von Balthasar*. Hyde Park, NY: New City, 2000.

Leamy, Katy. *The Holy Trinity: Hans Urs von Balthasar and His Sources*. Eugene, OR: Pickwick, 2015.

Levering, Matthew. *Sacrifice and Community: Jewish Offering and Christian Eucharist*. Oxford: Blackwell, 2005.

Lewis, Alan. *Between Cross and Resurrection: A Theology of Holy Saturday*. Grand Rapids: Eerdmans, 2001.

Lewis, C. S. *The Great Divorce*. San Francisco: Harper San Francisco, 2009.

de Lubac, Henri. "A Witness of Christ in the Church: Hans Urs von Balthasar." In *Hans Urs von Balthaasar: His Life and Work*, edited by David L. Schindler, 271–88. San Francisco: Ignatius, 1991.

Lubich, Chiara. *Mary: The Transparency of God*. Translated by Euzene Selzer, et al. Hyde Park, NY: New City, 2003.

Maas, Wilhelm. *Gott und die Hölle: Studien zum Descensus Christi*. Einsiedeln, Switzerland: Johannes Verlag, 1979.

MacKinnon, Donald. *Borderlands of Theology and Other Essays*. London: Lutterworth, 1968.

———. "A Master in Israel: Hans Urs von Balthasar" (An Introductory Essay). In *Engagement with God*, by Hans Urs von Balthasar, translated by John Halliburton, 1–16. London: SPCK, 1975.

———. *The Problem of Metaphysics*. Cambridge: Cambridge University Press, 1974.

———. "Some Reflections on Hans Urs von Balthasar's Christology with Special Reference to Theodramatik II/2 and III." In *The Analogy of Beauty: The Theology of Hans Urs von Balthasar*, edited by John Kenneth Riches, 164–74. Edinburgh: T. & T. Clark, 1986.

———. "Theology and Tragedy." *Religious Studies* 2, no. 2 (1967) 163–9.

de Maeseneer, Yves. "Review Symposium: Balthasar: A (Very) Critical Introduction by Karen Kilby." *Horizon* 40, no. 1 (2013) 100–6.

Martin, Jennifer Newsome. *Hans Urs von Balthasar and the Critical Appropriation of Russian Religious Thought*. Notre Dame, IN: University of Notre Dame Press, 2015.

Martini, Carlo. *Our Lady of Holy Saturday: Awaiting the Resurrection with Mary and the Disciples*. Translated by Andrew Tulluch. Liguori, MO: Liguori, 2001.

McInroy, Mark. *Balthasar on the Spiritual Senses: Perceiving Splendour*. Oxford: Oxford University Press, 2014.

McIntosh, Mark A. *Christology from Within: Spirituality and the Incarnation in Hans Urs von Balthasar*. Notre Dame, IN: University of Notre Dame Press, 1996.

———. *Mystical Theology: The Integrity of Spirituality and Theology*. Oxford: Blackwell, 1998.

Metz, Johann Baptist. "Suffering from God: Theology as Theodicy." *Pacifica* 5, no. 3 (1992) 274–87.

———. "Suffering Unto God." Translated by J. Matthew Ashley. *Critical Inquiry* 20, no. 4 (1994) 611–22.

Miles, Lois M. "Obedience of a Corpse: The Key to the Holy Saturday Writings of Adrienne von Speyr." PhD Diss., University of Aberdeen, 2013.

Moltmann, Jürgen. *The Trinity and the Kingdom: The Doctrine of God*. Translated by Margaret Kohl. Minneapolis: Fortress, 1993.

Moss, David, and Lucy Gardner. "Something like Time; Something like the Sexes—an Essay in Reception." In *Balthasar at the End of Modernity*, edited by Lucy Gardner, et al., 69–137. Edinburgh: T. & T. Clark, 1999.

Moss, David, and Edward T. Oakes, eds. *The Cambridge Companion to Hans Urs von Balthasar*. Cambridge: Cambridge University Press, 2004.

Mother Teresa. *Come Be My Light: The Private Writings of the Saint of Calcutta*. Edited by Brian Kolodiejchuk. New York: Crown, 2007.

Murphy, Francesca Aran. "Immaculate Mary: The Ecclesial Mariology of Hans Urs von Balthasar." In *Mary: The Complete Resource*, edited by Sarah Jane Boss, 300–313. London: Continuum, 2007.

Murray, Paul. *I Loved Jesus in the Night: Teresa of Calcutta, a Secret Revealed*. London: Darton, Longman & Todd, 2008.

Neuhaus, Richard John. *Death on a Friday Afternoon: Meditations on the Last Words of Jesus from the Cross*. New York: Basic, 2000.

Nicolas of Cusa. *Excitationes* 10. Basel: Heinrich Petri, 1565.

Nichols, Aidan. *Divine Fruitfulness: A Guide Through Balthasar's Theology Beyond the Trilogy*. Washington, DC: Catholic University of America Press, 2007.

———. "Introduction." In *Mysterium Paschale, The Mystery of Easter*, by Hans Urs von Balthasar, translated by Aidan Nichols, 1–10. San Francisco: Ignatius, 2000.

———. "Marian Co-redemption: A Balthasarian Perspective." *New Blackfriars* 95, no. 1057 (2014) 249–62.

Nouwen, Henri J. M. *With Burning Hearts: A Meditation on the Eucharistic Life*. Maryknoll, NY: Orbis, 2003.

Oakes, Edward T. "*Descensus* and Development: A Response to Recent Rejoinders." *International Journal of Systematic Theology* 13, no. 1 (2011) 3–24.

———. "'He Descended into Hell': The Depth of God's Self-Emptying Love on Holy Saturday in the Thought of Hans Urs von Balthasar." In *Exploring Kenotic Christology: The Self-Emptying of God*, edited by C. Stephen Evans, 218–45. Oxford: Oxford University Press, 2009.

———. *Infinity Dwindled to Infancy: A Catholic and Evangelical Christology*. Grand Rapids: Eerdmans, 2011.

———. "The Internal Logic of Holy Saturday in the Theology of Hans Urs von Balthasar." *International Journal of Systematic Theology* 9, no. 2 (2007) 184–99.

Oakes, Edward T., and David Moss, eds. *The Cambridge Companion to Hans Urs von Balthasar*. Cambridge: Cambridge University Press, 2004.

Oakes, Edward T., and Alyssa Lyra Pitstick. "Balthasar, Hell and Heresy: An Exchange." *First Things* 168 (2006) 25–29.

———. "More on Balthasar, Hell, and Heresy." *First Things* 169 (2007) 16–18.

O'Byrne, Máire. *Model of Incarnate Love: Mary Desolate in the Experience and Thought of Chiara Lubich*. Hyde Park, NY: New City, 2011.

O'Collins, Gerald. *Catholicism: A Very Short Introduction*. Oxford: Oxford University Press, 2008.

O'Donnell, John. *Hans Urs von Balthasar*. London: Continuum, 1991.

O'Donoghue, Noel. *Mystics for Our Time: Carmelite Meditations for a New Age*. Edinburgh: T. & T. Clark, 1989.

Oglesby, Les. *C. G. Jung and Hans Urs von Balthasar: God and Evil—A Critical Comparison*. London: Routledge, 2013.

O'Hanlon, Gerard. *The Immutability of God in the Theology of Hans Urs von Balthasar*. Cambridge: Cambridge University Press, 1990.

———. "Theological Dramatics." In *The Beauty of Christ: An Introduction to the Theology of Hans Urs von Balthasar*, edited by Bede McGregor and Thomas Norris, 92–111. Edinburgh: T. & T. Clark, 1994.

O'Regan, Cyril. *The Anatomy of Misremembering: von Balthasar's Response to Philosophical Modernity, Vol. 1: Hegel*. Chestnut Ridge, NY: Crossroad, 2014.

———. "Hegel, Theodicy, and the Invisibility of Waste." In *The Providence of God*, edited by Francesca Aran Murphy and Philip G. Ziegler, 75–108. London: Continuum, 2009.

Phan, Peter C. "Mystery of Grace and Salvation: Karl Rahner's Theology of the Trinity." In *The Cambridge Companion to the Trinity*, edited by Peter C. Phan, 192–207. Cambridge: Cambridge University Press, 2011.

———. "What is Old and What is New in the Catechism?" In *Introducing the Catechism of the Catholic Church*, edited by Berald L. Marthaler, 56–71. London: SPCK, 1994.

Phan, Peter C., ed. *The Cambridge Companion to the Trinity*. Cambridge: Cambridge University Press, 2011.

Pitstick, Alyssa Lyra. *Christ's Descent into Hell: John Paul II, Joseph Ratzinger, and Hans Urs von Balthasar on the Theology of Holy Saturday*. Grand Rapids: Eerdmans, 2016.

———. "Development of Doctrine, or Denial? Balthasar's Holy Saturday and Newman's Essay." *International Journal of Systematic Theology* 11, no. 2 (2009) 129–45.

———. *Light in Darkness: Hans Urs von Balthasar and the Catholic Doctrine of Christ's Descent into Hell*. Grand Rapids: Eerdmans, 2007.

Pitstick, Alyssa Lyra, and Edward T. Oakes. "Balthasar, Hell, and Heresy: An Exchange." *First Things* 168 (2006) 25–29.

———. "More on Balthasar, Hell, and Heresy." *First Things* 169 (2007) 16–18.

Poole, Adrian. *Tragedy: Shakespeare and the Greek Example*. Oxford: Blackwell, 1987.

Quash, Ben. "Christianity as Hyper-Tragic." In *Facing Tragedies*, Vol. 2, edited by Christopher Hamilton, et al., 77–88. Wien, Austria: LIT, 2009.

———. "Four Biblical Characters: In Search of a Tragedy." In *Christian Theology and Tragedy: Theologians, Tragic Literature and Tragic Theory*, edited by Kevin Taylor and Giles Waller, 15–34. Farnham, UK: Ashgate, 2011.

————."Hans Urs von Balthasar." In *The Modern Theologians: An Introduction to Christian Theology Since 1918*, 3rd ed., edited by David Ford, 106–23. Cambridge: Blackwell, 2005.

————. "Real Enactment: The Role of Drama in the Theology of Hans Urs von Balthasar." In *Faithful Performances: Enacting Christian Tradition*, edited by Trevor A. Hart and Steven R. Guthrie, 13–32. Aldershot, UK: Ashgate, 2007.

————. *Theology and the Drama of History*. Cambridge: Cambridge University Press, 2005.

Rahner, Karl. *Karl Rahner in Dialogue: Conversations and Interviews, 1965–1982*. Edited by Paul Imhof and Hubert Biallowons. Translated by Harvey D. Egan. New York: Crossroad, 1986.

————. *The Trinity*. Translated by Joseph Donceel. London: Burns & Oates, 1970.

Rambo, Shelly. *Spirit and Trauma: A Theology of Remaining*. Louisville, KY: Westminster John Knox, 2010.

Ratzinger, Joseph. *Eschatology: Death and Eternal Life*. Translated by Michael Waldstein. Washington, DC: Catholic University of America Press, 2004.

————. *Introduction to Christianity*. Translated by J. R. Foster. San Francisco: Ignatius Press, 2004.

————. *The Spirit of the Liturgy*. Translated by John Saward. San Francisco: Ignatius Press, 2000.

Ratzinger, Joseph, and Hans Urs von Balthasar. *Mary: The Church at the Source*. Translated by Adrian Walker. San Francisco: Ignatius, 2005.

Ratzinger, Joseph, and Christoph Schönborn. *Introduction to the Catechism of the Catholic Church*. San Francisco: Ignatius, 1994.

Reid, Alcuin. *The Organic Development of the Liturgy: The Principles of Liturgical Reform and Their Relation to the Twentieth Century Liturgical Movement Prior to the Second Vatican Council*. Farnborough, UK: Saint Michael's Abbey, 2004.

Reno, R. R. "Was Balthasar a Heretic?" *First Things*, October 15, 2008. http://www.firstthings.com/web-exclusives/2008/10/was-balthasar-a-heretic.

Richards, I. A. *Principles of Literary Criticism*. London: Routledge, 2001.

Riches, John Kenneth, ed. *The Analogy of Beauty: The Theology of Hans Urs von Balthasar*. Edinburgh: T. & T. Clark, 1986.

The Roman Missal. Translated by International Commission on English in the Liturgy Corporation. London: Catholic Truth Society, 2010.

Roten, Johann. "The Two Halves of the Moon: Marian Anthropological Dimensions in the Common Mission of Adrienne von Speyr and Hans Urs von Balthasar." In *Hans Urs von Balthasar: His Life and Work*, edited by David L. Schindler, 65–86. San Francisco: Ignatius, 1991.

Sara, Juan M. "*Descensus ad Infernos*, Dawn of Hope." In *Love Alone is Credible: Hans Urs von Balthasar as an Interpreter of the Catholic Tradition*, edited by David L. Schindler, 209–40. Grand Rapids: Eerdmans, 2008.

Sartre, Jean-Paul. *No Exit and Three Other Plays*. Translated by Stuart Gilbert and Lionel Abel. New York: Vintage, 1989.

Saward, John. *The Mysteries of March: Hans Urs von Balthasar on the Incarnation and Easter*. Washington, DC: Catholic University of America Press, 1990.

————. "Youthful unto Death: The Spirit of Childhood." In *The Beauty of Christ: An Introduction to the Theology of Hans Urs von Balthasar*, edited by Bede McGregor and Thomas Norris, 140–60. Edinburgh: T. & T. Clark, 1994.

Scherer, Bruno. *Tragik vor dem Kreuz: Leben und Geisteswelt Reinhold Schneiders.* Kißlegg-Immenried: Christiana-Verlag, 2017.

Schindler, David L., ed. *Hans Urs von Balthaasar: His Life and Work.* San Francisco: Ignatius, 1991.

————. *Love Alone is Credible: Hans Urs von Balthasar as an Interpreter of the Catholic Tradition.* Grand Rapids: Eerdmans, 2008.

Schindler, David L., and Nicholas J. Healy. "For the Life of the World: Hans Urs von Balthasar on the Church as Eucharist." In *The Cambridge Companion to Balthasar,* edited by Edward T. Oakes and David Moss, 51–63. Cambridge: Cambridge University Press, 2004.

Schneider, Reinhold. *Briefe an einen Freund (Otto Heuschele). Mit Erinnerungen von Otto Heuschele.* Köln: Hegner, 1961.

————. *Der Christliche Protest.* Zurich: Arche, 1954.

————. *Rechenschaft: Worte zur Jahrhundertmitte.* Einsiedeln, Switzerland: Johannes Verlag, 1951.

————. *(Lebensbericht) Schulfunk (22.9.1953).* Manuscript in Karlsruhe (Reinhold-Schneider-Archiv der Badischen Landesbibliothek).

————. *Tagebücher 1930–1935.* Frankfurt: Insel, 1983.

Schönborn, Christoph, and Joseph Ratzinger. *Introduction to the Catechism of the Catholic Church.* San Francisco: Ignatius, 1994.

Schoonenberg, Piet. *Man and Sin: A Theological View.* Translated by Joseph Donceel. London: Sheed & Ward, 1965.

Schuster, Ekkehard, and Reinhold Bochert-Kimmig. *Hope Against Hope: Johann Baptist Metz and Elie Wiesel Speak out on the Holocaust.* Translated by J. Matthew Ashley. New York: Paulist, 1999.

Servais, Jacques. "A Response from Jacques Servais." *New Oxford Review* 69, no. 8 (2002) 36–42.

Seymour, Charles Steven. *A Theodicy of Hell.* Vol. 20 of Studies in Philosophy and Religion. Dordrecht, The Netherlands: Kluwer Academic, 2000.

Shimomura, Kihachi. *Ikirareta Kotoba: Rainhoruto Shunaida no Shogai to Sakuhin (The Words That Have Been Lived: the Life and Works of Reinhold Schneider).* Tokyo: Choeisha, 2014.

Speyr, Adrienne von. *Confession.* Translated by Douglas W. Stott. San Francisco: Ignatius, 1985.

————. *Handmaid of the Lord.* Translated by E. A. Nelson. San Francisco: Ignatius, 1985.

————. *Korinther I.* Einsiedeln, Switzerland: Johannes Verlag, 1956.

————. *Kreuz und Hölle I: Die Passionen.* Vol. 3 of *Die Nachlasswerke.* Einsiedeln, Switzerland: Johannes Verlag, 1966.

————. *Kreuz und Hölle II: Auftragshöllen.* Vol. 4 of *Die Nachlasswerke.* Einsiedeln, Switzerland: Johannes Verlag, 1972.

————. *Mary in the Redemption.* Translated by Helena M. Tomko. San Francisco: Ignatius, 2003.

————. *The Passion from Within.* Translated by Sister Lucia Wiedenhöver. San Francisco: Ignatius, 1998.

————. *Three Women and the Lord.* Translated by Graham Harrison. San Francisco: Ignatius, 1993.

Speyr, Adrienne von, and Hans Urs von Balthasar. *To the Heart of the Mystery of Redemption*. Translated by Anne Englund Nash. San Francisco: Ignatius, 2010.

Steiner, George. *The Death of Tragedy*. New York: Hill & Wang, 1968.

———. *Real Presences: Is There Anything in What We Say?* London: Faber and Faber, 1989.

———. "Tragedy Reconsidered." In *Rethinking Tragedy*, edited by Rita Felski, 29–44. Baltimore: Johns Hopkins University Press, 2008.

Sutton, Matthew Lewis. "Does God Suffer? Hans Urs von Balthasar's Theology of Holy Saturday." In *On Suffering: An Interdisciplinary Dialogue on Narrative and Suffering*, edited by Nate Hinerman and Matthew Lewis Sutton, 171–83. Oxford: Inter-Disciplinary, 2012.

———. *Heaven Opens: The Trinitarian Mysticism of Adrienne von Speyr*. Minneapolis: Fortress, 2014.

Tallon, Philip. *The Poetics of Evil: Toward an Aesthetic Theodicy*. Oxford: Oxford University Press, 2012.

Taylor, Kevin. "Hans Urs von Balthasar and Christ the Tragic Hero." In *Christian Theology and Tragedy: Theologians, Tragic Literature and Tragic Theory*, edited by Kevin Taylor and Giles Waller, 133–48. Farnham, UK: Ashgate, 2011.

———. *Hans Urs von Balthasar and the Question of Tragedy in the Novels of Thomas Hardy*. London: Bloomsbury, 2013.

Taylor, Kevin, and Giles Waller, eds. *Christian Theology and Tragedy: Theologians, Tragic Literature and Tragic Theory*. Farnham, UK: Ashgate, 2011.

Thérèse of Lisieux. *Collected Letters*. Edited by Abbé Combes. Translated by F. J. Sheed. New York: Sheed & Ward, 1949.

———. *Story of a Soul: The Autobiography of St. Thérèse of Lisieux*. Translated by John Clark. Washington, DC: Institute of Carmelite Studies, 1976.

Vanstone, W. H. *The Stature of Waiting*. New York: Morehouse, 2006.

Vatican II Council. *Lumen Gentium*. November 21, 1964. http://www.vatican.va/archive/hist_councils/ii_vatican_council/documents/vat-ii_const_19641121_lumen-gentium_en.html.

Waller, Giles. "Freedom, Fate and Sin in Donald MacKinnon's Use of Tragedy." In *Christian Theology and Tragedy: Theologians, Tragic Literature and Tragic Theory*, edited by Kevin Taylor and Giles Waller, 101–18. Farnham, UK: Ashgate, 2011.

Waller, Giles, and Kevin Taylor, eds. *Christian Theology and Tragedy: Theologians, Tragic Literature and Tragic Theory*. Farnham, UK: Ashgate, 2011.

Walls, Jerry L. *Hell: The Logic of Damnation*. Notre Dame, IN: University of Notre Dame Press, 1992.

Ward, Graham. "Kenosis: Death, Discourse and Resurrection." In *Balthasar at the End of Modernity*, 15–68. Edinburgh: T. & T. Clark, 1999.

———. "Tragedy as Subclause: George Steiner's Dialogue with Donald MacKinnon." *The Heythrop Journal* 34, no. 3 (1993) 274–87.

Williams, Rowan. "Afterword: Making Differences." In *Balthasar at the End of Modernity*, edited by Lucy Gardner, et al., 173–79. Edinburgh: T. & T. Clark, 1999.

———. "Balthasar and the Trinity." In *The Cambridge Companion to Hans Urs von Balthasar*, edited by Edward T. Oakes and David Moss, 37–50. Cambridge: Cambridge University Press, 2004.

———. *The Wound of Knowledge: Christian Spirituality from the New Testament to St. John of the Cross*. London: Darton, Longman & Todd, 1990.

Index of Names

CPSIA information can be obtained
at www.ICGtesting.com
Printed in the USA
FSHW021252230720
72410FS